T0296048

Controlling the Capital

Controlling the Capital

Political Dominance in the Urbanizing World

Edited by

Tom Goodfellow
and
David Jackman

OXFORD
UNIVERSITY PRESS

Great Clarendon Street, Oxford, OX2 6DP,
United Kingdom

Oxford University Press is a department of the University of Oxford.
It furthers the University's objective of excellence in research, scholarship,
and education by publishing worldwide. Oxford is a registered trade mark of
Oxford University Press in the UK and in certain other countries

© Oxford University Press 2023

The moral rights of the authors have been asserted

Some rights reserved. No part of this publication may be reproduced, stored in
a retrieval system, or transmitted, in any form or by any means, for commercial purposes,
without the prior permission in writing of Oxford University Press, or as expressly
permitted by law, by licence or under terms agreed with the appropriate
reprographics rights organization.

This is an open access publication, available online and distributed under the terms of a
Creative Commons Attribution – Non Commercial – No Derivatives 4.0
International licence (CC BY-NC-ND 4.0), a copy of which is available at
http://creativecommons.org/licenses/by-nc-nd/4.0/.

Enquiries concerning reproduction outside the scope of this licence
should be sent to the Rights Department, Oxford University Press, at the address above

Published in the United States of America by Oxford University Press
198 Madison Avenue, New York, NY 10016, United States of America

British Library Cataloguing in Publication Data

Data available

Library of Congress Control Number: 2023905815

ISBN 978–0–19–286832–9

DOI: 10.1093/oso/9780192868329.001.0001

Printed and bound by
CPI Group (UK) Ltd, Croydon, CR0 4YY

Links to third party websites are provided by Oxford in good faith and
for information only. Oxford disclaims any responsibility for the materials
contained in any third party website referenced in this work.

MIX
Paper | Supporting
responsible forestry
FSC® C013604

Acknowledgements

This book brings together the research undertaken as part of a project entitled 'Cities and Dominance: Urban strategies for political settlement maintenance and change', funded by the Effective States and Inclusive Development (ESID) Research Centre based at the University of Manchester. The project evolved through a series of workshops in 2018 and 2019, with most of the fieldwork thankfully being undertaken before the world was hit by the Covid-19 pandemic. During the periods of lockdown and crisis we gradually managed to bring the book together—with world events constantly providing new food for thought about the book's topic—though always battling against other priorities, delays, and the challenges of that period which are now all too well known. We are very grateful to all of the chapter authors for their patience, thoroughness in responding to reviews, and continued support for the book project throughout this period.

The editors would like to thank ESID for funding the research, and particularly Sam Hickey for creating the opportunity for this project to come into being and supporting us along the way. We are also indebted to the wider ESID support team who in various ways supported the research, workshops, and production of working papers, including Kat Bethell, Julia Brunt, Clare Degenhardt, Chris Jordan, and Julie Rafferty. We are very grateful to Adrienne LeBas for joining us for our second project workshop to act as discussant, and for providing extremely sharp and valuable comments on our emerging analytical framework. We would like to thank all the anonymous peer reviewers for their comments on each of the working papers on which the case study chapters of this book are based, which have helped to strengthen these chapters in many important ways. We are grateful also to Tim Kelsall for his comments on an early iteration of our cross-cutting conclusions, which were very helpful in sharpening our comparative analysis.

We would like to thank all the participants in our project workshops who were external to the project, as well as audience members at conference panels showcasing early findings, who offered thoughtful comments that pushed forward our collective thinking. The chapter authors have also engaged with the book's evolving framework in creative and constructive ways throughout the project, which again has been invaluable in strengthening the book and its overall framing and analysis.

At OUP we would like to thank Adam Swallow for commissioning the book and dealing with all our various queries, and Vicki Sunter for helping us pull everything together in the final stages in order to get the book finally into production.

Tom Goodfellow and David Jackman
November 2022

This document is an output from a project funded by UK Aid from the UK Government for the benefit of developing countries. However, the views expressed and information contained in it are not necessarily those of, or endorsed by, the UK Government, which can accept no responsibility for such views or information, or for any reliance placed on them.

Contents

List of figures and tables

Figures

Table

The contributors

Kudzai Chatiza is a researcher and local governance student with experience in decentralization, development planning, citizen participation, housing policy and practice. He also has housing, social movement building, water and sanitation, resilience, evaluation, and slum-upgrading expertise. Kudzai studied at the University of Zimbabwe, UZ (Bachelor, 1992 and Master, 1995), and Swansea University (PhD, 2008). He teaches and supervises research students at UZ and Midlands State University. Kudzai advises state and non-state development organizations on devolved governance, and pro-poor land, agrarian, and housing governance in Africa in his current role of Director at the Development Governance Institute (www.degi.co.zw) based in Harare.

Eyob Balcha Gebremariam is a Research Associate at the Perivoli Africa Research Centre (PARC) at the University of Bristol. He completed his PhD in Development Policy and Management at the University of Manchester in 2018. Before joining PARC, Eyob was a Fellow at the London School of Economics and Political Science (LSE), where he convened and taught postgraduate courses on African Development and the African Political Economy. His areas of research and teaching are the politics of knowledge production in, on, and about Africa, decolonial knowledge production, African political economy, the politics of development, and young people's engagement in politics. He has published articles in the *Journal of Northeast*

African Studies and *IDS Bulletin*, and policy papers in the *Horn of Africa Bulletin*, *Tana Papers*, and *Chaliot Papers*. Eyob is the winner of the 2022 Thandika Mkandawire Prize for Outstanding Scholarship in African Political Economy.

Tom Goodfellow is a Professor of Urban Studies and International Development at the University of Sheffield. His research focuses on the comparative political economy of urban development in Africa, particularly the politics of urban land and transportation, conflicts around infrastructure and housing, migration, and urban institutional change. He is author of *Politics and the Urban Frontier: Transformation and Divergence in Late Urbanizing East Africa* (Oxford University Press, 2022) and co-author of *Cities and Development* (Routledge, 2016). He sits on the Editorial Boards of *African Affairs* and the *International Journal of Urban and Regional Research* and is Treasurer of the IJURR Foundation.

Marja Hinfelaar, PhD, is Director of Research and Programmes at the Southern African Institute for Policy and Research (SAIPAR), Lusaka, Zambia. Marja received her PhD in History in 2001 from the University of Utrecht, the Netherlands, where her dissertation focused on the history of women's organizations in Zimbabwe. She is the co-editor of *One Zambia, Many Histories: Towards a History of Post-colonial Zambia* (Brill, 2008), co-author of *Governing Extractive Industries: Politics, Histories,*

Ideas (Oxford University Press, 2018), and co-editor of *Democracy and Electoral Politics in Zambia* (Brill, 2020). Marja has been resident in Zambia since 1997.

David Jackman is a Leverhulme Early Career Research Fellow at the University of Oxford. His research interests lie in the political economy of crime and violence in South Asia, with a focus on Bangladesh, where he has worked since 2010. His work on gangsterism, labour politics, party–police relations, and beggar bosses have been published in journals such as *Development and Change, Modern Asian Studies*, and the *Journal of Contemporary Asia*. His current project examines the pirates of the Sundarbans in Bangladesh and West Bengal.

JoAnn McGregor is Professor of Human Geography in the School of Global Studies, University of Sussex. She has published widely on Zimbabwe politics, history, and urban transformations. Her research on urban governance in Zimbabwe has been conducted in collaboration with the Development Governance Institute (DEGI) and Dialogue on Shelter, both based in Harare. The research has a comparative frame across four cities in Africa and South Asia, through the projects 'Migrants on the Margins' funded by the Royal Geographical Society and more recently an ESRC-funded project on Inclusive Urban Infrastructure.

Paul Isolo Mukwaya holds a PhD in Geography from Makerere University in Kampala, Uganda. He received his BA in Geography from Makerere University and a Master of Philosophy degree in Social Change (specializing in Geography) from the Norwegian University of Science and Technology in Trondheim, Norway. His research

interests are grounded in geography but are frequently interdisciplinary, with expertise at the interface of geography and society, urban and regional sciences, transport policy and planning, human–environment interactions, environmental planning and design, institutional aspects of environmental change, climate change adaptation/mitigation, transport planning, and local economic development.

Nansozi K. Muwanga is the Executive Director of the Julius Nyerere Leadership Centre (JNLC), a presidential initiative at Makerere University in Kampala, Uganda. A Ugandan national, she holds a PhD in Political Science from the University of Toronto, Canada. She was the recipient of the Rockefeller Foundation's African Dissertation Internship Award (ADIA) for her PhD research on the politics of education reforms. Dr Muwanga was the first woman to head the Department of Political Science and Public Administration at Makerere University. A Fulbright New Century Scholar (NCS) at Stanford University, Dr Muwanga has over thirty years of research, teaching, and administrative experience.

Iromi Perera is a Colombo-based researcher and activist. She is the founder and Director of the Colombo Urban Lab and works on post-war urban development and spatial justice in Sri Lanka. Her research and policy work looks at the lived experiences of communities affected by large-scale infrastructure projects and development masterplans, focusing on housing, livelihood, public space, and social protection. Iromi is a member of the People's Alliance for Right to Land, and from 2008 to 2017 she was a Senior Researcher at the Centre for Policy Alternatives in Sri Lanka, leading its survey research work.

Danielle Resnick is a David M. Rubenstein Fellow at the Brookings Institution, in the Global Economy and Development Program. Key research areas include the political economy of development, decentralization, urban governance, and democratization, with a regional specialization in sub-Saharan Africa. She has lived, conducted fieldwork, and engaged in policy outreach in more than a dozen African countries. Among other publications, she is the author of *Urban Poverty and Party Populism in African Democracies* (Cambridge University Press, 2014) and co-editor of *Political Economy of Food System Transformation: Pathways to Progress in a Polarized World* (Oxford University Press, 2023).

Sishuwa Sishuwa is a Senior Lecturer in History at Stellenbosch University and an Honorary Research Affiliate in the Institute for Democracy, Citizenship and Public Policy in Africa at the University of Cape Town. Previously, Sishuwa was a Lecturer in African History at the University of Zambia. He works on southern Africa's political history during the twentieth and twenty-first centuries and his research emphasises a historical approach to understanding contemporary issues. Sishuwa obtained his doctorate in Modern History from the University of Oxford, where he studied as a Rhodes Scholar.

Jonathan Spencer is an anthropologist based at the University of Edinburgh, who has been researching in Sri Lanka since the 1980s. His recent work has focused on urban housing and on the history of dissent.

1
Introduction

Tom Goodfellow and David Jackman

Calmness and civility in urban history is the exception not the rule. The only interesting question is whether the outcomes are creative or destructive.

David Harvey (2003: 939)

Some people think that being in government for a long time is a bad thing. But the more you stay, the more you learn. I am now an expert in governance.

Ugandan president, Yoweri Museveni, 2012

In 2018—when the idea for the research project leading to this book was conceived—cities across the world were alive with protest. In Europe, France saw the start of the '*gilets jaune*' (yellow vest) movement, Spain felt constitutional crisis in Catalonia, and students internationally began to strike from school in response to the climate crisis and the example of Greta Thunberg. Meanwhile major unrest was seen on the streets of Iran, labour unions in Jordan pushed for legislative changes, students shut down much of Bangladesh's capital, Dhaka, and Nicaragua saw the rise of a university movement in response to state injustice. Armenia and Sudan saw revolution, while Ethiopia saw a new regime come to power following years of unrest across the country. This is to name only a few examples. Despite the scale of these protests, 2018 was in many ways unexceptional. These events took place against a backdrop of upheaval in North Africa and the Middle East in the so-called 'Arab Spring' several years earlier, and the period since has seen major protests even in the face of—and sometimes in response to—Covid-19 lockdowns, which shone new light on police brutality in many parts of the world. The persistence of protests has led some commentators to claim we are living in the age of a

Tom Goodfellow and David Jackman, *Introduction*. In: *Controlling the Capital*. Edited by: Tom Goodfellow and David Jackman, Oxford University Press. © Oxford University Press (2023). DOI: 10.1093/oso/9780192868329.003.0001 'mass protest' (Brannen et al. 2020), playing out primarily on the streets of cities and towns.

The issues raised by these movements are varied and complex, yet they generally reflected a concern with the hollowing-out of democratic institutions and the sense of creeping authoritarianism. In some cases, the response to the recent 'authoritarian turn' has taken the form of citizens in relatively democratic states raising their voice and expressing anger at not being listened to by governments they perceive as elite, aloof, and out of touch with contemporary needs and concerns. In others, these explosions of grievance are responding to more dramatic closures of democratic space and concerted efforts by governing regimes to secure long-term political dominance of the political arena. Authoritarianism is nothing new, and nor is the dialectic between attempts to secure political dominance and the varying modalities through which this is resisted. Yet the late twentieth century was characterized by widespread optimism about the prospects for progressive democratization globally—and, by some accounts, the process of urbanization unfolding across the majority of the world should be supporting this consolidation of democracy (Dima et al. 2011; Wallace 2014; Glaeser and Steinberg 2017). In reality, however, the early twenty-first century has been characterized by reassertions of authoritarianism and the proliferation of hybrid or 'semi-authoritarian' rule. According to Freedom House (2021), democracy has been in decline for the past fifteen years and is 'under siege'. This trend was compounded by Covid-19, which for some has revealed weaknesses in democratic responses to the pandemic, and offered opportunities for authoritarian moves to control the lives of citizens more tightly (Cooper and Aitchison 2020; Finn and Kobayashi 2020; Goodfellow and Jackman 2020; Valizadeh and Iranmanesh 2021; Simandan et al. 2023).

The fact that urbanization, authoritarian tendencies, and vigorous political protest are accelerating simultaneously in many parts of the world should perhaps not surprise us. Despite many reasons to believe that urbanization and democracy *ought* to be mutually reinforcing, existing research on the relationship between the two is very limited, and the evidence is contested (Dyson 2013; Glaeser and Steinberg 2017; Dorward and Fox 2022). The very same factors that help explain the democratic tendencies associated with cities—namely, population density and diversity, heightened potential for collective action, and generally higher levels of education—often also produce efforts to dominate cities through authoritarian practices (Scarnecchia 2008: LeBas 2011). It is thus far from clear that urbanization produces democracy in the short to medium term, even if it tends to over the *longue durée*. Meanwhile, in much of the world urbanization is being accompanied by a range of authoritarian strategies on the part of leaders seeking to stave off the threat of democracy.

This tension between the urban democratic impulse and the authoritarian urge to control cities from the top down dates back millennia. What is different in the twenty-first century is the sheer scale of cities, the pace of their growth in many parts of the world, and the breaking of the link between mass urbanization and the generation of urban economic opportunities (Fox 2012; Davis 2016). In this context, the clash between democratic and authoritarian impulses in cities often leads to an escalation of urban political violence. It has been argued that, globally, violence has become markedly more urban, and we have turned from the 'peasant wars of the 20th century' (Wolf 1969) to the 'urban wars' (Beall 2006) and 'slum wars' (Rodgers 2007) of the twenty-first. As one commentator puts it, 'urban areas have become lightning conductors for our planet's political violence' (Graham 2011: 16). In the context of rapid demographic changes, major cities have emerged as key sites within which struggles over the legitimacy and survival of regimes are played out, and opposition movements seek to gain support and influence (Resnick 2014a). All of this has also become increasingly visible, as social media and other platforms enable efficient and ubiquitous coverage of events, demonstrations, and reprisals, often in highly public and symbolic spaces, such as large squares and junctions (Karduni and Sauda 2020; Stokols 2022). Meanwhile, recent literature has critiqued linear ideas of 'urbanization of violence', arguing that it is more helpful to see heightened political violence and protest in cities as mutually entangled with violence at different scales and geographies (Kniknie and Büscher 2023).

The centrality of cities in both producing and resisting authoritarianism raises critical questions for the study of authoritarian politics. Recent decades have seen the emergence of a rich literature attempting to explain the nature of transitions to authoritarianism, the institutional heterogeneity such regimes exhibit, and their varying durability (Policzer 2009; Levitsky and Way 2010; Slater 2010; Svolik 2012; Lachapelle et al. 2020). With a few exceptions, however, non-democratic regimes and practices have been analysed at the national scale, with little attention to the key roles played by particular subnational places.[1] What political role do cities—and, in particular, capital cities—play in contemporary authoritarian contexts? Answers to such a

---

[1] The most notable exceptions here are probably Synder (2001, 2006), Gibson (2013), and Sidel (2014). Note, however, that this literature is primarily concerned with the authoritarian subnational tendencies within countries that are democratic to a significant extent at the national scale. Nor does this literature centre cities specifically within its analysis. In contrast, we are concerned not with subnational authoritarianism within broader democratic polities, but with the hardening of authoritarianism at the national scale and how this manifests within the specific context of capital cities.

question are surprisingly difficult to find, yet in some respects feel obvious. Images of the urban protest inspired by the Arab Spring around the world, or similarly of democracy movements in Hong Kong or Caracas, highlight the campaigns of brutal repression unleashed on cities. Scenes of armed and uniformed security agencies heavy-handedly repressing citizens on city streets are unfortunately too commonplace, but also risk leaving a simplistic impression about both urban politics and the ways that political regimes to seek and establish dominance.

If we move beyond headline-grabbing scenes of open urban protest and repression, it is clear that in many cities the work of establishing political dominance over cities happens behind the scenes or in ways that stifle or co-opt dissent before it becomes visible. As well as asking how urban protests emerge and how they are responded to, we need to consider a range of other questions if we are to understand the nexus between urban opposition and urban control. How do some authoritarian regimes prevent urban protests from happening in the first place? What levers of power do they command beyond coercion? What role do forms of longer-term repression and manipulation of opposition forces play? How do some regimes manage to co-opt substantial proportions of the urban population—or even convince them of their legitimacy—even as their authoritarian practices increase? This book addresses these questions, and in so doing hopes to open up a more complex story about how authoritarian regimes seek and sustain power, and the place of cities within these processes in the early twenty-first century.

1.1 Political dominance in the twenty-first century

Only a small minority of the world's population live in societies seen as broadly adhering to the values of democracy and liberalism. In the estimation of Freedom House (2021), less than 20 per cent of the world live in a 'free' society, while for the Economist Intelligence Unit's Democracy Index a measly 8 per cent live in a 'full democracy' (EIU 2021). Understanding the character of what is broadly termed 'authoritarianism' is for obvious reasons, therefore, crucial to appreciating the nature of contemporary politics globally, and part of addressing many of the world's challenges, from poverty reduction and human rights to climate change. Yet the term 'authoritarianism' is slippery. It is commonly applied not only to political systems, but also to characters and practices (Glasius 2018; Wallace 2019), and we hear it used in radically different contexts. For many, this undermines the analytical utility of the term, and hence academia is replete with concepts intended to distinguish and define political contexts more precisely. We hear, for example, of dominant-party regimes (Magaloni and Kricheli 2010), illiberal democracy and electoral authoritarianism (Gandhi 2008), hybrid regimes (Diamond 2002; Prempeh 2008), and competitive authoritarianism (Levitsky and Way 2010).

A key question that animates the study of such regimes is the question of authoritarian durability, and the ways that ostensibly democratic institutions often enable this. What helps an authoritarian regime survive? Answers to this question emphasize different factors, though many revolve around the strength of party and state institutions, and the relationship between them. For some, the strength of dominant parties lies in rulers' capacity to bargain with elites and mobilize the masses (Magaloni and Kricheli 2010), or in the politicization of the public purse for electoral campaigns and inducements (Greene 2010). Another strand of thought finds that regime durability really rests not with patronage, but with the identities formed through violent struggle and the ideological basis that this can bring to a regime (Levitsky and Way 2012). Similarly, for Lachapelle et al. (2020) the real key to durability lies in regime origins. Regimes with their roots in violent revolution tend to bring elite cohesion, loyal and strong military and coercive apparatus, and the diminishment of political alternatives. Within this reading, the design of authoritarian institutions matters less, and durability is largely preordained. Others have argued that the strength of political parties crucially depends on the character of contentious politics that political elites face, and which can mobilize them towards concerted collective action (Slater 2010).

Despite advancing our understanding of authoritarianism, there are number of weaknesses and omissions that remain in the mainstream literature on authoritarian durability. A first is that some of the leading explanations based on large n cross-national studies simply do not account for the durability of certain regimes over others in the contemporary global South. For example, the idea that the most durable regimes are founded through violent social revolutions, such as those in Russia, China, and Cuba (Lachapelle et al 2020), is of little use in explaining differences within sub-Saharan Africa or South Asia, where revolutions of this kind have been relatively rare and where, even in cases where they have occurred (such as Ethiopia in 1974), the durability of incoming regimes has been limited. Second, in focusing primarily on different forms of institutions within the party and state that can both repress dissent and deploy patronage to bolster support, many explanations overlook the ways in which such institutions are dependent on more fundamental political and economic relations in society (Pepinsky 2014).

It is for this reason that we have decided to frame the analysis in our book primarily in relation not to institutions of *authoritarianism*, but to the processes that produce and sustain the *dominance* of a particular ruling coalition, in terms of its ability to maintain power not just within political institutions but in relation to the wider sociopolitical context.

Third, and of particular relevance to this book, the existing literature largely neglects questions of how dominant regimes seek, sustain, and lose power within particular subnational places and geographies. Of particular interest here, there are many reasons to believe that cities, and especially capital cities, are crucial sites in the production of authoritarian dominance and the politics of maintaining it, as well as sites of popular resistance (Wallace 2014; Glaeser and Steinberg 2017). While some literature acknowledges cities as important in understanding authoritarian durability (for example, Slater 2010), the ways in which ruling elites and their broader coalitions *strategize* to build and maintain urban dominance are not directly examined. More generally, as Allen writes in his book *Lost Geographies of Power*, much of the literature on authoritarianism loses sight of the ways in which 'power is inherently spatial and, conversely, spatiality is imbued with power' (Allen 2003: 3). This concern is particularly pertinent in parts of the global South in which, for historical reasons, the state often has limited territorial 'reach' (Putzel and Di John 2012). For example, in much of Africa and some other postcolonial regions, the presence of internationally protected borders since independence has limited the incentive to invest in extending power fully across territories (Herbst 2014), leading to 'a centre-periphery divide in which the coercive capacity of states was uneven—high in the capital cities (the centre) but declining with every step into the rural hinterland (the periphery)' (Cheeseman 2015: 17).

Our intention in this volume is, then, to introduce a focus on capital cities as central sites in the study of political dominance, in this way contributing to the study of authoritarianism within political and the broader social sciences (Gandhi 2008; Levitsky and Way 2010; Magaloni and Kricheli 2010; Slater 2010; Pepinsky 2014), as well as contributing to the study of how urban power is constituted and contested (Branch and Mampilly 2015; Therborn 2017; Goodfellow 2018, 2022; Collord et al. 2021). Unlike much of the existing literature on authoritarianism, this book does not focus primarily on political parties or state institutions per se, or on classifying and scrutinizing the extent to which institutions in a given setting are authoritarian or democratic. Our focus is more on what authoritarian regimes *do* in the pursuit of political dominance and how this relates to the broader structure of power relations and contestation within societies and, particularly, cities. We focus, then, on the strategies and tactics deployed in authoritarian contexts, the material and discursive aspects to these, and the ways in which they can be seen in political life. In this sense, we respond to calls for a deeper examination of how authoritarian regimes seek and maintain control (Frantz 2018: 89) and the 'political *practices*' of authoritarianism (Glasius 2018: 521, italics in the original) in the ongoing pursuit of political dominance.[2]

Our understanding of political dominance is informed by the political settlements approach (PSA), which has been rapidly evolving over the past decade (Khan 2010, 2018; Whitfield et al. 2015; Pritchett et al. 2017; Gray 2018; Kelsall et al. 2022).[3] As noted above, a weakness in some of the mainstream political science approaches is to analyse authoritarian institutions without sufficient attention to the underlying structure of power relations among social and economic groups. A political settlement refers to the 'distribution of organizational power ... [which] reproduces itself over time', including through the deployment of formal and informal institutions that support that power distribution (Khan 2018: 641). Various approaches to political settlement analysis now exist, and our intention here is not to reconcile wider debates in this field (Kelsall 2018; Khan 2018), or to engage in depth with the concept or advance any particular theory of political settlements. Rather, we simply draw on the ideas from this approach to conceptualize political dominance in relation to the broader balance of power in society, facilitating our focus on how strategies for dominance target and impact particular urban groups through different kinds of intervention. It is the PSA's attention to historically constituted groups in society with different amounts of bargaining power, and how this constellation of power shapes strategies of rule and patterns of investment, that differentiates it from a more conventional focus on 'regime type'.

A key concept we adopt from the political settlements literature is the notion of a 'ruling coalition' (North et al. 2009; Khan 2010). While the concepts of *government* and political *regime* highlight the roles of explicitly political actors (whether associated with the apparatus of the state or the party) in the construction of political authority, the concept of a 'ruling coalition' draws attention to the wider set of actors on which the authority

[2] Marlies Glasius (2018) has argued that authoritarianism is too often defined in opposition to democracy rather than on its own terms. For example, it is seen as an absence of elections meeting a criterion around being 'free and fair'. As such, we lack a positive sense of the 'political *practices*' (ibid. 521, italics in the original) of authoritarianism, which—in this formulation—play a role in '*sabotaging accountability*' (ibid. 525, italics in the original).

[3] It has been similarly noted that the literature on political settlements and regime types has been poorly integrated with work on the geography and spatiality of political power, instead taking the nation state as the given unit of analysis (Meehan and Goodhand 2018).

of a particular government or regime rests.[4] A coalition incorporates diverse actors, important among whom are those commonly characterized as 'elites', which typically include leaders in the fields of politics, business, and religion. Yet ruling coalitions also extend beyond elites, incorporating a range of organizations and individuals that function at different hierarchical levels of society, from the national down to the street corner—sometimes characterized as the 'social foundation' of a political settlement (Kelsall et al. 2022). The constituent elements of a ruling coalition have very different organizational characters, which differ spatially between and within cities, as well as regionally (Jackman 2018a). When in power, the ruling elite has privileged access to a range of rent streams which can be distributed to politically significant groups through both formal and informal institutions, enabling the broader ruling coalition to accrue resources from a wide range of processes (Goodfellow 2018; Jackman 2018b; Khan 2018).

Notwithstanding the importance of party structures in many contexts, to understand why a certain coalition of actors is able to dominate political institutions and limit the power of rivals over time requires, then, going beyond a focus on parties, particularly since parties have historically often been weakly institutionalized in many parts of the global South (Randall and Svåsand 2002; LeBas 2011). The coalition of actors that consolidates control in a given country may, even if constituted within a given party, draw much of its power from organizational sources beyond the party. The concepts of political settlement and ruling coalition help to inform the study of political dominance in this broader sense, by enabling analyses of political systems without either resting on assumptions about the strength of parties or resorting to crude distinctions between authoritarianism and democracy—distinctions that are of diminishing utility in a world where most governing regimes constitute various forms of hybrid (Diamond 2015; Wintrobe 2018).

1.2 Cities, power, and state-building

We now turn to the second area of literature to which this book contributes: the study of urban politics and the construction and contestation of urban power, particularly in capital cities. There is no shortage of debate on the ways in which state power is *resisted* in contemporary cities. The visibility of

---

[4] Here we draw on the distinction made by Whitfield et al. (2015: 24): '*ruling elites* refers to the group of people who wield power as a result of their position in government, where they occupy offices in which authoritative decisions are made. *Ruling coalition* refers to the ruling elites as well as the groups and individuals behind the rise of the ruling elites to power and/or those groups or individuals that keep the ruling elite in power by organizing political support for it, typically in exchange for benefits.'

protests across the world has increased dramatically since the birth of social media and smartphones; grainy and rare images from iconic moments of confrontation between authoritarian regimes and citizens, such as Tiananmen Square's lone protestor, have been replaced with constant streams of images and footage. A protest in Myanmar or Hong Kong can be closely tracked on the other side of the world through tweets, posts, and video, sometimes even despite internet blackouts and surveillance. Such images bring cities and other urban spaces to the fore. Streets, squares, parks, and other quotidian urban sites become stages for marches, banners, speeches, battles, and coups. While more visibly globally now, the nature of such urban resistance and mobilization has long been a relatively common theme of research, not least through the sizeable literature on urban social movements (Castells 1983; Pickvance 2003; Tilly and Tarrow 2007; Nicholls 2008; Uitermark et al. 2013; Mitlin 2018). Despite this, there is a distinct lack of research into the role of urbanization in promoting or undermining democracy, and recent scholarship has called for this to be the subject of future work (Fox and Bell 2016; Glaeser and Steinberg 2017; Dorward and Fox 2022).

There is also a lack of systematic analyses of how cities are used to construct and maintain the power of dominant coalitions in the first place, and how forms of urban opposition both respond to and help to shape the urban strategies of ruling elites.[5] As urban populations continue to expand across Africa and Asia in particular, deepening our understanding of the relationship between cities and political dominance is a pressing concern. There is thus a need to interrogate the role played by urban political interventions in whether regimes fall or persist, as well as the urban dimensions of 'structural threats that regimes face and their strategic response to those threats' (Wallace 2014: 18).[6] While cities are 'privileged places for democratic innovation' (Borja and Castells 1997: 251), they also hold opportunities for ruling elites attempting to consolidate their control and thwart the potential for effective resistance. It is here that our book makes its primary contribution. We make no apology for focusing primarily on the strategies of ruling elites in their efforts to dominate cities because, in contrast with questions of social movements and protest, the literature is very underdeveloped in this area and our collection seeks to address this gap.

---

[5] This is not to deny the attention paid in recent decades to the exercise of state power in cities of the global South more broadly, including the use of planning as a tool of control (Njoh 2009; Watson 2009; Yiftachel 2009) and the exclusion and dispossession caused by certain forms of urban investment (Goldman 2011; Gillespie 2016).

[6] For Koren (2017) the neglect of the political salience of capital cities stems from the tendency to focus on national rather than subnational levels, a lack of data, and an overreliance on news media and non-government organization reporting.

The importance of understanding the constitution of urban power for broader questions of stability, state-building and development is well evidenced by historically focused studies. The centrality of cities to the evolution and consolidation of states in Europe, for example, is deep-rooted (Tilly 1992). Tilly argues that through European history, state formation stemmed from the accumulation and concentration of both capital and coercion within cities, which had the potential to disrupt and contest the power of emerging public authorities. Power-holders seeking to fight wars to consolidate territorial control had to develop relations with urban elites—including by taxing them to fund these wars in exchange for protection, which in turn fuelled the development of state bureaucracies. Thus the relationship between cities, taxation, and conflict fuelled the rise of modern states. As centres of government, loci of powerful economic and social organizations, and places of geographic importance (for example, industrial centres or ports), cities—and particularly capital cities—have been pivotal sites in revolutions, as well as wider forms of contentious politics. As Traugott's (1995) analysis of French revolutions suggests, the importance of a capital city is a function of a national system of governance. Where administration and politics have not been centralized into a modern nation state, the centre of governance can shift without undermining the claim of the ruler to command the territory. When a capital embodies a nation, however, this is not possible. Controlling and dominating capital cities have thus been key objects of war, revolutions, and regime changes.

The place of capital cities in state-building processes in much of the world diverges from the European context in fundamental ways. Schatz (2004: 114) summarizes this difference as such: 'Simply put: in Europe, capitals emerged as part and parcel of state and nation building; elsewhere, capitals emerged after legal claims to territoriality had been established.' The relationship between states, cities, and conflict in many developing countries has thus been shaped by the role of European empire-building and externally driven state formation, as well as by the globalization of capital flows that fundamentally change the nature of bargaining between holders of capital and wielders of coercive power (Beall et al. 2013). In many colonized regions, although there were some urban areas with precolonial histories that functioned as sites of capital, coercion and early state-building, the experience of extended colonial domination transformed the logic of cities. Many of the major cities of Africa and Asia today either were created for, or became defined by, the extraction of resources and the development of infrastructure geared towards the export of primary products, as well as military protection of colonial regimes (Beall et al. 2013; Fox and Goodfellow 2022).

Consequently, in many colonized contexts, states and cities were created concurrently through a logic of external domination and unequal global integration (Getachew 2019), rather than co-evolving and becoming entwined through a dynamic relationship over time. However, crucially, in this colonially driven state-city relationship, the state was dominant: instead of a productive interdependence and bargaining process between the two, the city was primarily a site for the projection of state domination (Myers 2003; Njoh 2009).[7] Capital cities were particularly significant in this regard, because it was in colonial capitals that government bureaucracies, regulatory regimes, and systems of policing were largely constructed. Meanwhile, the economic foundations of colonial cities were often weak. In the early postcolonial period, experiments with import-substitution industrialization were short-lived – particularly in Africa – and not accompanied by the anticipated expansion of productive capacities and urban employment, particularly after international pressure to open economies intensified from the 1980s (Mkandawire 2005; Whitfield et al. 2015). Consequently, in many parts of Africa and Asia, rapid urbanization proceeded with neither a substantial urban capitalist class nor an industrial working class that could organize at a large scale to confront the state (Fox and Goodfellow 2022).

Capital cities thus embody state authority in distinctive ways in postcolonial contexts, with the stark dualities created in what were initially 'nationally alien capitals' persisting through forms of planning, zoning, architecture, and patterns of service provision (Therborn 2017: 145; see also Njoh 2009; Watson 2009). In countries that managed to resist colonialism, meanwhile, the kinds of rule needed to effectively stave off encroachment by colonizing powers involved a kind of 'reactive modernization' from above, which replicated some of the urban effects of colonial domination within the context of a global system of racialized sovereign inequality (Therborn 2017: 147; Getachew 2019). Thus, Therborn argues, cities in non-colonized states ranging from Thailand to Ethiopia were shaped by top-down modernization projects that preserved greater historical continuity than colonial capitals, but were nevertheless marked by state domination and strong dualities between ruling and subservient classes (Therborn 2017).

This is the urban backdrop against which we need to understand strategies employed by ruling coalitions to assert dominance in much of the world. Major urban centres, being economic hubs, will play a central role in the political economy of any political settlement, due to the significant resources

---

[7] It has also been argued that the other key element in Tilly's account of statebuilding—namely coercion, or more specifically war—has contributed to eroding democracy in states where war has been a significant feature of the postcolonial period (Cheeseman et al 2018).

they embody, and the ways in which different groups attempt to capture and exploit these. Selectively providing access to valuable urban land and property, as well as lucrative trading opportunities, is one of the most powerful levers that ruling elites possess in terms of shoring up their broader coalition in such contexts (Goodfellow 2018, 2022). Distributing urban benefits in this way is often a complex process, particularly in terms of the management of opportunities in often unruly urban economies. Distribution of resources often operates through 'horizontal' ties among urban elites as well as hierarchical structures of patron–client relations (Collord et al. 2021), which often involve networks of higher- and lower-level 'brokers' that ruling elites have to work continually to keep onside in the face of the threat of defection or factional splits (Stokes et al. 2013; Themnér and Utas 2016; McGregor and Chatiza 2019).

In addition to the question of how political dominance can be built through urban economies, capital cities specifically are 'containers' of national sovereignty (Beall et al. 2013); hence demonstrating territorial authority within them is an important signifier for broader sovereign authority, to the extent that in civil wars, control of the capital is often synonymous with victory (ibid.). This significance is no less relevant in peacetime, not only due to the need to protect government assets and elite resources, but also because of the extreme visibility of capital cities, which plays a significant role in efforts to attain and secure dominance. Given their disproportionate representation in national and international media, capital cities are spaces in which development, security, and dominance itself are regularly performed, which is part of the process through which dominance is maintained (Goodfellow and Smith 2013; Rollason 2013; Amarasuriya and Spencer 2015). They are, to use Putzel and Di John's (2012: 13) term, not just territory, but 'significant territory'; even if formal dominance of institutions in capital cities is challenged by powerful opposition forces, as is often the case, the symbolic demonstration of power and more informal exercise of authority are crucially important. We now turn to the question of urban opposition and how this factors into elite strategies for controlling the capital.

1.3 Opposition and political ferment

Capital cities' dual function as hubs of economic opportunity and 'containers' of sovereignty makes them central rallying points for opposition struggle and contentious claims (Beall et al. 2013), as well as sites of 'spectacular' violence and resistance (Goldstein 2004). The roles of cities in fostering revolution have been documented by studies of Western contexts such as

France (Traugott 1995) and the USA (Carp 2007), and have also been evident in recent years in the events of the 'Arab Spring' and the wave of urban uprisings linked to austerity and economic crisis (Allegra et al. 2013; Branch and Mampilly 2015). Given that they are places particularly associated with the state, it is unsurprising that they should also be primary sites of resistance to it, and theatres of violent contentious politics. This takes different forms. Being densely populated can mean cities are 'conduits where movements connect and develop' (Uitermark et al. 2013: 2549), and where ideas and discourse ferment. Urban populations tend to be more highly educated, and notions and claims of citizenship have most often originated in urban contexts (Heater 2004; Holston and Appadurai 1996).

At the same time, capital cities are also the object of extreme forms of political violence. Using the Political Instability Task Force (PITF) Worldwide Atrocities data from 1996 to 2009, Koren (2017: 327) argues that 24 per cent of 'atrocities against civilians perpetrated by insurgents' occur in capital cities, despite these often housing a far smaller percentage of national populations and representing only a tiny percentage of national territory. This spectacular violence serves different purposes, and can be a means of 'elite coercion', 'popular intimidation', or 'international persuasion' (ibid.). Where public policy and investment are perceived to have an 'urban bias', this can increase the likelihood of such symbolic attacks on cities (Pierskalla 2016). Greater levels of inequality between urban and rural areas have hence been argued to increase the probability of 'high-intensity civil war' (Nedal et al. 2020: 1147) on account of both the opposition born from rural neglect, and also the fact that politically significant territory becomes more concentrated in urban spaces which conventional militaries are ill equipped to defend (ibid.). Mkandawire (2002), meanwhile, has argued that many rural-based rebellions in Africa are rooted in 'urban malaise', in the sense that they are often led by rebel leaders who feel excluded from urban power and retreat into the countryside in order to build a base from which to launch on the city. These dynamics all underscore the fundamental importance of capital cities to the political settlement in many contexts.

The great political irony of capital cities in much of the world is that despite being so central to the dominance of ruling coalitions, they are often opposition strongholds (Diouf 1996; Lambright 2014; Resnick 2014b). When opposition parties come to control municipal authorities, the ensuing situation of 'vertically divided authority' can lead ruling elites to engage in various forms of 'strategies of subversion' to protect their interests in the city (Resnick 2014b). These involve actions to limit the autonomy of municipal authorities, while also ensuring that local authorities take the blame for poor service delivery (Resnick 2014b; see also Gore and Muwanga 2014). But regardless of whether opposition parties achieve power, opposition forces make their presence known in distinctive ways in urban areas, exploiting the visibility of urban space for protests, riots, and demonstrations, and invoking shared issues of urban collective consumption to realize their critical mass as a force able to challenge the central authority of the state (Branch and Mampilly 2015; Golooba-Mutebi and Sjögren 2017; Asante and Helbrecht 2018). In response, ruling elites mobilize the apparatus of the state to respond, often violently, to assert their dominance visibly. It is not in the extremely authoritarian states that these patterns of urban protest and violent state response are most pronounced, but in hybrid regimes—in other words, those in which democratic forces enable some expression of grievance and mobilization of urban opposition, even while authoritarian tendencies generate persistent repression (Fox and Hoelscher 2014; Goodfellow 2014; Dorward and Fox 2022).

For Wallace (2014), large urban centres pose particular threats to ruling coalitions for two key reasons: first, because they are more likely to have effective collective action events; and, second, because high levels of urban concentration can lead to a dominant city overwhelming other political forces. Fox and Bell (2016) likewise demonstrate statistically that city size (rather than level of urbanization) is correlated with urban protest globally. These features of large cities can sometimes foster developmental progress through the state's responses to these perceived threats. Based on the experience of China, Wallace argues that threats to regime stability stemming from cities led not only to coercion, and limits to where people can and cannot live, but to more positive forms of state response including subsidies and improved urban living conditions. This resulted in an 'urban bias' in China's public policy,[8] which through improving urban conditions and the relaxation of the *hukou* policy further incentivized rural–urban migration. Over time, this bolstered threats to the regime, given the propensity for urban growth to foment political opposition. Wallace thus posits a 'Faustian bargain hypothesis', which he elaborates thus: 'while urban bias might have short-term benefits for leaders, its long-term effects—namely inducing urban concentration—are self-undermining for regimes' (ibid. 44).

These ideas about the potential for urbanization to weaken or even break the dominance of entrenched ruling coalitions are echoed elsewhere. For

---

[8] It is important, however, to note that urbanization, even when rapid, does not in itself necessarily promote 'urban bias' (Jones and Corbridge 2010). Where regimes in power have a strong rural base, and particularly where they have evolved out of rural guerrilla struggles, they may be much more concerned to appease rural constituencies than urban ones. Even as urbanization gathers pace, it can be some time before a tipping point is reached that results in more concerted efforts to distribute urban benefits. There is significant evidence that this was the case in Uganda, for example, where the capital suffered decades of neglect prior to a major turnaround in priorities from 2010 (Gore and Muwanga 2014; Goodfellow 2022).

Glaeser and Steinberg (2017), there are three possible routes by which urbanization can undermine authoritarian dominance. First is the idea that population density facilitates collective action. Cities increase the likelihood of opposition forces meeting each other; the risk associated with protesting is reduced in large, dense urban spaces as the likelihood of being caught is lower; the geography of cities can offer advantages for mobilizing opposition; any protest will be visible nationally and perhaps internationally; and these factors are magnified when we focus on capital cities. Second, urbanization can increase innovation and trade, which over time are generally threatened by dictatorship, hence leading to support for democracy. Third, cities can promote 'civic capital': the ability of citizens to push for higher-quality government.

While these democratizing features of cities are generally well known, in reality the relationship between cities and democratization is far from straightforward. As well as the heightened presence of urban opposition often prompting authoritarian counter-moves by the state, it can threaten a range of elites who fear reprisals or demands for redistribution, which in turn can incentivize such elites to increase support for repressive states in return for protection (Slater 2010: 44). These 'protection pacts' may have a state-building function, but can also inhibit democracy and cement authoritarian dominance. Indeed, while these processes could in theory begin to echo those described by Tilly (1992) in relation to early modern Europe, it is important to remember the highly elitist and exclusionary nature of politics in European city states, where the pressures also to appeal to a wider public in the context of democratic elections were absent. Controlling the capital under conditions in which political elites are attempting both to protect elite interests *and* to build support among the urban majority in the context of democratic pressures is in many respects more complex, requiring more multifaceted strategies for dominance than in periods of historical state-building.

Recognizing the centrality of capital cities to political contention and control opens up questions about the role that cities play in maintaining wider arrangements of state authority—the strategies and forms of governance that ruling elites utilize in urban settings in order to limit the potential for dissension and unrest. It is these complex and multifaceted strategies that we unpack in this volume. This focus resonates closely with the argument of Uitermark et al. (2013: 2546) that

> the city is a generative space of mobilisations and, because of this, it is also the frontline where states constantly create new governmental methods to protect and produce social and political order, including repression, surveillance, clientelism, corporatism, and participatory and citizenship initiatives.

Contention and control, these authors go on to argue, exist in a 'dialectic' (ibid. 2552), dynamically interacting as governments deploy strategies to mitigate the particular threat posed by urban contentious politics. This dialectic is one that should be understood over time, with interaction shifting power within coalitions, altering the forms of contention and control possible, and potentially even shaping the national political settlement. As the quotation from President Museveni at the start of this chapter indicates, elite strategies for dominance need to evolve in response to new threats and popular practices, but also through the process of learning how to dominate: 'the more you stay, the more you learn'. Yet this learning can itself be undone in the face of the dynamism and fluidity of urban politics: the more you stay, the more complex the urban threats you face. In sum, capital cities have a unique importance to national political settlements and studying them can offer deeper insights into the critical question of how settlements are maintained (or unravelled) over time.

1.4 Research design, cases and contexts

This project emerged from the Effective States and Inclusive Development Research Centre (ESID) at the University of Manchester. This centre was established with a broad agenda to explore the relationship between politics and development in the 'global South', in part responding conceptually to the idea of a political settlement as originally developed by Mushtaq Khan. The editors of this volume designed the initial conceptual scope and agenda for this project, identified country cases, and worked collaboratively with research teams to hone this further through a workshop in Manchester in 2018. This set the basis for the research itself, much of which was conducted in the same year and the following year, drawing in many instances from other relevant research and work by the country teams. We have been very fortunate that each case has been produced by an academic or academic collaboration with expertise and rich experience in their context. These studies thus build on years of ethnographic and qualitative research studying urban politics.

This volume draws from six studies of the strategies adopted by ruling elites to dominate and control capital cities, and how these efforts to dominate have been resisted, contested, modified or sometimes actively co-created by urban social groups. These cases come from Africa (Addis Ababa, Harare, Kampala, and Lusaka) and South Asia (Colombo and Dhaka).

There were several rationales for focusing on these regions. Most significantly, both regions are rapidly urbanizing, with some of the largest emerging cities in the world, and associated challenges such as intense congestion, (un)employment, infrastructure provision, and dysfunctional and contested urban governance. Indeed, the pace of urbanization in Africa (especially sub-Saharan Africa) and Asia (particularly South Asia, now the continent's most rapidly urbanising region) is the highest in the world, far exceeding other global regions; hence our styling of the geographic focus of this volume as 'the urbanizing world'. As regions particularly associated with the conditions of 'late urbanization' (Fox and Goodfellow 2022), the political challenges associated with governing large cities are particularly acute in sub-Saharan Africa and South Asia. Secondly, both regions have also seen a marked shift towards authoritarianism in recent decades, offering opportunities to contribute not only to the theoretical agenda set out above, but to better understanding of these political transitions and contexts. Each chapter thus offers valuable insight into its country context, as well as speaking to broader trends within these regions. It is furthermore very rare that we find comparative research projects between sub-Sahraran Africa and South Asia, despite the two regions symbolizing and sharing some of the major development challenges facing the world today.

The project began with four country cases designed to represent a continuum in the nature of political dominance, in terms of both the duration of dominant-party rule and the degree of hold that the dominant ruling coalition has on society. Together this continuum was intended to enable us to offer a comparative analysis of how forms of governance and contention emerge in capital cities at different stages of dominance, from situations of firm and enduring urban control to more fluid and dynamic contexts. At one end of this continuum, representing well-established dominant political settlements, were Ethiopia (until the disintegration of the Ethiopian People's Revolutionary Democratic Front (EPRDF) regime in 2018, the year this project began) and Uganda, where a dominant-party settlement under Yoweri Museveni's National Resistance Movement has been in place since 1986, but with strong resistance to political domination at the city level. Bangladesh represents a case of a new dominant-party settlement with significant uncertainty around the ability for dominance to persist. Finally, the case of Zambia initially represented a case where there were signs of a dominant-party settlement emerging, with President Edgar Lungu attempting to consolidate power. We later added two further cases—Harare (Zimbabwe) to examine attempts to control a city that has been opposition-supporting for decades, and Colombo (Sri Lanka), where the capital had played a less significant role in the country's politics historically, but where efforts to dominate it had ramped up since 2009, with very mixed outcomes. Together these cases offer a comparative analysis of contention and control not only at different stages of dominance but also at different scales, with the Bangladesh case in particular offering a capital city far larger than the African cases. The historical periods of political dominance, and within this the period of particular interest studied in our chapters, are listed in Table 1.1.

Methodologically, we did not impose on the individual case study research teams a strict research design or focus: each responded to the particular histories and dynamics in their case to draw out the most pertinent examples of strategies deployed by ruling coalitions to build and/or consolidate urban dominance. Each team was asked to choose two or three empirical domains on which to focus, which could take the form of specific institutions, policy initiatives, sectors of urban society, or even 'critical events' that would illuminate dominance strategies particularly well in that context. As a result, the six cities studied offer a rich breadth of insight into the strategies and interventions deployed in attempts to garner and consolidate political support, repress political opposition, and manipulate institutions and coalitions. Domains examined range across legal manoeuvres to control municipal governance, the politicization of cooperatives, appeals to the middle class, urban

Table 1.1 Historical periods of interest by country case

Country	Capital city	Period of dominance
Zimbabwe	Harare	1980–present (particularly 2000–20) Under ZANU-PF
Ethiopia	Addis Ababa	1991–2018 (particularly 2005–18) Under the Ethiopian People's Revolutionary Democratic Front
Uganda	Kampala	1986–present (particularly 2010–21) Under the leadership of Yoweri Museveni and the National Resistance Movement
Sri Lanka	Colombo	2005–15 and 2019–22 Under the leadership of Mahinda and Gotabaya Rajapaksa
Bangladesh	Dhaka	2009–present Under the leadership of Sheikh Hasina and the Awami League
Zambia	Lusaka	2011–21 Under the leadership of Michael Sata and Edgar Lungu and the Patriotic Front

beautification schemes, new modalities of surveillance, and the urban legacies of politicized gangsters – to name just a few. This allows us to speak to the
rich variety of strategies deployed by political elites in their attempts to dominate capital cities, and to explore the complex ways in which diverse aspects of
urban life have important political resonances. We developed a first iteration
of our analytical framework for the project and presented this for discussion
at a workshop in 2019 with all of the researchers/research teams. This led to
lively debate on the framework and several adaptations to it, as well as the
weaving of a shared conceptual language into the written case studies that
subsequently emerged.

Since this project began, some of our cases have seen dramatic political
change. Though all these chapters were intended, then, to speak to contemporary politics, in some instances they now speak primarily to recent political
history. However, the changes that have unfolded since the research was
undertaken have in all cases proved very interesting in terms of this book's
core themes, and where possible have been folded into the analysis. First of
all, in the year the project began (2018), the EPRDF government in Ethiopia
unravelled as Prime Minister Hailemariam Desalegn was forced out of office
and replaced by Abiy Ahmed, who began a programme of reform under
his new Prosperity Party. The case study in this book focuses primarily on
the period of EPRDF dominance, which ended not because of events in the
capital city (indeed, as Chapter 4 will show, the capital was quite effectively
dominated), but through a collapse of the broader political settlement. Abiy's
own capacity to dominate Ethiopia politically is far more uncertain in the
context of the civil war that subsequently broke out in late 2020.

Major changes and reversals have also unfolded in some of our other cases,
most dramatically in Sri Lanka. Unlike our other cases, Colombo has played a
marginal role in the national political settlement through much of the country's history, serving instead as a site for spectacular violence and—more
recently under the Rajapaskas—politically charged beautification. Yet economic instability and widespread claims of mismanagement led to dramatic
urban protest in 2022, the eventual occupation of the presidential palace,
and the resignation of the Rajapaksa brothers as president and prime minister. This turn of events indicates both that their strategies for political
control had failed and that, following several decades of intense urbanization, the city could indeed be the source of major historical ruptures. Our
case from Zambia initially spoke to the rising climate of authoritarianism
and the configuration of this within the capital, Lusaka, under Edgar Lungu
and the Patriotic Front (PF). Even at the time of this research, it was clear
that this attempt by the PF to maintain its political dominance was faltering,

and events certainly demonstrated this to be the case when the opposition's Hakainde Hichilema was elected as president by a landslide in 2021. All of these changes illustrate not only the dynamism of the subject under study and the fact that even the most concerted and authoritarian quests for dominance can collapse through means other than a coup or civil war, but also the gravity of what is at stake in the quest for political dominance.

1.5 Organization of the book

The book to come is organized as follows. Chapter 2 by Tom Goodfellow and David Jackman sets out the conceptual framework that was developed iteratively in conversation with the empirical case material. This guided aspects of the analysis, but was also further developed and refined in response to early presentations of the case material. The framework outlines an array of strategies deployed by political elites in their attempts to dominate. In particular, two overlapping modalities of intervention are proposed: those which are *generative* by design and those which are *repressive* by design. The chapter then presents a typology of strategies that cut across these spheres of intervention and examines an array of relevant literature which has explored these in diverse contexts. These include co-optation, legitimizing discourses, legal manoeuvres, coercive distribution, and violent coercion. The chapter thus offers a way of approaching the study of political control in capital cities.

Chapter 3, by Nansozi K. Muwanga, Paul I. Mukwaya, and Tom Goodfellow, studies the contentious politics of Uganda's capital city, Kampala, under Yoweri Museveni's National Resistance Movement (NRM). It examines how, despite the NRM's three and a half-decade-long grip on power, Kampala has stubbornly remained a source of opposition support. Museveni's government has developed a suite of strategies to control the city, ranging from legal manoeuvres to infiltrating urban informal workers and courting urban youth; yet this has generated a situation in which neither the ruling coalition nor opposition forces can effectively dominate the city. Instead, what has been reproduced repeatedly is a situation of national dominance that has evolved in character but still been vigorously resisted, and which has undermined democratic institutions in the city and fuelled state–society violence.

Chapter 4, by Eyob Gebremariam, examines the politics of dominating Addis Ababa, the capital of Ethiopia, under the EPRDF regime. Studying the period between 2005 and 2018 in particular, the chapter explains the dominance of the party as rooted in its developmentalist aspirations and generative interventions, against a backdrop of heavy repression. In particular, the party carefully managed the city's poor and unemployed youth, partly by co-opting people through cooperatives and employment programmes. Focusing in detail on the Urban Consumers' Cooperatives and successive youth employment schemes, it examines how these were designed to ensure that basic needs were met through party-political channels, as well as exploring the different ways in which city-dwellers themselves engaged (and sometimes helped initiate) these schemes.

Chapter 5, by David Jackman, examines the political dominance of Dhaka under the present Awami League government. The capital of Bangladesh has long been at the centre of political upheaval, a site of coup, mass protest, and often violent party-political confrontations. Since 2015, however, the opposition Bangladesh Nationalist Party (BNP) has largely failed to disrupt the city and the ruling party has achieved an unprecedented degree of control. This chapter traces this development to the empowerment of domestic security agencies and new forms of surveillance, which have eroded the opposition—whose ranks were also depleted by the decline in gangsters in the early 2000s. The city is also at the centre of a campaign by the ruling party to cast itself as a source of development and prosperity.

Chapter 6, by Marja Hinfelaar, Danielle Resnick, and Sishuwa Sishuwa, tracks how the PF sought to dominate Zambia's capital, Lusaka, during its terms in office between 2011 and 2021, following a very successful effort to build urban support from 2006. Lusaka was long a site for major political upheaval and became particularly important as a base for the PF. The chapter examines the PF's shifting strategies to control three important urban constituencies—the urban poor, civil society, and the middle class—strategies which veered between co-optation and repression, sometimes of the very same groups. Ultimately, this led to a massive failure to sustain the support of urban groups over time, leading to the PF losing power in the 2021 election.

Chapter 7, by JoAnn McGregor and Kudzai Chatiza, examines the politics of Harare's periphery. It argues that, rather than view capital cities as monolithic, we need to be attentive to the political importance of specific spaces. Moreover, in critically engaging with the book's analytical framework they argue that, rather than viewing dominance in terms of strategies implemented from the top down, we need to appreciate how political authority can be mutually constituted by governing elites and urban communities within certain 'dominated locales'. The chapter then traces the strategies of the ruling ZANU(PF) in the face of pressure from the Movement for Democratic Change (MDC). In the face of an opposition-supporting capital, the chapter highlights the importance of opportunities for 'generative' patronage related to land and new settlements on the city's peripheries, alongside a range of forms of repression.

Chapter 8, by Iromi Perera and Jonathan Spencer, studies the politics of Sri Lanka's capital, Colombo, in the context of the rise and reign of the Rajapaksa brothers through the 2000s and 2010s. Colombo is another opposition-leaning city, which in many ways has been marginal to the political dominance of ruling parties through the country's history, except as a site of spectacle. Under the Rajapaksas it became a site of politically targeted beautification, intended to speak to the Sinhala Buddhist new middle classes of the suburbs. Here, urban development became organized under the newly created Ministry of Defence and Urban Development, in which military capacity built from decades of civil conflict became repurposed towards politically charged urban redevelopment. This clearly delivered political dividends in the urban suburbs, as evidenced by Gotabaya Rajapaksa's success in the 2019 election, though this has subsequently proved to be a weak foundation for securing long-term political dominance.

Chapter 9, by Tom Goodfellow and David Jackman, draws together these cases to offer some broader reflections on the nature of authoritarianism and political dominance in the context of capital cities in Africa and South Asia. It returns to the question of why capital cities matter so much politically and how this varies depending on political geography, before considering the role of spaces, institutions and coalitions in strategies for urban control, and the ways in which dominance can be co-constituted by elites and urban populations. It introduces a distinction between 'persistent' and 'episodic' strategies of dominance, and considers the varying effects of external versus intra-coalitional threats to dominance. Finally, it reflects on the broader implications of the book's findings in the context of urbanization alongside rising authoritarianism worldwide, and the challenges they pose to ideas and practices of 'development'.

References

Allegra, M., Bono, I., Rokem, J., Casaglia, A., Marzorati, R., and Yacobi, H. (2013). Rethinking cities in contentious times: The mobilisation of urban dissent in the 'Arab Spring'. *Urban Studies* 50(9): 1675–1688.

Allen, J. (2003). *Lost Geographies of Power*. New York: John Wiley & Sons.

Amarasuriya, H., and Spencer, J. (2015). 'With that, discipline will also come to them': The politics of the urban poor in postwar Colombo. *Current Anthropology* 56(S11): S66–S75.

Asante, L. A., & Helbrecht, I. (2018). Seeing through African protest logics: A longitudinal review of continuity and change in protests in Ghana. *Canadian Journal of African Studies* 52(2): 159–181.

Beall, J. (2006). Cities, terrorism and development. *Journal of International Development* 18(1): 105–120.

Beall, J., Goodfellow, T., and Rodgers, D. (2013). Cities and conflict in fragile states in the developing world. *Urban Studies* 50(15): 3065–3083.

Borja, J., and Castells, M. (1997). *Local and Global: The Management of Cities in the Information Age.* London: Earthscan.

Branch, A., and Mampilly, Z. (2015). *Africa Uprising: Popular Protest and Political Change.* London: Zed Books.

Brannen, S. J., Haig, C. S., and Schmidt, K. (2020). *The Age of Mass Protests: Understanding an Escalating Global Trend.* Centre for Strategic and International Studies (CSIS), March 2020 report.

Carp, B. L. (2007). *Rebels Rising: Cities and the American Revolution.* Oxford: Oxford University Press.

Castells, M. (1983). *The City and the Grassroots: A Cross-cultural Theory of Urban Social Movements.* Berkeley, CA: University of California Press.

Cheeseman, N. (2015). *Democracy in Africa: Successes, Failures, and the Struggle for Political Reform.* Cambridge: Cambridge University Press.

Cheeseman, N., Collord, M., & Reyntjens, F. (2018). War and democracy: the legacy of conflict in East Africa. *The Journal of Modern African Studies* 56(1): 31–61.

Collord, M., Goodfellow, T., and Asante, L. A. (2021). Uneven development, politics and governance in urban Africa: An analytical literature review. African Cities Research Consortium, Working Paper no. 2, University of Manchester.

Cooper, L., & Aitchison, G. (2020). The dangers ahead: Covid-19, authoritarianism and democracy. LSE Conflict and Civil Society Research Unit, London School of Economics and Political Science.

Davis, D. E. (2016). Reflections on the relations between development and urbanization: Past trajectories and future challenges. *International Journal of Urban Sciences* 20(1): 1–14.

Diamond, L. (2002). Elections without democracy: Thinking about hybrid regimes. *Journal of Democracy* 13(2): 21–35.

Diamond, L. (2015). Facing up to the democratic recession. *Journal of Democracy* 26(1): 141–155.

Dima, B., Leitao, N. C., and Dima, S. (2011). Urbanization and democracy in the framework of modernization theory: recent empirical evidences. *Actual Problems of Economics* 10: 390–398.

Diouf, M. (1996). Urban youth and Senegalese politics: Dakar 1988–1994. *Public Culture* 8(2): 225–249.

Dorward, N., and Fox, S. (2022). Population pressure, political institutions, and protests: A multilevel analysis of protest events in African cities. *Political Geography* 99: 102762.

Dyson, T. (2013). On demographic and democratic transitions. *Population and Development Review* 38: 83–102.

EIU (2021). Democracy Index 2021: The China Challenge. London: Economist Intelligence Unit.

Finn, B. M., & Kobayashi, L. C. (2020). Structural inequality in the time of COVID-19: Urbanization, segregation, and pandemic control in sub-Saharan Africa. *Dialogues in Human Geography* 10(2), 217–220.

Fox, S. (2012). Urbanization as a global historical process: Theory and evidence from sub-Saharan Africa. *Population and Development Review* 38(2): 285–310.

Fox, S., and Bell, A. (2016). Urban geography and protest mobilization in Africa. *Political Geography* 53: 54–64.

Fox, S., and Hoelscher, K. (2012). Political order, development and social violence. *Journal of Peace Research* 49(3): 431–444.

Fox, S., and Goodfellow, T. (2022). On the conditions of 'late urbanisation'. *Urban Studies* 59(10), 1959–1980.

Frantz, Erica. (2018). Authoritarian politics: Trends and debates. *Politics and Governance* 6(2): 87–89.

Freedom House (2019). *Democracy in Retreat: Freedom in the World 2019*. New York and Washington, DC: Freedom House.

Gandhi, J. (2008). *Political Institutions under Dictatorship*. Cambridge: Cambridge University Press.

Gibson, E. L. (2013). *Boundary Control: Subnational Authoritarianism in Federal Democracies*. Cambridge: Cambridge University Press.

Getachew, A. (2019). *Worldmaking after Empire*. Princeton: Princeton University Press.

Gillespie, T. (2016). Accumulation by urban dispossession: Struggles over urban space in Accra, Ghana. *Transactions of the Institute of British Geographers* 41(1): 66–77.

Glaeser, E. L., and Steinberg, B. M. (2017). Transforming cities: Does urbanization promote democratic change? *Regional Studies* 51(1): 58–68.

Glasius, M. (2018). What authoritarianism is … and is not: A practice perspective. *International Affairs* 94(3): 515–533.

Goldman, M. (2011). Speculative urbanism and the making of the next world city. *International Journal of Urban and Regional Research* 35(3): 555–581.

Goldstein, D. M. (2004). *The Spectacular City: Violence and Performance in Urban Bolivia*. Durham, NC: Duke University Press.

Golooba-Mutebi, F., and Sjögren, A. (2017). From rural rebellions to urban riots: Political competition and changing patterns of violent political revolt in Uganda. *Commonwealth and Comparative Politics* 55(1): 22–40.

Goodfellow, T. (2014). Legal manoeuvres and violence: Law making, protest and semi-authoritarianism in Uganda. *Development and Change* 45(4): 753–776.

Goodfellow, T. (2018). Seeing political settlements through the city: A framework for comparative analysis of urban transformation. *Development and Change* 49(1): 199–222.

Goodfellow, T. (2022). Politics and the urban frontier: Transformation and divergence in late urbanizing east Africa. Oxford University Press.

Goodfellow, T., and Smith, A. (2013). From urban catastrophe to 'model' city? Politics, security and development in post-conflict Kigali. *Urban Studies* 50(15): 3185–3202.

Goodfellow, T., and Jackman, D. (2020) Ghost towns and crackdowns: the politics of urban Covid-19 control. Effective States and Inclusive Development Research Centre, University of Manchester. Available at: http://www.effective-states.org/ghost-towns-andcrackdowns-the-politics-of-urban-covid-19-control/. Accessed 4 May 2023.

Meehan, P., and Goodhand, J. (2018). Spatialising political settlements. *Accord* 4: 14–19.

Gore, C. D., and Muwanga, N. K. (2014). Decentralization is dead, long live decentralization! Capital city reform and political rights in Kampala, Uganda. *International Journal of Urban and Regional Research* 38(6): 2201–2216.

Graham, S. (2011). *Cities under Siege: The New Military Urbanism*. London and New York: Verso.

Gray, H. (2018). *Turbulence and Order in Economic Development: Institutions and Economic Transformation in Tanzania and Vietnam*. Oxford: Oxford University Press.

Greene, K. F. (2010). A resource theory of single-party dominance. In M. Bogaards and F. Boucek (eds), *Dominant Political Parties and Democracy: Concepts, Measures, Cases and Comparisons*. London: Routledge, pp. 155–174.

Harvey, D. (2003). The right to the city. *International Journal of Urban and Regional Research* 27(4): 939–941.

Heater, D. (2004). *A Brief History of Citizenship*. Edinburgh: Edinburgh University Press.

Herbst, J. (2014). *States and Power in Africa: Comparative Lessons in Authority and Control*. Princeton, NJ: Princeton University Press.

Holston, J., and Appadurai, A. (1996). Cities and citizenship. *Public Culture* 8: 187–204.

Jackman, D. (2018a). The decline of gangsters and politicisation of violence in urban Bangladesh. *Development and Change* 50(5): 1214–1238.

Jackman, D. (2018b). Violent intermediaries and political order in Bangladesh. *European Journal of Development Research* 31(4): 705–723.

Jones, G. A., and Corbridge, S. (2010). The continuing debate about urban bias: The thesis, its critics, its influence and its implications for poverty-reduction strategies. *Progress in Development Studies* 10(1): 1–18.

Karduni, A., and Sauda, E. (2020). Anatomy of a protest: Spatial information, social media, and urban space. *Social Media + Society* 6(1): 2056305119897320.

Kelsall, T. (2018). Towards a universal political settlement concept: A response to Mushtaq Khan. *African Affairs* 117(469): 656–669.

Kelsall, T., Schulz, N., Ferguson, W. D., vom Hau, M., Hickey, S., and Levy, B. (2022). *Political Settlements and Development: Theory, Evidence, Implications.* Oxford University Press.

Khan, M. H. (2010). *Political Settlements and the Governance of Growth-Enhancing Institutions.* London: SOAS.

Khan, M. H. (2018). Political settlements and the analysis of institutions. *African Affairs* 117(469): 636–655.

Kniknie, S., & Büscher, K. (2023). Rebellious Riots: Entangled Geographies of Contention in Africa. In *Rebellious Riots.* Brill, pp. 1–22.

Koren, O. (2017). Why insurgents kill civilians in capital cities: A disaggregated analysis of mechanisms and trends. *Political Geography* 61: 237–252.

Lachapelle, J., Levitsky, S., Way, L. A., and Casey, A. E. (2020). Social revolution and authoritarian durability. *World Politics* 72(4): 557–600.

Lambright, G. M. (2014). Opposition politics and urban service delivery in Kampala, Uganda. *Development Policy Review* 32(s1): s39–s60.

LeBas, A. (2011). *From Protest to Parties: Party-building and Democratization in Africa.* Oxford: Oxford University Press.

Levitsky, S., and Way, L. A. (2010). *Competitive Authoritarianism: Hybrid Regimes after the Cold War.* Cambridge: Cambridge University Press.

Levitsky, S., and Way, L.A. (2012). *Competitive Authoritarianism: Hybrid Regimes after the Cold War.* Cambridge University Press.

McGregor, J., and Chatiza, K. (2019). Frontiers of urban control: Lawlessness on the city edge and forms of clientelist statecraft in Zimbabwe. *Antipode* 51(5): 1554–1580.

Magaloni, B., and Kricheli, R. (2010). Political order and one-party rule. *Annual Review of Political Science* 13: 123–143.

Mitlin, D. (2018). Beyond contention: Urban social movements and their multiple approaches to secure transformation. *Environment and Urbanization* 30(2): 557–574.

Mkandawire, T. (2002). The terrible toll of post-colonial 'rebel movements' in Africa: towards an explanation of the violence against the peasantry. *The Journal of Modern African Studies* 40(2): 181–215.

Mkandawire, T. (2005). Maladjusted African economies and globalisation. *Africa Development* 30(1): 1–33.

Myers, G. A. (2003). *Verandahs of Power: Colonialism and Space in Urban Africa*. Syracuse, NY: Syracuse University Press.

Nedal, D., Stewart, M., and Weintraub, M. (2020). Urban concentration and civil war. *Journal of Conflict Resolution* 64(6): 1146–1171.

Nicholls, W. J. (2008). The urban question revisited: The importance of cities for social movements. *International Journal of Urban and Regional Research* 32(4): 841–859.

Njoh, A. J. (2009). Urban planning as a tool of power and social control in colonial Africa. *Planning Perspectives* 24(3): 301–317.

North, D. C., Wallis, J. J., and Weingast, B. R. (2009). *Violence and Social Orders: A Conceptual Framework for Interpreting Recorded Human History*. New York: Cambridge University Press.

Pepinsky, T. (2014). The institutional turn in comparative authoritarianism. *British Journal of Political Science* 44(3): 631–653.

Pickvance, C. (2003). From urban social movements to urban movements: A review and introduction to a symposium on urban movements. *International Journal of Urban and Regional Research* 27(1): 102–109.

Pierskalla, J. H. (2016). The politics of urban bias: Rural threats and the dual dilemma of political survival. *Studies in Comparative International Development* 51: 286–307.

Policzer, P. (2009). *The Rise and Fall of Repression in Chile*. Notre Dame, IN: University of Notre Dame Press.

Prempeh, H. K. (2008). Progress and retreat in Africa: presidents untamed. *Journal of Democracy* 19(2): 109–123.

Pritchett, L., Sen, K., and Werker, E. (eds) (2017). *Deals and Development: The Political Dynamics of Growth Episodes*. Oxford: Oxford University Press.

Putzel, J., and Di John, J. (2012). *Meeting the Challenges of Crisis States*. CSRC Report. London: Crisis Studies Research Centre, LSE.

Randall, V., and Svåsand, L. (2002). Political parties and democratic consolidation in Africa. *Democratization* 9(3): 30–52.

Resnick, D. (2014a). *Urban Poverty and Party Populism in African Democracies*. Cambridge: Cambridge University Press.

Resnick, D. (2014b). Urban governance and service delivery in African cities: The role of politics and policies. *Development Policy Review* 32(s1): s3–s17.

Rodgers, D. (2007). Slum wars of the 21st century: The new geography of conflict in Central America. Working Paper no. 10, series 2, Crisis States Research Centre, LSE.

Rollason, W. (2013). Performance, poverty and urban development: Kigali's motari and the spectacle city. *Afrika Focus* 26(2): 9–29.

Scarnecchia, T. (2008). *The Urban roots of Democracy and Political Violence in Zimbabwe: Harare and Highfield, 1940–1964*. Rochester, NY: University of Rochester Press.

Schatz, E. (2004). What capital cities say about state and nation building. *Nationalism and Ethnic Politics* 9(4): 111–140.

Sidel, J. T. (2014). Economic foundations of subnational authoritarianism: Insights and evidence from qualitative and quantitative research. *Democratization* 21(1): 161–184.

Simandan, D., Rinner, C., and Capurri, V. (2023). The academic left, human geography, and the rise of authoritarianism during the COVID-19 pandemic. *Geografiska Annaler: Series B, Human Geography*, 1–21.

Slater, D. (2010). *Ordering Power: Contentious Politics and Authoritarian Leviathans in Southeast Asia*. Cambridge: Cambridge University Press.

Snyder, R. (2001). Scaling down: The subnational comparative method. *Studies in Comparative International Development* 36(1): 93–110.

Snyder, R. (2006). Beyond electoral authoritarianism: The spectrum of nondemocratic regimes. In A. Schedler (ed.), *Electoral Authoritarianism: The Dynamics of Unfree Competition*. Boulder, CO: Lynne Rienner Publishers, pp. 219–231.

Stokes, S., Dunning, T., Nazareno, M., and Brusco, V. (2013). *Brokers, Voters and Clientelism: The Puzzle of Distributive Politics*. Cambridge: Cambridge University Press.

Stokols, A. (2022). From the square to the shopping mall: New social media, state surveillance, and the evolving geographies of urban protest. *Urban Geography* (online first): https://doi.org/10.1080/02723638.2022.2056366.

Svolik, M. W. (2012). *The Politics of Authoritarian Rule*. Cambridge: Cambridge University Press.

Themnér, A., and Utas, M. (2016). Governance through brokerage: Informal governance in post-civil war societies. *Civil Wars* 18(3): 255–280.

Therborn, G. (2017). *Cities of Power: The Urban, the National, the Popular, the Global*. London: Verso.

Tilly, C. (1992). *Coercion, Capital and European States, AD 990–1992*. Oxford: Blackwell Publishing.

Tilly, C., and Tarrow, S. G. (2007). *Contentious Politics*. Oxford: Oxford University Press.

Traugott, M. (1995). Capital cities and revolution. *Social Science History* 19(1): 147–168.

Uitermark, J., Nicholls, W., and Loopmans, M. (2013). Cities and social movements: Theorizing beyond the right to the city. *Environment and Planning A* 44: 2546–2554.

Valizadeh, P., and Iranmanesh, A. (2021). Covid-19: Magnifying pre-existing urban problems. *Fennia-International Journal of Geography* 199(2): 260–272.

Wallace, J. (2014). *Cities and Stability: Urbanization, Redistribution, and Regime Survival in China*. Oxford: Oxford University Press.

Wallace, J. (2019). Authoritarian turnover and change in comparative perspective. *Oxford Research Encyclopedias: Politics*. Available at: https://doi.org/10.1093/acrefore/9780190228637.013.636, accessed 31 March 2023.

Watson, V. (2009). 'The planned city sweeps the poor away …': Urban planning and 21st century urbanisation. *Progress in Planning* 72(3): 151–193.

Whitfield, L., Therkildsen, O., Buur, L., and Kjær, A. M. (2015). *The Politics of African Industrial Policy: A Comparative Perspective*. Cambridge: Cambridge University Press.

Wintrobe, R. (2018). An economic theory of a hybrid (competitive authoritarian or illiberal) regime. *Public Choice* 177(3–4): 217–233.

Wolf, E. (1969). *Peasant Wars of the Twentieth Century*. New York: Harper and Row.

Yiftachel, O. (2009). Theoretical notes on 'gray cities': The coming of urban apartheid? *Planning Theory* 8(1): 88–100.

2

Generativity and repression

Strategies for urban control

Tom Goodfellow and David Jackman

2.1 Conceptualizing dominance strategies

The literature on authoritarian rule is replete with examples of the different strategies and tactics used by authoritarian regimes to attempt to achieve and maintain dominance. Some forms of the exercise of power work through the explicit threat of negative sanctions or the use of violence, while others involve forms of suggestion, persuasion, and manipulation, sometimes with intent concealed (Allen 2003). Authoritarian rulers have always experimented with different combinations of repressive measures and material and symbolic benefits, with varying degrees of depth and success (Cheeseman 2015). Attempts to conceptualize across the diverse strategies and tactics deployed in authoritarian regimes to seek and sustain political dominance are rare, though a few recent contributions are worthy of note. Cheeseman and Klaas (2018) examine the variety of tactics in the authoritarian 'toolbox' in the context of elections, but given their specific focus on election-rigging they do not explore the broader dimensions of the production and maintenance of political dominance. Slater and Fenner (2011) see authoritarian durability as resting on four 'infrastructural mechanisms' used for political control. These are: coercion, both violent and subtle; revenue extraction; systems for 'registering citizens', thereby making citizens 'legible'; and finally cultivating dependence in the form of patronage or state services (ibid. 20–24). More fundamentally, a common approach to conceptualizing strategies for dominance is to subsume a wide range of political interventions within two overarching categories of 'co-optation' and 'repression'. The former refers to the securing of support (or at least acquiescence) through distributing benefits, and the latter encompasses any interventions involving force, the threat of force, or the withholding of benefits (see e.g. Kelsall et al. 2022). For Gerschewski (2013), strategies of legitimation

Tom Goodfellow and David Jackman, *Generativity and repression*. In: *Controlling the Capital*. Edited by: Tom Goodfellow and David Jackman, Oxford University Press. © Oxford University Press (2023). DOI: 10.1093/oso/9780192868329.003.0002 constitute a third 'pillar of authoritarian stabilization', alongside co-optation and repression.

We draw to varying extents on these approaches, but in our focus on building and maintaining dominance in capital cities we seek to provide a more granular and tailored typology, while also highlighting dynamics of dominance that have particular resonance in urban areas. Clearly the range of strategies and tactics deployed in pursuit of dominance includes blunt methods, such as violence and intimidation, and co-optation through public, private, and 'club' goods provision. But it also involves more subtle forms of cooperative and symbolic appeals to particular groups, legal and administrative changes that manipulate the institutional environment in which opposition groups must contend, the mobilization of discourses to legitimize dominance and discredit the very idea of competitive politics, and overt as well as covert forms of surveillance. In this sense, while the distinction between co-optation and repression is useful as a starting point, it does not adequately capture the full range of more nuanced and hybrid forms of dominance-building, or some of the distinctive ways in which co-optation and repression can intersect and overlap.

Recognizing the value of the co-optation/repression binary as a 'high level' starting point for analysis, we too begin with a two-way distinction but frame this instead in terms of two overlapping modalities of intervention that we term *generative* and *repressive*. In using 'generative' instead of 'co-optive', we relegate co-optation to a specific strategy within a broader range of generative approaches (as defined below). Yet we also seek to highlight more directly the creative versus destructive intentionality that lies behind strategies for dominance, as well as how in practice some strategies can both generate support and repress opposition simultaneously. We define these terms in the following ways:

- *Generative* interventions involve efforts actively to create or bolster sources of support through explicit or implicit appeals to certain groups of urban residents: for example, through including them in a political party position, making public investments to win over an urban constituency, distributing selective 'club' goods or private goods, mobilizing particular discourses, and fostering new coalitions or new forms of symbolic recognition for particular groups.
- *Repressive* interventions are explicitly intended to destroy or undermine some source of opposition. This broadly captures forms of expulsion and population dispersal, surveillance, closure of political space, legislation against political activism, arbitrary arrest, and state-sanctioned violence used to undermine political opposition.

These are 'ideal types', and we need to qualify their use a number of ways. First, they are not mutually exclusive and in practice the strategies and actions deployed by ruling elites can often incorporate elements of each (Gerschewski 2013), hence we see them as overlapping spheres that allow for hybrid forms. A particular social group such as an armed militia or vigilante association may be co-opted and bolstered as part of a generative strategy, while being put to use for the express purpose of repressing another group. Second, while the terms 'generative' and 'repressive' are ways of characterizing strategies, the *outcomes* of these are rarely straightforward and are experienced differentially by different groups. For example, a generative strategy designed to co-opt the elite within a particular social group or economic sector may have the effect of repressing other members of that group. Alternatively, a campaign to repress a particular social minority may have the consequences (intended or otherwise) of generating support among a different group. A repressive intervention for one actor can then be generative with respect to another. The effect of such actions may also change over time—for example, what appears to be a generative intervention can take a markedly more repressive turn as it plays out.

Third, it is important to acknowledge also that the objects of such repressive and generative interventions are not only actors outside the ruling coalition— that is, those we might collectively term 'opposition' groups. Lower-level actors *within* a coalition can attempt to disrupt elites or others to improve their status, and elites in the coalition may rely on repressive or generative interventions to contain lower-level actors. Ruling elites will use these in differing measures and combinations, depending on the 'disruptive potential' of groups both inside and outside the ruling coalition (Kelsall et al. 2022). In fact, as Kelsall et al. (2022: 52) note, the 'social foundation' underpinning a given political settlement often involves groups that are repressed and co-opted in roughly equal measure. Both supporters and opponents of a given ruling coalition can therefore be subject to generative and repressive measures at given points in time, depending on their relative power and the nature of the threat they pose to the ruling coalition's dominance.

Despite these important qualifications, distinguishing between interventions primarily targeted at building new support and those focused on undermining opposition can be analytically useful, since this distinction has real-world implications for urban development outcomes and how they are perceived and experienced. It is, however, important to continually subject such dichotomies to scrutiny and – having set them up as an overarching logic – break them down in ways that align more with reality. A two-way distinction is insufficient to capture the range of forms of intervention that are commonly seen in the pursuit of dominance, particularly given the above caveats. We therefore present five strategies for dominance that embody and sometimes transect generativity and repression, while also going beyond the three-way distinction offered by Gerschewski (2013). We feel it is important to introduce several further categories for two main reasons. First, unlike Gerschewski, we are not concerned with authoritarian stability but rather with dominance—and some of the strategies we outline can be quite destabilizing, even as they work to increase dominance. Second, given our particular focus on urban contexts, the institutional complexity and nature of goods provision in urban areas motivates us to introduce further categories to maximize the utility of our framework as an interpretive tool for exploring how strategies for dominance play out in urban space.

The five types of dominance strategy in our typology are *violent coercion*, *coercive distribution*, *co-optation*, *legal manoeuvres*, and *legitimizing discourses*. As noted above, we see some of these as corresponding to more 'purely' generative forms (such as co-optation) and some that are overwhelmingly repressive in intent (violent coercion). In between these poles, however, are strategies that contain elements of both generativity and repression, or do not easily sit within either of these modalities. Below we outline each of these five strategies in turn, and in so doing we discuss some of the more specific tactics and approaches deployed within each.

2.2 Violent coercion

A key repressive strategy utilized to contain rivals is violence, and specifically the use or threat of violence to coerce people into acquiescing to the rule of a particular group or coalition. People are coerced in varied ways, which differ in 'intensity' (Levitsky and Way 2010), including through direct intimidation and acts, but also through techniques such as surveillance, government programmes, and urban design. Coercion need not always be violent—or, at least, the violence that underpins it need not be enacted. The threat of violence is often itself sufficient to coerce (Tilly 2003), and at times even this may not be necessary, where violence can exist 'latent' in society (Jackman 2019). Although central to political dominance, the organization of coercive institutions and actors is often highly intricate and rarely explored in depth (Greitens 2016; Khisa and Day 2020; Tapscott 2021). In our framework, we distinguish between 'violent coercion'—which, even where violence need not be explicitly enacted, involves force or the threat of it as a purely repressive measure to generate fear, subservience, and acquiescence—and 'coercive distribution' (discussed in Section 2.3), in which the repressive element of coercion is *combined* with a generative element of public goods provision.

We know surprisingly little about how violence is organized in authoritarian settings, and even less about the varied and specific forms this can take in socio-economically and institutionally complex urban areas. The nature of urban violence in authoritarian contexts is in part shaped by the character of 'violence specialists', the political economy in which they are embedded, and the available ways in which violence can be deployed by elites to achieve dominance (LeBas 2013; Jackman 2018a). Cities typically contain a wide array of actors using violence entrepreneurially to seek power at different scales. These range from gangsters and mafia, to militia, defence forces, political factions, and state security agencies. Very often, such figures are interlinked and interdependent, such that even ostensibly criminal actors such as gangsters can in fact be considered part of the ruling coalition (Jackman 2018a), although it is acknowledged that such relationships differ widely between contexts (Arias 2017). At times, ruling coalitions need to deploy, empower, and disempower such actors strategically in specific combinations, in order to confront opposition or neutralize potential threats. Attention then needs to be given to who precisely within the ruling coalition is the source of violence and coercion, and how the organization of this changes. At the same time, where the state enrols violence specialists in the form of urban gangs, vigilantes, and ethnic militias, it is important to recognize that these organizations are also local in the way that they operate, with gangs' local 'social sovereignty' often coexisting with state sovereignty (Rodgers 2006). As LeBas (2013) notes, shared ethnic identity, popular legitimacy, or other forms of embedding in local culture can act as constraints on local armed actors' behaviour, though it is precisely these that are undermined, the more that such groups are drawn into national political struggles.

The coercive tools deployed by state agencies and the range of specialists they enrol may be clear and blunt, in the form of arrests, intimidation, disappearances, killings, and the suppression of protestors; yet they are often more complex, and can involve surveillance, community policing, and the design of cities themselves. The threat of urban violence, and particularly terrorism, has created worldwide what Graham (2011) describes as a 'military urbanism', a militarized response to controlling urban spaces, involving the 'radical ratcheting-up of techniques of tracking, surveillance and targeting' (ibid. 21). As modes of warfare have shifted with the growth of terrorism and insurgency, cities have become a primary battleground, such that contemporary warfare increasingly 'takes place in supermarkets, tower blocks, subway tunnels, and industrial districts rather than open fields, jungles or deserts' (ibid. 14–15; Konaev and Spencer 2018). Even where open urban warfare seems remote, ruling coalitions have a heightened awareness of the opportunities that urban areas provide for opposition forces to mobilize revolt. The state response to the threat of urban insurrection has been to blur the traditional boundaries between military, intelligence, and policing. New technologies are developed to track potential threats, at times building on existing datasets and technologies used for corporate and transport purposes (Graham 2011: 25). Even without the use of extensive high-tech instruments, the deployment of local institutions and involvement of a range of non-state actors and organizations in gathering intelligence and generalizing the threat of coercion is sometimes highly effective in maintaining dominance, as the case of urban Rwanda demonstrates (Lamarque 2020).

At times, coercion is even built into the design of a city itself. Urban planning can be explicitly used to counter the threat of insurgency and unrest. In nineteenth-century Paris, barricades of rubbish, furniture, and street paving became a common tool in the repertoire of contentious politics, sheltering the city's many narrow streets and alleyways against the authority of the state (Traugott 1995; Scott 1998). In response, much of the city was rebuilt in the now classic Haussmannian boulevards, which were harder to barricade, thus making it easier to assert state power (Scott 1998: 60–61). Following the Mumbai riots in the early 1990s, when the Muslim community effectively barricaded a neighbourhood, new infrastructure was built to counter this (Gupte 2017). In Cairo's Tahrir Square, which was occupied by tens and later hundreds of thousands of protestors prior to the 2011 revolution, blockades and gates now guard key entry points and government offices have been relocated (Beier 2018). Across the colonized world more generally, the use of wide streets and the elimination of many narrow alleyways, as well as construction of domineering architectural forms for government buildings, have been used by imperial powers to limit the scope for clandestine political mobilization while also projecting the threat of coercion (Myers 2003; Njoh 2009). These examples form part of a more general pattern of 'infrastructural violence', through which urban infrastructures are part of the repertoire of urban coercion (Rodgers and O'Neill 2012). Forms of administration, such as censuses, can similarly support the ability of a ruling coalition to track and manipulate its population (Scott 1998; Wallace 2014), countering the inherent complexity of cities, which by virtue of architecture and density can offer places to hide and mobilize.

2.3 Coercive distribution

To provide for nuanced analyses of the ways in which coercion can play out in strategies for dominance, we distinguish between violent coercion itself and forms of what have been termed 'coercive distribution' (Albertus et al. 2018). This is the idea that authoritarian states often deploy widespread distribution of resources as a means of bolstering their strength, having the effect of 'cultivating dependence and curtailing subjects' exit options' (ibid. 2). This is distinct from the forms of violence identified above, because it does not necessarily involve acts of violence, or even the threat of violence, and—importantly—has a generative as well as repressive dimension. Forms of administration such as censuses and surveillance (increasingly through digital means), as noted above, can also provide the foundations for coercive distribution, by enabling the state to 'know' its population in greater detail and thereby target forms of distribution that could engender dependency on, for example, dominant-party institutions. In some cases, security provision itself can also be seen as a form of coercive distribution, with the 'public good' of urban security effectively depending on party membership or allegiance. Social policies, including for example targeted social assistance and youth livelihood programmes, can be used to this effect (Gebremariam 2017; Esen and Gumuscu 2021).

Recent work on 'globalized authoritarianism' similarly argues that ostensibly inclusive urban development programmes targeting the urban poor can in fact serve as the means to control potentially disruptive urban constituencies, and adapt the population and geography of cities to neoliberal globalization and authoritarian rule (Bogaert 2018). In the Moroccan context, slums had been a source of violence and contentious politics, and in response, attempts at urban renewal have been implemented, partly in partnership with international donors. Bogaert argues that such programmes have two aims: first, to control a potentially dangerous population group; and, second, to create a citizen in the image of a neoliberal entrepreneurial figure. As such, they constitute a technique of government control. State authoritarianism, then, not only is constituted by more conventional sources of authority and loyalty, such as patrimonialism, but also 'lies in the class projects of urban renewal, slum upgrading, poverty alleviation, gentrification, structural adjustment, market liberalization, market integration, foreign capital investment, and the creation of a good business climate' (ibid. 253).

In Turkey, meanwhile, the slide from democracy into authoritarianism under the Justice and Development Party (AKP) involved not only heightened repression but also the distribution of public resources in ways that reduced the costs of repression, because the recipients of these resources fear the loss of benefit flows if there is regime change (Esen and Gumuscu 2021). Thus, the tools of coercive distribution represent an important additional instrument for the consolidation of dominance—and one which is often facilitated by the context of a 'liberalized' economy and the movement of foreign capital. These examples from Morocco and Turkey also illustrate the ways in which coercive distribution is often associated with the urban poor, whose dual qualities as potential mobilizers of opposition and constituents in need of livelihood opportunities and cash are particularly pronounced.

2.4 Co-optation

Violence and coercion are costly for ruling coalitions, with significant potential consequences for their perceived legitimacy, both domestically and abroad. While forms of coercive distribution that attempt to lever certain groups into the 'social foundation' of a ruling elite's dominance can help to address this legitimacy deficit, a softer strategy used to placate potential opposition involves outright co-optation. This essentially refers to a 'purer' generative process by which some benefit is conferred on a potentially threatening group, incentivizing them to cooperate. As Kelsall (2018: 7–8) argues,

> Assuming the repression of large groups is costly, we hypothesise that the broader and deeper the society's potentially disruptive groups, the more likely it is that the government will make co-optation its dominant strategy.

Co-optation (also known as co-option) takes many different forms, relating to factors including the character of the actors or groups involved, the ways in which they organized, whether the threat they pose is manifest or potential, and what precisely they can bring to the coalition. Co-optation can, then, include processes as diverse as the distribution of formal political power through the creation of government jobs, ideological concessions relating to the place of religion in society, and the informal 'buying off' of key groups with disruptive potential through promises of future benefits and favours. Again, in distinguishing this from coercive distribution above it is important to note that these benefit flows need not always be linked to threats of coercion, to party membership, or to the institutionalization of dependency.

A fundamental tool for co-optation, even in authoritarian states, is the electoral process, which can provide an opportunity for the redistribution of access to state and market resources to actors, by bringing them into the ruling coalition. Even beyond elections, the elevation of people from key constituencies into positions of power to create a sufficiently inclusive 'elite bargain' to maintain stability is an often crucial modality of co-optation (Lindemann 2008). As the organizational power of groups shifts over time, such adjustments can be made necessary to ensure balance within the ruling coalition. This occurs at different scales, relating to micro negotiations within political constituencies, as well as large political parties or ethnic groups. However small, such negotiations can be crucial, as coalitions are built of such groups and these negotiations ultimately have wider affects within the coalition. Policy concessions can also represent an important tool for co-optation (Gandhi and Przeworski 2006), and one form these can take is placating particular ideological interests—for example, appealing to a religious or ethnic group by promoting their beliefs and identity in public ways.

Others have directly measured co-optation in terms of government spending (Fjelde and De Soysa 2009), and this does represent a prominent and often relatively transparent way in which advantages can be conferred onto specific groups. This is particularly important in urban areas where demands for services are greater, as also is the need for coercive force and the bureaucracy to sustain it. In addition to official social protection programmes, such as those in Ethiopia and Rwanda (Lavers and Hickey 2016), facilitating access to other kinds of private and 'club' goods can also operate as effective means of co-optation. In the urban context, the provision of housing accessible to particular groups, for example, can help to maintain a political settlement (Croese 2017; Planel and Bridonneau 2017). Given the potential threat that the broader 'public' pose to the ruling coalition, capable of mobilizing independently on the streets or providing new support to potential opposition, public policy driven towards improving general life conditions (be they economic, health, security, and so on) can have the effect of co-opting key elements of the population.

A concept closely related to that of co-option is clientelism,[1] which is central to the achievement and maintenance of dominance in many, if not most, states the world over. Clientelism is a system through which benefits are conferred by people in positions of political power, conditional on recipients returning these favours with votes or some other form of political support (Stokes et al. 2013). It thus involves particularistic institutions of reciprocal exchange based on asymmetric power relations (Kitschelt 2000; Hicken 2011). Despite its ubiquity, we do not include clientelism as a strategy for dominance, because it is an institutional modality of reciprocal exchange,

---

[1] Some literature uses the two terms virtually interchangeably (see e.g. Cross 1998).

rather than a *strategy* as such. Indeed, as noted by Josua (2016: 36), 'clientelism cannot be seen as being equivalent to co-optation, as the former denotes a general pattern of social organization (patron–client relations), while the latter is a strategy of political rule'. Clientelism can involve the mutual construction of legitimate authority at community level rather than necessarily being driven from above (Paller 2019). Co-optation is thus a strategy that can generate new forms of clientelism, but the two are conceptually distinct.

Reflecting on the relationship between co-optation and clientelism serves as a reminder that the nature of the power relations in a patron–client relationship can vary substantially, with very different degrees of leverage for the client group and varying degrees of active agency in constructing the patron–client relationship. In some cases, the client group itself plays a significant role in initiating a clientelistic relationship, which it uses to try and leverage benefits from politicians (Goodfellow and Titeca 2012). Often the benefits leveraged may not be in the form of financial resources, but rather 'forbearance'—defined as the 'intentional and revocable nonenforcement of law' (Holland 2016), through which politicians withhold sanctions and facilitate the breach of regulations in their pursuit of political support. Indeed, co-optation as a generative modality need not take the form of active 'handouts'—for example, of cash, benefits, or jobs—but often takes the form 'negative inducements' (Post 2018), such as the selective suspension of the law, and various forms of 'discretionary enforcement' of policies and regulations.[2]

The question of differing degrees of agency in initiating a clientelistic relationship also leads us to draw a distinction within the 'co-optation' category between *passive co-optation* and *cooperative empowerment*. Definitions of co-optation usually imply a degree of assimilation by the ruling elite—that is, that the co-opted person or group should use their resources 'in line with the ruling elite's demands' (Gerschewski 2013: 22). Co-optation therefore refers to a situation in which the initiators 'do not want the advice of the co-opted, merely his or her endorsement' (Kotter and Schlesinger 1979: 111). Co-optation is also often used to refer to the 'buying off' of other elites, or the leaders of particular groups (Gerschewski 2013), rather than to more subaltern groups with less institutionalized power. In all these cases, the people being co-opted are themselves relatively passive in the process. Yet in some cases a clientelist relationship is co-created both by a ruling elite strategizing to co-opt new groups into its coalition and by a group seeking to gain greater

---

[2] See Collord et al. (2021) for an extensive discussion of these different modalities of clientelism.

voice or access to resources. Moreover, the latter may succeed in building their power or resources through this process, albeit within a situation of fundamental unequal power relations. The idea of 'cooperative empowerment' thus attempts to capture situations in which those targeted by a strategy are not only assimilated or 'bought off' by the ruling elite, but actually manage to gain some increased leverage for their own agendas through this interaction. This could involve the group in question playing a significant role in initiating a cooperative endeavour with the ruling coalition, which is possible by virtue of the potential power or value that it represents to the coalition. In this regard, rather than being brought into the coalition and *losing* independent power in the process, both the ruling coalition and the group in question gain in power through this process.

There is thus a subtle but important difference between 'passive co-optation', in which those co-opted yield to the co-opters' agenda in exchange for continued access to benefits, and these more empowering and agenda-shaping forms of cooperation. Both can be broadly thought of as primarily generative, rather than repressive strategies, in that they create opportunities and bring groups into a broader coalition, rather than merely repressing opposition forces.[3] The point is to allow for a distinction between subsuming people into an existing elite agenda and actually building on shared interests between dominance-seeking elites and groups whose support they desire and who possess some degree of power, often latently by virtue of their numbers and/or disruptive potential. In some cases, the exertion of interests by a client group might be highly informal, resulting in 'forbearance' by savvy elites seeking votes through favours; in others, cooperative empowerment may be more formal—for example, where an organized urban group lobbies for and manages to gain inclusion in particular decision-making or gain access to certain resources.

2.5 Legal manoeuvres

The above categories demonstrate the extent to which coercion and co-optation are broad and encompass a wide range of forms, as well as overlapping through 'coercive distribution'. Yet, despite this breadth, there are other varieties of dominance strategy that require a distinct conceptualization and analysis. The law is used in many different ways in the pursuit of dominance, most obviously through forms of repression (such as legal constraints on

---

[3] We do accept, however, that clientelism as an institutional form can be thought of as having repressive aspects (Auyero 2001; Wood 2003).

freedom of assembly) and generative inducement (such as the changing of land laws to benefit a particular group or the strengthening of a particular minority's rights). However, our category of 'legal manoeuvres' is intended also to capture the dimension of legal and formal institutional processes that go beyond measures obviously intended either to repress or to co-opt. Legal processes and instruments sometimes constitute hybrid strategies that, through repressing or threatening particular social groups, intentionally give out political signals to bolster support among other groups. In some cases, it has been argued that particular laws and the public debates around them have been deployed to stimulate resistance or violence on the part of certain groups, in order to stigmatize them (Goodfellow 2014). Moreover, strategies for dominance may also utilize legislative processes to shift the balance of legal powers between different tiers of the state under conditions of decentralization, and between legislative and executive arms (Prempeh 2008). This can be particularly relevant in urban areas that have many tiers of government present simultaneously, some of them often controlled by opposition.

This subcategory of legislative processes to restructure institutional relations is a distinctive aspect of the broader category of legal manoeuvres, and one which is neither necessarily coercive nor co-optive; instead, such a strategy aims specifically at *manipulating the political arena* by creating obstacles, delays, and institutional frustration that limit the organizational capacities of rival coalitions without overt repression. This can involve central governments attempting to sow confusion about roles and responsibilities and to disable and discredit local authorities run by political opposition. Drawing on Resnick's (2014b) analysis of 'strategies of subversion', these kinds of manoeuvres can be political (e.g. central governments increasing their ability to place central appointees in positions of power over local authorities), administrative (central governments divesting local authorities of responsibilities previously decentralized to them), and fiscal (limiting the tax-raising capacities, and therefore the authority, of opposition-run councils).

Some legal manoeuvres operate in more nuanced ways, seeking to produce outcomes indirectly, with their political intent concealed behind official discourses. As demonstrated in the case of Uganda, legal manoeuvres can involve the use of the legislative process itself, and other democratic institutions, to enact carrot-and-stick modalities of control (Makara 2010; Goodfellow 2014; Collord 2016). This involves allowing an element of democratic process and debate, which can influence the political climate, before ultimately attempting to exert authoritarian control over the process (albeit incompletely given limited party institutionalisation) (LeBas 2011; Collord 2016; Khisa 2019). Affording some democratic 'voice' through legislative processes that are then undermined through informal structures of power can constitute an important means of manipulating, and thus weakening, groups that threaten the ruling coalition. This resonates with studies of the use of law in authoritarian settings that emphasize the 'malleable, situational, and plural nature of legal power' (Chua 2019: 355), which often contributes not just to harsh forms of legal repression but also to forms of 'soft authoritarianism' (Mohamed Nasir and Turner 2013). Again, capital cities provide especially fertile terrain for such manoeuvres given the complex overlapping spheres of legal-institutional authority and multiple tiers of government.

The decision to grant certain urban areas the administrative status of 'city' can also serve political functions, creating new patronage opportunities or administrative levers as well as an enhanced legal commitment to infrastructure and services in those areas. At the more dramatic end of this kind of intervention is the surprisingly common decision by elites to entirely move a nation's capital, often to a distant and remote location. It is estimated that worldwide since the First World War, such an event takes place on average every six years, with examples from every continent, as diverse as Myanmar, Brazil, Tanzania, and Kazakhstan (Campante et al. 2015: 6–7). Up to 30 per cent of capital cities are today outside of society's largest city (Potter 2017). The rationale for moving capital cities differs for many developing nations, but often centres around the imperative to marginalize or disempower rivals and consolidate authority through patronage networks in the process of state-building. Recent econometric analyses have also suggested a relationship between capital cities and the concentration of intrastate violence; hence an occasional strategy deployed by fearful governments is to move the capital itself in order to reduce violent threats to the regime, often to a remote and secure location (Campante et al. 2015). Given the association between cities and opposition groups, an outcome of relocating capital cities away from a society's primary city can be the weakening of the hold that interest groups associated with that city have on state power, and equally the empowerment of other groups within society, increasing the ability of a state to resolve civil conflict. It has been argued that there is a correlation between this arrangement and reduced civil conflict (Potter 2017), and an association between moving capital cities and authoritarianism (Schatz 2004: 118).

2.6 Legitimizing discourses

Achieving dominance requires the weakening of the organizational power of rivals to the extent that they are unable to challenge the ruling coalition significantly. The capacity for coercion is necessary, but insufficient, for this—indeed, 'No government exclusively based on the means of violence has ever existed' (Arendt 1969: 50)—and combinations of coercion and co-optation may also not do the job on their own. Crucially, dominance also requires discourse and ideology to render an elite's rule moral, and thereby provide a legitimacy to its actions—as is increasingly noted in the 'authoritarian durability' literature (Ngoun 2022). This is not to relegate the importance of ideology to simply bolstering the organizational power of a coalition, but to recognize that this is one important role it can play. We therefore include a category of 'legitimizing discourses', in recognition of the significance of such discourses for the maintenance of dominance, and in so doing are building on Gerschewski's (2013) call to reincorporate a focus on legitimation into the study of authoritarian rule. Too often, legitimacy is associated specifically with democratic legitimacy, when in fact no governing coalition can survive for long without a legitimation strategy.

In some respects, the more authoritarian the governing regime, the more legitimation is required, because of the absence of the legitimating meta-narrative of democracy itself – although many authoritarian states continue to deploy the veneer of democracy to legitimize their rule (Cheeseman and Klaas 2018). In many parts of the postcolonial global South, governments were bequeathed quite limited coercive capacity over their territories, and leaders of both one-party states and military dictatorships therefore often seek to tap various forms of popular legitimacy as one way of overcoming this limitation (Cheeseman 2015: 39). This resonates with Bertrand de Jouvenel's claim that 'The king, who is but one solitary individual, stands far more in need of the general support of society than any other form of government' (de Jouvenel 1952: 98). For the purposes of our conceptual framework, we identify three particularly prominent legitimizing discourses beyond that of democracy—sometimes deployed in combination, with different target audiences—that ruling elites commonly make recourse to, in seeking to justify and normalize their strategies for dominance.

The first is a discourse of developmentalism. This is particularly prominent in states which, for structural/historical reasons, find themselves in situations where they urgently need to generate developmental progress (Leftwich 1995; Doner et al. 2005). The extensive literature on 'developmental states' explores in depth the conditions under which regimes are motivated vigorously to pursue goals of inclusive economic growth, as well as the reasons why these approaches have for the most part been highly authoritarian.[4] The point here is that this *association* of rapid developmental success with authoritarianism also provides a basis on which to justify authoritarian behaviour, regardless of the likelihood of such behaviour actually producing developmental

---

[4] See, for example, Amsden (1989), Doner et al. (2005) and Leftwich (2000).

outcomes. Focusing on positive development outcomes (or the aspiration to achieve them) provides a powerful discourse of 'output legitimacy' (Schmidt 2013), thus distracting from a lack of democratic 'input' into government.

A second legitimizing discourse in the pursuit of dominance is that of populism. This can in some regards can be contrasted with developmentalism, given that the latter accords substantial importance to elite leadership, expertise, and formal institutions—the very things that populist discourses reject. Populism can be defined as a political strategy based on anti-elite rhetoric, an appeal to the masses, and the pursuit or exercise of power by a personalistic leader based on direct, unmediated support from mostly unorganized followers (Weyland 2001: 14). In this discourse, direct, personal connection takes precedence over concrete developmental outcomes. Populism is by no means confined to the sphere of authoritarian rule, and many democratizing developing countries are drawn to populist strategies to build support through democratic means (Boone 2009; Resnick 2014a). Yet the ideas underpinning populism do not depend on democratic processes or institutions, so they exert substantial appeal for authoritarian rulers seeking to legitimize their strategies. They can also be effective in urban areas with highly informalized economies, where collective mobilization against elites and the wealthy gain a particular resonance, due to the latter's proximity and visibility.

The third legitimizing discourse of particular relevance here is that of securitization. This is relevant in contexts afflicted by major civil conflict, where 'conflict fatigue' has placed a large premium on the goal of securing territory, but can also be powerful in societies where urban areas are affected by high levels of violent crime. While securitization is central to the legitimizing narratives of many military dictatorships, it can also be used to great effect by civilian governments, particularly in cases where crime, sectional or gang warfare are used to justify heavy levels of repression and aggressive policing. Even everyday elements of urban life, such as informal street trading, are commonly cracked down on by governments in the name of enhancing 'security', when often the motives are as much about dispersing potential opposition (Goodfellow 2013; Resnick 2019).

In trying to understand how regimes seek to achieve and maintain dominance, the role of legitimizing discourses such as the three highlighted above is central. Such discourses are not mutually exclusive, but can be combined; it is common, for example, to find the rhetoric of developmentalism and securitization employed concurrently by ruling elites seeking to maintain dominance against a backdrop of both devastating violence and deep poverty (Goodfellow and Smith 2013). It is also not particularly helpful to reduce legitimizing discourses to being either repressive or a form of co-optation.

They can in many cases be both, but they may not be accurately characterized as either if the purpose of the discourse is to obfuscate or even to disincentivize competitive politics without actively repressing or appealing to specific groups. As will be explored in our empirical cases, the nature of the threats to ruling coalitions in urban areas shapes, and is shaped by, the discourses that ruling elites deploy to accompany other forms of repressive and generative intervention.

2.7 Towards an urban dominance framework

The five categories through which we can understand strategies for dominance are summarized in Fig. 2.1. While—as noted in Chapter 1—our focus is primarily on the top-down strategizing and tactical actions of ruling elites, it also important to highlight the value in seeing these not only as strategies for dominance but as relational categories that can inform our understanding of the dialectic between control and contention. In other words, groups who mobilise from below to contest dominance can themselves also employ forms of violent coercion (e.g. through street battles, riots and destruction of state property), coercive distribution (such as gang-based goods provision), legal manoeuvres (through petitioning and symbolic law-breaking), co-optation (e.g. in relation to bringing in other excluded groups), and the mobilization of discourses to legitimize their contentious actions. Indeed, the ways in which ruling elites deploy the strategies for dominance set out above can influence the choice of modalities of contention, and vice versa. As such, the above can

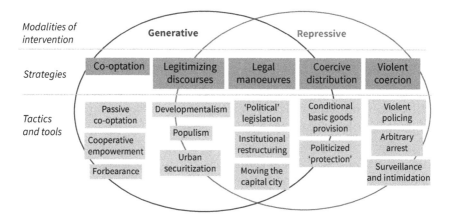

Fig. 2.1 Strategies for urban dominance

be seen not only as top-down strategies, but *as terrains of negotiation* in the dialectic between the ruling coalitions and rival groups.[5]

The question of which particular groups are targeted for these various strategies is not one we have explicitly addressed this chapter. How specific groups and factions are repressed, co-opted, and otherwise drawn into or excluded from ruling coalitions is a central concern of political settlements analysis (Khan 2010; Kelsall et al. 2022), and must be central to understandings of authoritarian dominance in specific settings. Yet our purpose in laying out the framework in this chapter is to provide a conceptual framework for describing and interpreting dominance in *any* possible urban—and especially capital city—setting. Through the inductive approach of the research project underpinning this book, we sought not to set out a theory of dominance for testing, but to offer a framework for the interpretation of empirical case material, which can then lead us towards hypotheses about why particular groups are targeted with certain interventions and how this plays out over time. It is to these empirical explorations that the following case study chapters are devoted, before we attempt some deeper explanatory propositions in Chapter 9.

To summarize the book so far, the opening chapters have aimed to make two primary contributions to the study of authoritarian dominance. First, we have argued that there is need for closer analysis of the role of capital cities in the evolution and maintenance of dominance in political settlements, particularly in places where rapid urban growth is coinciding with the rise and persistence of authoritarian forms of government, as the case in many parts of the urbanizing world. Second, we have offered a framework for exploring how ruling coalitions seek to gain and perpetuate their dominance through actions within capital, developing a conceptual 'toolbox' and analytical language intended to inform empirical exploration and inductive analysis. This is rooted in a distinction between the two overlapping modalities of generative and repressive intervention, and a typology of five categories of strategy that transect these and which can in turn be broken down into particular approaches, tools, and tactics.

Through our framework, empirically interrogating different strategies of dominance, how they change, and how they are deployed in different combinations is a way of deepening analysis of the various shades of 'semi-authoritarianism' that analysts now suggest characterize most regimes (Ottaway 2003; Tripp 2010; LeBas 2011). Yet it is also a route to deepening our

[5] We are grateful to Adrienne LeBas for this point.

understanding of the drivers of different forms of urban governance, given that the politics of dominance can have a huge influence on concrete urban outcomes, from the delivery of services to the capacity of different groups to exercise collective voice.

References

Albertus, M., Fenner, S., and Slater, D. (2018). *Coercive Distribution*. Cambridge: Cambridge University Press.

Allen, J. (2003). *Lost Geographies of Power*. New York: John Wiley & Sons.

Amsden, A. H. (1989). *Asia's Next Giant: South Korea and Late Industrialization*. Oxford: Oxford University Press.

Arendt, H. (1969). *On Violence*. Orlando, FL: Harcourt Books.

Arias, E. D. (2017). *Criminal Enterprises and Governance in Latin America and the Caribbean*. New York: Cambridge University Press.

Auyero, J. (2001). *Poor People's Politics: Peronist Survival Networks and the Legacy of Evita*. Durham, NC: Duke University Press.

Beier, R. (2018). Towards a new perspective on the role of the city in social movements. *City* 22(2): 220–235.

Bogaert, K. (2018). *Globalized Authoritarianism: Megaprojects, Slums, and Class Relations in Urban Morocco*. Minnesota, MN and London: University of Minnesota Press.

Boone, C. (2009). Electoral populism where property rights are weak: Land politics in contemporary sub-Saharan Africa. *Comparative Politics* 41(2): 183–201.

Campante, F. R., Do, Q.-A., and Guimaraes, B. (2015). Capital cities, conflict, and misgovernance. LIEPP Working Paper, no. 39, SciencesPo, Paris.

Cheeseman, N. (2015). *Democracy in Africa: Successes, Failures, and the Struggle for Political Reform*. Cambridge: Cambridge University Press.

Cheeseman, N., and Klaas, B. (2018). *How to Rig an Election*. New Haven, CT: Yale University Press.

Chua, L. J. (2019). Legal mobilization and authoritarianism. *Annual Review of Law and Social Science* 15: 355–376.

Collord, M. (2016). From the electoral battleground to the parliamentary arena: Understanding intra-elite bargaining in Uganda's national resistance movement. *Journal of Eastern African Studies*, 10(4): 639-659.

Collord, M., Goodfellow, T., and Asante, L. A. (2021). Uneven development, politics and governance in urban Africa: An analytical literature review. African Cities Research Consortium, Working Paper no. 2, University of Manchester.

Croese, S. (2017). State-led housing delivery as an instrument of developmental patrimonialism: The case of post-war Angola. *African Affairs* 116(462): 80–100.

Cross, J. C. (1998). Co-optation, competition, and resistance: State and street vendors in Mexico City. *Latin American Perspectives* 25(2): 41–61.

De Jouvenel, B. (1952). *Power: The Natural History of Its Growth*. London: Batchworth Press.

Doner, R. F., Ritchie, B. K., and Slater, D. (2005). Systemic vulnerability and the origins of developmental states: Northeast and Southeast Asia in comparative perspective. *International Organization* 59(2): 327–361.

Esen, B., and Gumuscu, S. (2021). Why did Turkish democracy collapse? A political economy account of AKP's authoritarianism. *Party Politics* 27(6), 1075–1091.

Fjelde, H., and De Soysa, I. (2009). Coercion, co-optation, or cooperation? State capacity and the risk of civil war, 1961–2004. *Conflict Management and Peace Sciences* 26(1): 5–25.

Gandhi, J., and Przeworski, A. (2006). Cooperation, co-optation, and rebellion under dictatorships. *Economics and Politics* 18(1): 1–26.

Gebremariam, E. B. (2017). The politics of youth employment and policy processes in Ethiopia. IDS Bulletin, 48(3): 33-50.

Gerschewski, J. (2013). The three pillars of stability: Legitimation, repression, and co-optation in autocratic regimes. *Democratization* 20(1): 13–38.

Goodfellow, T. (2013). The institutionalisation of 'noise' and 'silence' in urban politics: Riots and compliance in Uganda and Rwanda. *Oxford Development Studies* 41(4): 436–454.

Goodfellow, T. (2014). Legal manoeuvres and violence: Law making, protest and semi-authoritarianism in Uganda. *Development and Change* 45(4): 753–776.

Goodfellow, T., and Smith, A. (2013). From urban catastrophe to 'model' city? Politics, security and development in post-conflict Kigali. *Urban Studies* 50(15): 3185–3202.

Goodfellow, T., and Titeca, K. (2012). Presidential intervention and the changing 'politics of survival' in Kampala's informal economy. *Cities* 29(4): 264–270.

Graham, S. (2011). *Cities under Siege: The New Military Urbanism*. London and New York: Verso.

Greitens, S. C. (2016). *Dictators and Their Secret Police: Coercive Institutions and State Violence*. Cambridge: Cambridge University Press.

Gupte, J. (2017). 'These streets are ours': Mumbai's urban form and security in the vernacular. *Peacebuilding* 5(2): 203–217.

Hicken, A. (2011). Clientelism. *Annual Review of Political Science* 14: 289–310.

Holland, A. C. (2016). Forbearance. *American Political Science Review* 110(2): 232–246.

Jackman, D. (2018a). The decline of gangsters and politicisation of violence in urban Bangladesh. *Development and Change* 50(5): 1214–1238.

Jackman, D. (2018b). Violent intermediaries and political order in Bangladesh. *European Journal of Development Research* 31(4): 705–723.

Jackman, D. (2019). Towards a relational view of political violence. In: A. Riaz, Z. Nazreen and F. Zaman (eds.), *Political Violence in South Asia*. Abingdon: Routledge, pp. 26–37.

Josua, M. (2016). Co-optation reconsidered: Authoritarian regime legitimation strategies in the Jordanian 'Arab Spring'. *Middle East Law and Governance* 8(1): 32–56.

Karduni, A., and Sauda, E. (2020). Anatomy of a protest: Spatial information, social media, and urban space. *Social Media + Society* 6(1): 2056305119897320.

Kelsall, T. (2018). Towards a universal political settlement concept: A response to Mushtaq Khan. *African Affairs* 117(469): 656–669.

Kelsall, T., Schulz, N., Ferguson, W. D., vom Hau, M., Hickey, S., and Levy, B. (2022). *Political Settlements and Development: Theory, Evidence, Implications*. Oxford University Press.

Khan, M. H. (2010). *Political Settlements and the Governance of Growth-Enhancing Institutions*. London: SOAS.

Khisa, M. (2019). Shrinking democratic space? Crisis of consensus and contentious politics in Uganda. *Commonwealth & Comparative Politics*, 57(3): 343-362.

Khisa, M., & Day, C. (2020). Reconceptualising civil-military relations in Africa. *Civil Wars*, 22(2-3): 174-197.

Kitschelt, H. (2000). Linkages between citizens and politicians in democratic polities. *Comparative Political Studies* 33(6–7): 845–879.

Konaev, R. and Spencer, J. (2018). The era of urban warfare is already here. Foreign Policy Research Institute, https://www.fpri.org/article/2018/03/the-era-of-urban-warfare-is-already-here/.

Kotter, J. P., and Schlesinger, L. A. (1979). Choosing strategies for change. *Harvard Business Review* 57(2): 106–114.

Lamarque, H. (2020). Policing small communities: Rwandan law enforcement and the co-production of security. *Politique africaine* 160(4): 113–138.

Lambright, G. M. (2014). Opposition politics and urban service delivery in Kampala, Uganda. *Development Policy Review* 32(s1): s39–s60.

Lavers, T., and Hickey, S. (2016). Conceptualising the politics of social protection expansion in low income countries: The intersection of transnational ideas and domestic politics. *International Journal of Social Welfare* 25(4): 388–398.

LeBas, A. (2011). *From Protest to Parties: Party-building and Democratization in Africa*. Oxford: Oxford University Press.

LeBas, A. (2013). Violence and urban order in Nairobi, Kenya and Lagos, Nigeria. *Studies in Comparative International Development* 48(3): 240–262.

Leftwich, A. (1995). Bringing politics back in: Towards a model of the developmental state. *Journal of Development Studies* 31(3): 400–427.

Leftwich, A. (2000). *States of Development: On the Primacy of Politics in Development.* Cambridge: Polity.

Levitsky, S., and Way, L. A. (2010). *Competitive Authoritarianism: Hybrid Regimes after the Cold War.* Cambridge: Cambridge University Press.

Lindemann, S. (2008). Do inclusive elite bargains matter? A research framework for understanding the causes of civil war in sub-Saharan Africa. CSRC Discussion Paper no. 15, Crisis States Research Centre, LSE.

Makara, S. (2010). Deepening democracy through multipartyism: The bumpy road to Uganda's 2011 elections. *Africa Spectrum*, 45(2): 81-94.

Mohamed Nasir, K., and Turner, B. S. (2013). Governing as gardening: Reflections on soft authoritarianism in Singapore. *Citizenship Studies* 17(3-4), 339-352.

Myers, G. A. (2003). *Verandahs of Power: Colonialism and Space in Urban Africa.* Syracuse, NY: Syracuse University Press.

Ngoun, K. (2022). Adaptive authoritarian resilience: Cambodian strongman's quest for legitimacy. *Journal of Contemporary Asia* 52(1), 23–44.

Njoh, A. J. (2009). Urban planning as a tool of power and social control in colonial Africa. *Planning Perspectives* 24(3): 301–317.

Ottaway, M. (2003). *Democracy Challenged: The Rise of Semi-authoritarianism.* Washington, DC: Carnegie Endowment for International Peace.

Paller, J. W. (2019). *Democracy in Ghana: Everyday Politics in Urban Africa.* Cambridge University Press.

Planel, S., and Bridonneau, M. (2017). (Re)making politics in a new urban Ethiopia: An empirical reading of the right to the city in Addis Ababa's condominiums. *Journal of Eastern African Studies* 11(1): 24–45.

Post, A. E. (2018). Cities and politics in the developing world. *Annual Review of Political Science* 21: 115–133.

Potter, A. (2017). Locating the government: Capital cities and civil conflict. *Research and Politics*, October–December: 1–7.

Prempeh, H. K. (2008). Progress and retreat in Africa: presidents untamed. *Journal of Democracy* 19(2): 109–123.

Resnick, D. (2014a). *Urban Poverty and Party Populism in African Democracies.* Cambridge: Cambridge University Press.

Resnick, D. (2014b). Urban governance and service delivery in African cities: The role of politics and policies. *Development Policy Review* 32(s1): s3–s17.

Resnick, D. (2019). The politics of crackdowns on Africa's informal vendors. *Comparative Politics* 52(1): 21–51.

Rodgers, D. (2006). The state as a gang: Conceptualizing the governmentality of violence in contemporary Nicaragua. *Critique of Anthropology* 26(3): 315–330.

Rodgers, D., and O'Neill, B. (2012). Infrastructural violence: Introduction to the special issue. *Ethnography* 13(4): 401–412.

Rollason, W. (2013). Performance, poverty and urban development: Kigali's motari and the spectacle city. *Afrika Focus* 26(2): 9–29.

Schatz, E. (2004). What capital cities say about state and nation building. *Nationalism and Ethnic Politics* 9(4): 111–140.

Schmidt, V. A. (2013). Democracy and legitimacy in the European Union revisited: Input, output and 'throughput'. *Political Studies* 61(1): 2–22.

Scott, J. C. (1998). *Seeing Like a State: How Certain Schemes to Improve the Human Condition Have Failed*. Cambridge, MA: Yale University Press.

Slater, D., and Fenner, S. (2011). State power and staying power: Infrastructural mechanisms and authoritarian durability. *Journal of International Affairs* 65(1): 15–29.

Stokes, S., Dunning, T., Nazareno, M., and Brusco, V. (2013). *Brokers, Voters and Clientelism: The Puzzle of Distributive Politics*. Cambridge: Cambridge University Press.

Tapscott, R. (2021). *Arbitrary States: Social Control and Modern Authoritarianism in Museveni's Uganda*. Oxford: Oxford University Press.

Tilly, C. (2003). *The Politics of Collective Violence*. Cambridge: Cambridge University Press.

Traugott, M. (1995). Capital cities and revolution. *Social Science History* 19(1): 147–168.

Tripp, A. M. (2010). *Museveni's Uganda: Paradoxes of Power in a Hybrid Regime*. Boulder, CO: Lynne Rienner Publishers.

Wallace, J. (2014). *Cities and Stability: Urbanization, Redistribution, and Regime Survival in China*. Oxford: Oxford University Press.

Weyland, K. (2001). Clarifying a contested concept: Populism in the study of Latin American politics. *Comparative Politics* 34(1): 1–22.

Wood, G. 2003. Staying secure, staying poor: The 'Faustian bargain'. *World Development* 31(3): 455–471.

3

Carrot, stick, and statute

Elite strategies and contested dominance in Kampala

Nansozi K. Muwanga, Paul I. Mukwaya, and Tom Goodfellow

3.1 Introduction

President Yoweri K. Museveni seized power in 1986, following a protracted five-year guerrilla war in Uganda (Amaza 1998). For his first decade in power, his stated commitment to democracy through the Ten-Point Programme and a 'no-party' system in which anyone could stand for office under the National Resistance Movement (NRM) achieved wide international admiration (Mujagu and Oloka-Onyango 2000). So too did an apparently deep programme of political decentralization, aimed at transforming the 'resistance councils' that evolved during the civil war into a five-tier system of local government. As donor resources flowed in, Uganda became internationally renowned for radical improvements in governance (Hansen and Twaddle 1998). Yet by the early 2000s, perceptions of Museveni and the NRM government were changing. The 2001 and 2006 elections were marred by significant manipulation and violence, signalling that the regime was seeking to maintain its dominance of the political scene at all costs (Rubongoya 2007; Kobusingye 2010). Through a wide range of strategies and tactics, it has maintained its dominance electorally and institutionally in the face of an increasingly organized and youthful opposition. By 2022, having held power for thirty-six years, Museveni is among the longest-standing non-royal rulers in the world.

This undeniable dominance has, however, never fully extended to the capital city. Kampala has stubbornly resisted submitting to the NRM's political grip for over three decades, despite both overt and covert attempts to control it. The political and economic significance of Kampala, which is the administrative and political capital as well as the focal point of oppositional politics and youth organization, cannot be overstated. As the

Nansozi K. Muwanga, Paul I. Mukwaya, and Tom Goodfellow, *Carrot, stick, and statute*. In: *Controlling the Capital*. Edited by: Tom Goodfellow and David Jackman, Oxford University Press. © Oxford University Press (2023). DOI: 10.1093/oso/9780192868329.003.0003 city population has grown and Uganda has gradually continued to urbanize, the NRM has shifted from largely ignoring the city—focusing instead on its rural heartlands—to a range of strategies and tactics to increase its influence and control in Kampala, and increasingly also in the wider metropolitan area, including the districts of Wakiso and Mukono. Though present for over two decades now, threats to elite dominance in the city have become even more pronounced since 2017, with the emergence of Robert Kyagulanyi Ssentamu (aka Bobi Wine) as a major political figure with a strong urban support base, including the wider central region of Uganda.

Despite its failure to dominate the city electorally, the regime's challengers in Kampala have also never managed to weaken central control over urban governance and resources in any sustained way. In exploring the varying strategies that the ruling elite has used to try and dominate Kampala, this chapter therefore considers why the city remains a space of continually contested—but not substantially weakened—central control. We explore three particular strategic approaches to analyse the regime's efforts to control the city, and how these have been responded to by urban populations, with a particular focus on the decade 2010–20. The first involves a range of high-level efforts to co-opt and coerce opposition politicians, with growing attention to politicians whose key roles and support base are in the capital city. The second involves efforts to control the city by administrative means, deploying legislative manoeuvres and institutional restructuring to do so. The third focuses on the co-option and manipulation of urban youth, using money and other incentives to try and engineer support for the NRM. We explore the underlying rationale for these strategies as they have evolved over time, and examine how and why each approach has produced only limited gains, ultimately reproducing a situation of intensely contested control in which no single group or political force completely dominates the city.

This chapter is based on research involving a combination of methods, including: a review of relevant literature and policy and legal documents; analysis of international and international print and electronic media; and informant interviews with key actors and interest groups in the city in mid–late 2018 and early 2019, including MPs, city-level politicians and bureaucrats, the Uganda Police Force, *boda boda* (motorcycle taxi) drivers and specific youth groups in Kampala City and surrounding municipalities.

3.2 From democratic high hopes to entrenched dominance: the evolution of Uganda's national political settlement

Despite the continuing conflict in the north, the NRM's victory in 1986 and establishment of relative security elsewhere meant that, for the first decade of his rule, Museveni and the NRM were generally popular both abroad and with the war-weary population at home. His initial reconstruction programme—especially economic recovery measures, gender equality initiatives, education, and the fight against HIV/AIDS—met with considerable success and approval. Museveni provided donors seeking an 'African success story' with an intellectually sophisticated, yet compliant partner (Hansen and Twaddle 1998; Kuteesa et al. 2010; Tripp 2010). His invention of a 'no-party' system that involved democratic principles but without divisive party politics was innovative and initially widely accepted as sensible in the context of Uganda's violent recent past (Mujagu and Oloka-Onyango 2000; Carbone 2008). Meanwhile, the decision to restore most of the traditional kingdoms and chiefdoms in 1993, albeit in a purely 'cultural' role, also ensured support in central and western Uganda.

By the mid-1990s, however, there were signs that the 'honeymoon' period was over, as discontent grew over the no-party system, land reform, and continuing instability in northern Uganda. NRM hegemony was now firmly entrenched, alongside corruption, clientelism, and increased ethnic exclusion (Mwenda and Tangri 2005; Rubongoya 2007; Tripp 2010). The decade 1995–2005 typifies the 'push and pull' of politics under Uganda's 'hybrid' regime (Tripp 2010), whereby growing democratic capacities in society and the enhancement of some formal democratic institutions were simultaneously responded to by new forms of authoritarian manipulation and exclusion (Goodfellow 2014).

These tensions became even more apparent after 2005, when the opening-up of party competition was used by Museveni as a bargaining chip to remove presidential term limits, enabling him to stand for a third term in the 2006 elections. For many previous supporters, this was the ultimate betrayal of his early democratic promise (Kobusingye 2010) and seemed to confirm his intention to be 'president for life'. Museveni also found new ways to strengthen the hand of the executive, with parliamentary powers to vet ministerial appointments and censure ministers being reduced, and new presidential powers to dissolve Parliament introduced (Kasfir and Twebaze 2009; Keating 2011). With party competition now permitted, Museveni's main opposition within the NRM became the country's most powerful opposition force in the form of the Forum for Democratic Change (FDC) led by his former ally Kizza Besigye. In an election marred by violence and intimidation (including the arrest and temporary imprisonment of Besigye on charges of treason and rape), Museveni secured 59 per cent of the vote to Besigye's 37 per cent in 2006.

In 2011 Museveni stood yet again and was re-elected by a landslide, gaining 68 per cent of the vote against Besigye's 28 per cent. Alongside the drop in the opposition's share of the vote—including in Kampala—was the significant (and unexpected) decrease in pre-election violence. This demonstrated that the dominance of Museveni's ruling coalition was not only as strong as ever but did not rely on coercion alone, and that the NRM continued to enjoy widespread support across large parts of the country—even if much of this depended on rural vote-buying (Mwenda 2011). By the time of the 2016 elections, Museveni's ruling coalition was 'not even faking it anymore' (Abrahamsen and Bareebe 2016), with his victory a foregone conclusion. Predictable patterns of intimidation and misconduct were associated with an election that closely mirrored the 2006 result, with Museveni winning 61 per cent of the vote to Besigye's 35%. As in previous elections, the failure of the opposition to forge a sustained coalition contributed to its inability to dent the NRM's position (Beardsworth 2017). Following his 2016 election victory, Museveni wasted no time in moving to amend the constitution to remove the age limit of presidential candidates, paving the way for him to run for a sixth term in 2021. According to Article 105(2) of the 1995 Constitution, Museveni would have been able to run for a maximum of just two terms. Yet he repeatedly contradicted his early claim that he would not 'overstay' in power, removing the limit on presidential terms in 2005 and then the age limit for presidential candidates in 2017.

In the 2021 elections, and facing a new opponent in the form of Robert Kyagulanyi (discussed further below), Museveni won 59 per cent of the national vote, with Kyagulanyi winning 35 per cent. The relative stability of Museveni's vote share from 2006 to 2021 suggests that NRM dominance is deeply embedded, and that the political work of the ruling elite in achieving ongoing dominance is deep, highly sophisticated, and always evolving. The city level tells a specific story that we examine in detail in this chapter, but it is first important to acknowledge several processes underpinning this dominance at the national level.

Establishing dominance has been a well-calculated strategy on the part of the government, starting with the creation of the Local Council System that evolved out of the 'Resistance Councils' (RCs) established during the guerrilla war against the second Obote government. Originally designed as support structures for the NRA fighters, the RCs grew into a model for what was viewed as 'popular democracy' when the NRA transitioned into the NRM on coming to power in 1986 (HRW 1999). Yet they have also operated as tools of NRM control. Moreover, in 1996, the Uganda Parliament created a number of non-elected parliamentary seats, reserved for the army and other government sectors and special interest groups such as young people and persons with disabilities, as well as elected seats reserved specifically for women and, since 2021, for elderly persons. These 'strong' affirmative actions aimed at raising the profile of marginalized groups have tended to produce members of Parliament who are NRM-leaning. Appointed Resident District Commissioners (RDCs)—recently termed 'Uganda's sub-national presidents' by Muhereza and Hitchen (2022)—also play an important role in many districts, controlling the electoral colleges representing these special interest groups as well as administering the political mobilizers in each district and the party schools (HRW 1999). The Movement Act of 1997 further ensured that the NRM was represented at the lowest village levels, giving it a strong political advantage which put it well ahead of the pack when multi-party politics was reinstated in 2005. Alongside these measures, during its early years the Museveni government used '*Chaka-mchaka*', a political education and military science course primarily aimed at civil servants and graduating high-school students, as an additional tool to increase its political control.

In addition, the NRM has used election processes themselves to embed itself 'normatively and conceptually' as well as organizationally among the population at large, and to inculcate local cultures of securitization that consciously or unconsciously remind people of the chaos preceding it (Vokes and Wilkins 2016: 582). Meanwhile, Museveni's interweaving of formal and informal governance mechanisms is, in Hickey and Golooba-Mutebi's (2016) analysis, central to keeping different constituencies onside and continuing to win elections. The President explicitly reminds his critics during rallies that, being a good politician, he should keep changing tactics to outmanoeuvre adversaries.[1]

The opposition in Uganda has always been relatively fragmented and collectively weak, despite a range of opposition parties, many of which have long histories. With their origins in the last years of colonial rule, several of the 'traditional' opposition parties (such as the Democratic Party and Uganda People's Congress) have a strongly regional or religious character,

---

[1] Interview with a political commentator and journalist at one of Uganda's daily newspapers.

which has limited their effectiveness as national opposition movements—even when they have attempted to form coalitions for electoral purposes, as has been common (Beardsworth 2017). The prohibition of most party activity for two decades under the NRM was obviously a further hindrance, and civil society organizations have also generally been politically weak (Beardsworth 2017). Despite this, with the rise of the FDC under Besigye and, more recently, Bobi Wine's National Unity Platform and its strongly urban base, the strength of specifically *urban* opposition has surged. Our question in this chapter is therefore how the NRM's different strategies and manoeuvres come together in the context of Kampala, where the ruling coalition faces growing challenges to its rule and a distinct political environment requiring different strategies of dominance. In the next section, we consider Kampala's role within the national political context outlined above.

3.3 The role of Kampala

Although not the capital city during the colonial period (which was based in nearby Entebbe on Lake Victoria), Kampala was sited next to the historical capital of the Buganda kingdom at Mengo and had become the economic core of the Uganda Protectorate by the 1940s.[2] Kampala is the undisputed economic as well as administrative capital of Uganda. It was named the thirteenth fastest-growing city on the planet, with an annual population growth rate of 4.03 per cent for the period 2006–20 (City Mayors 2018). Greater Kampala boasts a population of 3.5 million and is growing fast, on account of both redevelopment within the city and expansion on the periphery (World Bank 2015). Around 80 per cent of the country's industrial and service sectors are located in the city, which also hosts an estimated 46 per cent of all Uganda's formal employment. Seventy per cent of Uganda's manufacturing plants are clustered in Kampala and it produces a third of Uganda's manufacturing gross domestic product (Lall et al. 2009; Gore et al. 2014). Under the NRM's celebrated decentralization policy, Kampala was designated the only official 'city' in Uganda in administrative terms, with Kampala City Council (KCC) being equivalent to a district (LC5).[3] As such, until the radical governance overhauls of 2011 discussed below, KCC had substantial autonomy under

[2] See Omolo-Okalebo et al. (2010) and Goodfellow (2022) for an extended historical discussion of the evolution of Kampala.

[3] This changed in 2010, when fifteen other areas were approved for official 'city' status.

Uganda's decentralized system. Eighty per cent of services were devolved to KCC; everything in the city except national roads and secondary and tertiary education was under its jurisdiction.

Given Kampala's complex heritage, its location within the Buganda kingdom, and its economic centrality, its governance since colonial times has been the focus of political contestation. The contestation has primarily involved three key poles of power: the national government, the opposition-dominated KCC (including a number of city mayors), and the governing authorities of the kingdom of Buganda. Moreover, these tensions were compounded over several decades by a lack of attention to the city's needs and challenges. Historically, national support for large cities in Uganda has been limited; poverty alleviation and development strategies have rarely mentioned cities, urban activities, or urban contributions to economic development (Gore 2009). While there was plenty of interest among politicians in Kampala's resources (including land), supporting the governance and infrastructure of the city was of little interest to the NRM until the 2000s. In the words of one political figure in 2009, Kampala was 'to put it crudely, the bastard child of nobody … it's just an orphan that no-one quite wants to deal with properly' (Goodfellow 2010: 7).

By the late 2000s Kampala was severely run down, its poor infrastructure and service delivery decried by the media on a daily basis—arguably reflecting a deliberate strategy to discredit the Democratic Party-dominated city council (Goodfellow 2013; Lambright 2014). Moreover, in 2005 MPs passed a government amendment to the Constitution that provided for the central government to take a greater role in the administration of Kampala. This was initially put on hold, but as the 2000s wore on and the sense of crisis in the city deepened, plans were made to realize this increased central government role. The move did not go uncontested, and opposition actors at the city level tried to resist and subvert the central government 'takeover' of Kampala in various ways.

Fig. 3.1 starkly illustrates the extent to which the government has failed to take control of Kampala electorally, with a deepening and geographic broadening of opposition in and around Kampala in 2021. In what follows, focusing particularly on the period from 2010 onwards, we analyse a series of overlapping strategies for dominance that were pursued by the NRM government in the face of mounting opposition. Each of these met with limited success, as efforts to contain opposition in one area led to new forms of contestation in others.

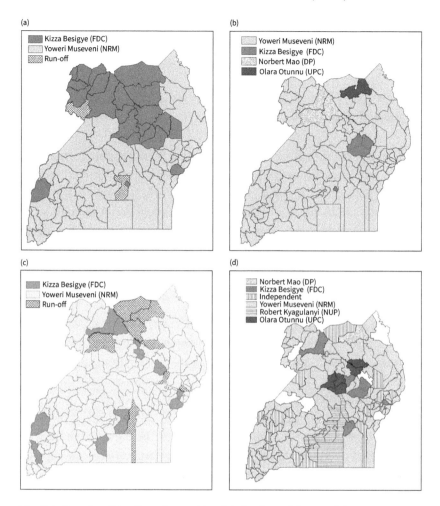

Fig. 3.1 Results of the Uganda presidential elections: (a) 2006; (b) 2011; (c) 2016; (d) 2021

Source: based on data from Uganda Electoral Commission.

3.4 Repression and co-optation of the opposition

Perhaps the most obvious way in which the ruling elite has sought to control the capital city is through the combination of high levels of repression and a strategy of political co-optation, picking off key opposition figures who pose a particular threat by making offers they find difficult to refuse. In this section we explore some of the ways in which coercion and co-optation are deployed by the NRM nationally, with attention to aspects that are particularly prominent in Kampala.

The iron fist: persecution, suppression, and containment of political dissent

The NRM regime uses a mix of security forces including the regular police, the military, plain-clothes security men and women, and unidentified male youth to crack down on any sign of protest. These forces are in a state of constant flux in type, numbers, and leadership. Yet Uganda's security architecture draws in an even wider array of players through aspects of surveillance and financing. Overall, the ruling coalition relies on a wide and growing security enterprise linked to intelligence outfits, prominent business personalities, print and electronic media outlets, Pentecostal pastors, and retired military figures.[4]

Any semblance of political opposition is treated with suspicion, and in many circumstances the above security organs are deployed to quell it including through the use of tear gas, sticks, and guns.[5] Vigilantes and plain-clothes militias such as the Black Mamba, Kibooko Squad, Kalangala Action Plan (KAP), Popular Intelligence Network, Arrow Boys, Amuka Group, Labeca Group, and Kifeesi Group have been created at different times to perform this task, many of them centred on Kampala. At the hands of these groups, most of which operate through highly informal processes, both opposition activists and people linked to civil society organizations (CSOs) engaged in political advocacy have been heavily surveilled, regularly detained, and even killed (HRW 2015; Mugabe 2018). In some cases, CSOs' work is rendered impossible by bank account closures, the confiscation of equipment, or full closure. Until recently, a key figure in the organization of violent repression and surveillance in Kampala was the Inspector General of Police, General Kale Kayihura. Under his command, the President's political opponents were in and out of jail and their public activities thwarted, often justified using the Uganda Public Order Management Act (2013). The police's aggressive crowd-control tactics earned Kayihura the nickname 'Mr Teargas'.

Since 2015, the most important group within this landscape of informal, overlapping organizations of violence specialists were the 'Crime Preventers'.

---

[4] Interview with Uganda Police Force official.
[5] Interview with a political scientist, columnist, student and teacher of politics and political development with a focus on contemporary Africa.

Loosely based on community policing principles and organized in large groups armed only with sticks, this organization was hugely expanded from 2015 in advance of the 2016 election. While the Ugandan police reportedly set a target of 1.6 million crime preventers, or around thirty in each of Uganda's 56,000 villages, details of their numbers and training are difficult to come by. The government itself reported recruiting over 1 million by the end of 2015 (Tapscott 2016). The methods of absorption and (re)deployment and rejection are also unclear, but they are civilian volunteers trained by the Ugandan police (sometimes referred to as a band of civilian vigilantes recruited by the government) for low-level community security. By some accounts, one recruitment tactic was the promise that they would later be recruited in the conventional police force, and Museveni met large numbers of them in person at Lugogo in Kampala to declare them a 'reserve force' of the UPDF (Ugandan Army). Interestingly, however, the crime preventers were not used exclusively to mobilize violence. Tapscott (2016: 694) argues that at different moments, political authorities described crime preventers in different ways: as agents of state violence, as benevolent citizens, and even as entrepreneurial young people. This ambiguity about their role created uncertainty and a lack of accountability, and also benefited the NRM during elections because it seemed to embody a promise to generate livelihood opportunities for large numbers of young people (Tapscott 2016).

The pattern in the use of intimidation, torture, arrests, and detentions by the police and other security operatives suggests that people who are able to expose brutality and those perceived to have political ambitions are particularly targeted, with the aim of incapacitating any attempts to mobilize Ugandans around a programme for change. Security as a central feature of the regime's legitimacy has been used to introduce an array of measures designed to prevent violent crimes and to heighten surveillance in the process. In addition to the violent kidnap, arrest, and torture of opposition politicians in safe houses, measures include the re-registration of SIM cards and installation of CCTV cameras across Kampala, the banning of hoodies, the recall and reassignment of crime preventers, and the revitalization of heavily armed Local Defence Units. It is alleged that there are over 40,000 armed men spread across Kampala overseeing ordinary people going about their business (Serunkuma 2019). Yet the increasingly aggressive repressive measures to curb opposition outlined above have been deployed alongside a series of 'generative' approaches towards dominating Kampala, which we now examine.

'More NRM than the NRM': the co-optation, infiltration, and dismantling of political opposition

The ability of the ruling elite to co-opt opposition figures can partly be explained by the aura of invincibility and permanence that Museveni has so effectively built around himself. The often-repeated praise of party stalwarts and sychophants suggesting that the country cannot exist without him has emboldened Museveni and enhanced his cult-like status.[6] Having seen off potential challenges from within the NRM in the form of generals like David Sejusa (alias Tinyefuza) and Henry Tumukunde, Museveni has worn out his ambitious former comrades, making it most likely that he will face a challenger who is younger than his own children (Sserunjogi 2018). He has taken great care to keep influential political and business figures in the city onside, including those from all the city's major religious institutions, and rarely misses important community functions in Kampala. Even people within the official opposition have been continuously courted in an attempt to co-opt them into the ruling coalition. Reaching out specifically to cash-strapped opposition members has also helped to draw a wedge between opposition forces to eliminate any possibility of unity and cohesion among opposition politicians.[7] At the national level, despite some political glitches President Museveni has largely been successful in what appears to be a long-term mission to decimate the opposition, which he frequently refers to as 'useless'.

The list of leading opposition figures who are working with or have worked with the NRM government is long. Most significant in terms of Kampala, when the President announced a new cabinet after the 2016 elections, newly co-opted members included former opposition politicians from the capital, such as Beti Kamya of the Uganda Federal Alliance (made Minister for Kampala and Metropolitan Affairs), Florence Nakiwala Kiyingi (made Minister for Youth and Children Affairs), Sarah Kanyike, a former personal assistant to the opposition Lord Mayor Erias Lukwago (appointed as Minister for the Elderly and Disability), and Joyce Nabbosa Ssebugwawo, the Deputy President of FDC and Mayor for Lubaga division (appointed as Minister of State for ICT and National Guidance). After her appointment as Minister for Kampala, Beti Kamya, a former FDC insider, promised to reverse the NRM's especially poor performance in Kampala in 2016 by delivering it 80 per cent of the city's vote by 2021. It was hoped that the deployment of Kamya, who

---

[6] Anonymous interview with one of the old guard in the NRM.
[7] Interview with Ms Betty Nambooze, member of Parliament and Democratic Party stalwart.

had been a very high-profile opposition figure and activist supporting the Buganda kingdom, would bridge divides and heal the wounds that had led to historical lows in NRM support in Kampala. However, as we explore below, it is far from clear that this was a winning strategy.

Officials in the army, the party, and State House are all armed with reasonable amounts of money to soften and recruit opposition politicians (Kaaya 2017). According to an NRM insider, the opposition is a 'nursery bed' of people who are frequently 'hobnobbing' with the NRM party stalwarts and camouflaging under the cover of darkness before joining the party.[8] It is difficult to know whether many people go into opposition politics as a façade—a deliberate route to eventually securing a powerful government position— or whether most start with a genuine opposition agenda but give up when they judge it to be futile or dangerous. The President himself has frequently referred to opposition politicians as 'political prostitutes' willing to sell themselves to willing buyers (Kaaya 2017). Even the Chief Opposition Whip has often complained about the way his colleagues are compromised, lamenting that many official members of the opposition appear to be two-faced, 'which has affected us in assigning them to committees. We have people who appear to be opposition yet they are more NRM than the NRM MPs.'

The ruling elite's tactics change periodically, and depending on the individuals being engaged, the NRM may use both the carrot and stick. For hard-line opposition politicians, if repeated efforts at co-optation fail then the government often opts to block their businesses and sources of income, as one prominent opposition politician notes:

> Carrots come in the form of job offers or cash, while the sticks include blocking access to jobs or businesses ... There have been cases where financial institutions have been forced to recall opposition politicians' loans, which forces them to run to Mr Museveni for help. If one hardens, they will use economic disempowerment or cripple one financially by making one either unemployable or if one is in business, they will be handed unusual tax assessments, dismantle any franchise holdings and business territory or set inflexible sales targets. If one is in a partnership with others, they will make your partners start feeling uncomfortable working with you.[9]

In the case of Robert Kyagulanyi (aka Bobi Wine, whose rise we explore below), his continued mobilization led to over 124 planned concerts being suspended or cancelled altogether by 2020, in defiance of the directive made

---

[8] Interview with one NRM insider and political commentator for Makindye West constituency in Kampala City.
[9] Interview with the Forum for Democratic Change (FDC) official.

by the Ugandan Parliament and the judiciary. Yet the immense popularity of Kyagulanyi indicates that these tactics have limited capacity to win over the population of Kampala. While co-optation of key opposition politicians and deployment of multiple security forces has enabled the NRM to maintain dominance across large swathes of rural Uganda, it has long been clear that it is not enough in Kampala. Moreover, these strategies and tactics can generate new forms of opposition even as they try to repress it. Consequently, alongside the above activities, over the past decade the NRM has engaged in a sustained battle to take control of the key levers of governance in the city, in order further to constrain the opposition's room for manoeuvre.

3.5 Legal manoeuvres and capital city reforms

The Kampala Capital City Act and its dysfunctions

Following its repeated failures to win a majority in Kampala and to control KCC, the NRM took steps to reclaim formal governance of the city in the late 2000s through some significant legal manoeuvres, specifically in the form of institutional restructuring. In June 2009, building on the foundations set in place by the 2005 constitutional amendment, the central government tabled the Kampala Capital City Bill, which was passed into law in 2010 amid huge controversy (Gore and Muwanga 2014). The Act provided for the creation a new national authority to oversee the administration of the city—the Kampala Capital City Authority (KCCA)—effectively taking administrative and decision-making authority away from a popularly elected council and Mayor (though these would continue to exist within KCCA), and empowering a technocratic administration that owed its loyalty to the President. The position of Mayor was effectively abolished and replaced with that of Lord Mayor with far fewer executive powers, and the city was to be led by an Executive Director supported by a team of ten directors appointed by the central government: an attempt to overcome the longstanding 'vertically divided authority' (Resnick 2014) in the city. The 2010 Act created two parallel structures (Fig. 3.2): a political arm headed by the Lord Mayor and the technical wing headed by Executive Director Jennifer Musisi, whom many saw as an urban reformer, known for her toughness during her tenure at the Uganda Revenue Authority. At the same time, the creation of the Ministry of Kampala and Metropolitan Affairs was further testimony to the shift in power away from the city to the central government.

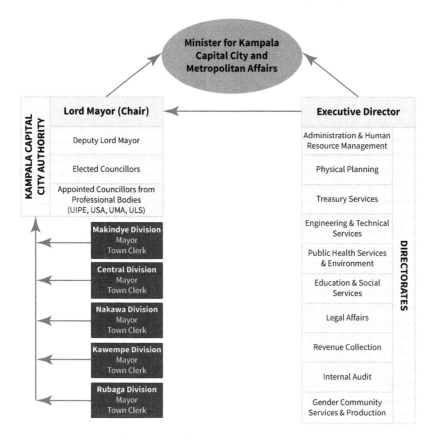

Fig. 3.2 Institutional structure of Kampala city
Source: UNAS (2017).

KCCA was ostensibly created to resolve the inefficiencies of KCC. In reality, however, the 2010 Act set out unclear institutional arrangements, with overlapping roles that impeded policy coordination. For example, the Act does not clearly delineate hierarchy between the administrative and political wings of the authority. Section 11(1) provides that the Lord Mayor shall be the political head of the capital city, while section 17(1) provides that the Executive Director shall be the chief executive of KCCA; no clarification, however, is provided on the difference between the capital city and the KCCA. The result has frequently been institutional paralysis and conflict.

Despite the role of Mayor being downgraded to that of Lord Mayor, Erias Lukwago—who was elected into that role after the creation of KCCA in 2011—ensured that opposition presence within KCCA remained strong, even as opposition parties lost their dominance of the KCCA council to the

NRM in the 2011 elections. The presence of strong opposition figures in the city after 2011, despite the formal disempowerment of the opposition, set the scene for further political battles that would draw in the President himself. Although city-level politicians were severely weakened under the 2010 Act relative to the Executive Director, Lukwago strongly contested this interpretation of the Act and frequently took to the streets to mobilize popular support in protest. He justified his campaign of resistance and obstruction with reference to the Act itself, and the aforementioned differing interpretations of roles and responsibilities. Frustrated by the failure to pass any KCCA business legally, the NRM-dominated KCCA council eventually impeached Lukwago in 2013, citing incompetence, misconduct, and abuse of office (Kafeero 2013). Lukwago's removal was the subject of contestation in the courts of law and debate in Parliament, media, and other public fora, not least because the Act offered no provision for how the Lord Mayor's functions would be performed in his absence. Consequently, while court battles raged on, three years of legal deadlock ensued during which KCCA ran without a Lord Mayor, until 2016 when fresh elections allowed Lukwago to stand—and win—again. However, an important development during his absence was that the government tabled an amendment to the 2010 Act, with the stated aim of solving the underlying problems that had led to the fallout between the Lord Mayor and the NRM-dominated KCCA (Kafeero 2013).

The rise of the Ministry of Kampala and Metropolitan Affairs

The KCCA Amendment Bill (2015) was introduced in the run-up to the 2016 elections. Its key provisions were for: a Metropolitan Physical Planning Authority to enable better planning in the Greater Kampala Metropolitan Area; removal of the borrowing cap for KCCA, subject to the Public Finance Management Act; and removal of ambiguity in the composition of the City Authority and nomenclature of institutions and offices. However, the bill's biggest controversy related to the proposed change to how the Lord Mayor is elected (from universal adult suffrage to an internal vote among KCCA councillors), and the transfer of the title of 'political head' of the city from the Lord Mayor to the Minister of Kampala and Metropolitan Affairs. In a situation where the ruling NRM dominated Council membership, any opposition mayoral candidate would now find it hard to win, despite widespread popular support. Unsurprisingly, Lukwago heavily criticized the bill as 'an underhand method designed to fight me out of office … because the ruling government knows they cannot beat us in Kampala' (quoted in Semakula et al. 2017).

Similar sentiments were raised in our interviews with other opposition figures, including the Shadow Minister for Local Government:

> The government brought a bill in bad faith to realign the leadership of Kampala City. Like in any other struggle for power, you cannot be taken to have success-fully won when you have not captured the capital city. This thing keeps haunting Museveni because he has never taken over Kampala politically. He has been trying everything to see that he chases the opposition out of the capital city. He wanted to do away with Lord Mayoral elections because of Erias Lukwago, a man he could neither defeat nor compromise.[10]

The manner in which the bill was introduced was also controversial; it was initially tabled when the KCC was not sitting, the office of the Lord Mayor was locked, and the chambers were locked, ensuring there was no input from Kampala's elected leadership. Moreover, under the KCCA structure proposed in the 2015 Amendment Bill, the Minister for Kampala and Metropolitan Affairs would assume all the executive functions currently vested in the office of the Lord Mayor, with elected councillors effectively becoming an advisory board helping to mobilize local revenue. In a highly political move, shortly after introducing the bill Museveni replaced Frank Tumwebaze as Minister for Kampala with Beti Kamya—a recently co-opted former opposition figure, as noted above. This turned the two-way power struggle between Musisi and Lukwago into three-way struggle between Musisi, Lukwago, and Kamya, with little if any common ground between them.

One of the 2015 bill's primary purposes was to transfer whatever executive powers then remained with the Lord Mayor to the Minister for Kampala and Metropolitan Affairs—initially described by many people as a 'Minister without a Ministry'. In essence, it proposed that Kampala be governed by ministerial orders and decrees, in contravention of the Local Government Act (1997). According to the former Executive Director of the National Planning Authority (NPA), Kisamba Mugerwa:

> There is no work to necessitate the office of Minister for Kampala. The NRM gov-ernment only created that office to politically counter Lukwago after failing to get their own candidate win in Kampala. I am sure if the elected Mayor was from the

---

[10] Interview with the Shadow Minister for Local Government.

ruling NRM, that office of Kampala Minister would not have been created. (quoted by Walakira 2018)

Another source noted that:

> The title of political head that is prevalent in the Act is irrelevant ... the Lord Mayor and Minister for Kampala and Metropolitan Affairs are bickering over a title that is useless because being a 'political head' is not a function.[11]

Given the many controversies affecting the bill, significant backtracking took place and it was shelved a number of times: first after it was introduced in 2015, and then again in 2017 amid fierce resistance from the Lord Mayor and Shadow Minister (then) for Local Government, Betty Nambooze Bakireke. By this time, the opposition's position in the city authority had again been strengthened by the 2016 election; Lukwago was re-elected but the opposition also won outright in the surrounding district of Wakiso (see Fig. 3.1)—a significant development that we discuss below. This weakening of the NRM position in terms of elected seats in 2016 led to a souring of the President's relationship with KCCA Chief Executive Jennifer Musisi, whose zeal for banishing street vendors he blamed for the NRM's poor electoral performance in Kampala. The new plan after 2016 was therefore to try and control Kampala centrally through the Minister for Kampala, Beti Kamya, rather than through Musisi, who eventually resigned in 2018, citing a lack of presidential support. The new line of conflict thus became that between Lukwago as Lord Mayor and Kamya as Minister for Kampala, as reflected in these comments from Lukwago:

> The current Minister for Kampala and Metropolitan Affairs is usurping my powers. She is posturing around as the political head of the city and there are litigations in court over the issue. Furthermore, stripping the powers of the Lord Mayor would disenfranchise and disempower the voters (the people of Kampala) and deny them a voice in the management and administration of the city. What took President Museveni to the bush was to return power to the people and democratic rule, but what is going on in Kampala shows that people shed their blood for nothing.[12]

The KCCA (Amendment) Bill was finally passed in 2019—though it was stripped of the controversial clauses changing the modality for electing the Lord Mayor and making the Minister for Kampala the city's 'political head'.

---

[11] Interview with the Chair of the Parliamentary Committee on Presidential Affairs, 11 October 2018.
[12] Interview with the Lord Mayor.

In this respect, the Lord Mayor's powers were reaffirmed; yet at the same time, from 2020 onwards the ministry became less of a 'shell' and started to develop more concrete roles and capacities (Goodfellow and Mukwaya 2021a). Moreover, the passing of the bill introduced yet more contradictions regarding who holds ultimate control over budgeting. The effective stalemate between city-level political forces and central control thus continues, particularly given that in 2021 Lukwago was again re-elected with a landslide victory (Goodfellow and Mukwaya 2021b).

These events illustrate how, over a decade, the ruling elite has adapted its approach to controlling city governance since its decision in 2009 to dominate the city administratively. The Lord Mayor's power remains highly constrained, with the opposition hemmed in by successive layers of legislation that exacerbate blurred lines of accountability and spheres of authority. Yet this decade of 'legal manoeuvres' also clearly illustrates the limitations of this strategy. Creating new figureheads for the city in the form of Musisi and Kamya, who were accountable upwards to a regime seen as brutal and corrupt rather than to the city population itself, ultimately backfired by bolstering Lukwago's popularity and the confidence of the opposition to shoot down key elements of the KCCA (Amendment) Bill. In the face of growing resentment towards the NRM-sponsored urban renewal project under Musisi, and the vigorous political mobilization by Lukwago, Besigye, and now Bobi Wine, new strategies of dominance were therefore also needed. One of these centred on courting Kampala's key constituency: the young.

3.6 Young people compromised: political manoeuvring with youth groups

Uganda has one of the youngest populations in the world and more than 70 per cent of the country's citizens have never known a president other than Museveni (The Atlantic 2018). Around half of young people are estimated to be unemployed, and a 2017 Sauti wa Wananchi survey, conducted by the NGO Twaweza, indicated that 78 per cent of Ugandans thought the government was not doing well at creating jobs. Young people are better educated than their parents, but less likely to find a job. This has given rise to an upsurge in resentment, creating a sense of hopelessness that provides fertile ground for politicians of every hue (Nantume 2018). The battle for young people has intensified since the growing influence of the 'People Power' movement under Robert Kyagulanyi (Bobi Wine), particularly in Kampala where Kyagulanyi has long been associated with the Kamwokya suburb in which he grew up, and in Wakiso district where he has been an MP since 2017. Bobi Wine's fifteen-year career as a pop musician has been associated with increasingly angry, politically charged, and anti-Museveni music (Osiebe 2020; Wilkins et al 2021).

The President's engagement with young people in Kampala goes as far back as the early 1990s, but the speed and magnitude of engagement increased after the 2001 presidential and parliamentary elections and has remained significant in every election since. In the run-up to the 2016 election and facing heightened hostility among urban youth, channelled by Wine's music, Museveni persuaded an impressive number of Uganda's leading pop stars to compose and record a song, 'Tubonga Nawe' ('We Are with You'), praising him and urging people to vote NRM (Schneidermann 2015). This was a misstep that ultimately backfired in an age of social media. Intense debate about the proper role of pop stars in politics ensued, with the media profiling stars who had refused to participate in Museveni's campaign song. Many young people, angered by the decisions of their favourite stars to participate in this stunt, responded by boycotting their music (Kagumire 2018).

As one of the biggest stars to refuse to join the campaign song, Kyagulanyi capitalized on this popular anger when standing in the 2017 by-election. His victory and subsequent success in putting forward winning candidates in a number of by-elections, under the banner of a vague but emotive 'People Power' movement, led to the President further stepping up efforts to win over urban youth—but this time primarily through cash and other influential personalities, rather than music, as well as parallel efforts to infiltrate and manipulate key informal economic sectors. While these strategies play out across the nation, they have particular significance in Kampala. The remainder of this section explores two specific approaches through which the ruling coalition has tried to manipulate and buy support among youth groups in Kampala over the past decade: (i) the distribution of cash among youth groups in selected areas of Kampala, and (ii) courting and manipulating informal workers with particular attention to *boda boda* motorcycle taxis.

Countering 'People Power' with cash

Cash is one of the biggest weapons in Museveni's armoury, and it has become commonplace for him to carry bags of money and brown envelopes.[13] In

---

[13] Interview with a member of Nakasero Market Vendors' Association.

the company of his ministers, the State House Controller, the former KCCA Executive Director, and many other government officials, the President regularly provides funds for young people, women, and other groups in Kampala and surrounding urban councils. The source of the money is unclear, though reference is sometimes made to the State House Community Donations Budget and the Consolidated Fund. Unconfirmed reports indicate that a State House-commissioned 'Ghetto Fund' of Shs1.8 billion was set up to bribe young people into supporting the NRM prior to the 2021 elections. Speculation is widespread that such funds involve diversions from productive government projects to ensure there is a steady supply (Khisa 2018b).

During campaign time, rather than rely on his lieutenants, Museveni has taken to handing out the cash himself. Some observers believe this actually helps to reduce financial malfeasance, with money for poverty reduction finally reaching the poor;[14] the President is very aware that entrusting cash to formal channels for distribution results in much of the money being pocketed along the way.[15] In other cases, State House and the Internal Security Organization (ISO) have enlisted obscure 'socialites-turned-philanthropists' as emissaries to divert urban youth from opposition politicians, again echoing Kyagulanyi's own philanthropic activities (Osiebe 2020). These philanthropists appear and disappear mysteriously. A recent example is Brian White (Brian Kirumira), who has moved around the country under the guise of helping young people and women out of poverty. He has been seen handing out bicycles, seeds, medicine, and school equipment, as well as large amounts of cash. In many ways, these practices have underlined the increasing commercialization of elections, where people expect 'something small' in exchange for their vote.

In Kampala specifically, another way in which the NRM has sought to counter the threat posed by Kyagulanyi is through the creation of large numbers of youth projects, organized through their own Savings and Credit Cooperative Organizations (SACCOs). These have been visited by the President and State House handlers, including in Kamwokya suburb (Kyagulanyi's base). Six 'ghetto youth groups' were created in Kamwokya in 2018 and registered to receive funds from the President. No consistent criteria were used to select the beneficiaries, or determine how funds should be spent.[16]

An important point to note in terms of the clearly political nature of these funds is that they operate beyond the purview of the official Youth Livelihood

---

[14] Interview with a beneficiary of youth funds in Kamwokya.
[15] Interview with a political scientist.
[16] Interview with one of the officials from the Ministry of Finance, Planning and Economic Development and a regular columnist in one of Uganda's major newspapers.

Fund, overseen by the Ministry of Gender, Labour and Social Development (MGLSD). Many of the groups that have received the cash handouts in Kampala were not in the MGLSD database for registered youth groups in the period prior to the 2021 election, and were hastily assembled just for the purposes of receiving cash. Moreover, in 2019–20 official youth funds were moved from MGLSD to State House, resulting in a Shs130 billion State House Youth Livelihood Fund (Daily Monitor 2019), which clearly heightens the risk of such funds being politicized. State House operations are almost beyond public scrutiny, with limited parliamentary oversight. However, this ease of distribution without the need for complex bureaucratic procedure is precisely why some people defend placing this fund under direct presidential control.[17]

The extent to which these activities have focused on Kampala is striking, with an NRM candidate from Arua, northern Uganda, noting that 'in Kampala money is being distributed like beans'.[18] Yet despite such efforts to win the favour of Kampala's young people, the 2021 election result demonstrated that they had failed to secure NRM votes on a significant scale. Our research shows that the attention lavished on opposition-supporting areas such as Kamwokya led former NRM supporters to complain of neglect:

> We are tired of being neglected. The habit of bypassing party structures must stop. We know Kampala and all the groups that work within the city. Why do you rely on State House officials who do not even know anything about the people of Kampala and leave out the NRM leaders?[19]

The President often likens his poverty reduction struggle in urban areas to the five-year protracted bush war he fought in an area known as the Luweero triangle to oust the Obote II regime. In a significant development, he has placed increasing emphasis on Wakiso, the district that almost entirely surrounds Kampala and which (as illustrated in Fig. 3.1) was lost to the opposition for the first time in 2016. Even in advance of this election, he announced in 2015 that 'Wakiso District … is going to be my Luweero to liberate the urban poor from poverty. If we earmark this area and injected like Shs100m, this place can become paradise.'[20] In 2018, with Kyagulanyi building momentum from

---

[17] Director of Uganda Media Centre, quoted in 'Cabinet endorses Museveni's donation budget', *Daily Monitor*, 29 January 2019. Available at: https://mobile.monitor.co.ug/News/Cabinet-endorses-Museveni-donation-budget/2466686-4956718-format-xhtml-xg5rmbz/index.html, accessed 1 July 2019.

[18] Quoted in 'NRM Tiperu warned the ruling party against people power', InfoUganda, available at https://info256.com/nrm-tiperu-warned-the-ruling-party-against-people-power/, accessed 17 July 2019.

[19] Interview with NRM youth leader, central Kampala.

[20] Quoted in 'Museveni goes back to the Bush', RadioSimba.ug, available at https://www.radiosimba.ug/museveni-goes-back-to-the-bush/, accessed 17 July 2019.

his constituency in Wakiso, the government unveiled a 'Wakiso Grand Plan', with promises that employment opportunities would follow.

There are several other programmes such as 'Entandikwa'[21] and a slew of other 'wealth creation' initiatives that have been implemented through Museveni's bags of cash. Their long-term impact on beneficiary communities is unclear: few if any beneficiary groups had plans about how to use the donated money. Moreover, one Kamwokya-based youth group claims that the Shs100 million given to youth clubs and SACCOs in the area had never reached them, but rather was diverted by officials who were not members of their car-washing business.[22] The group also accused officials of registering the wrong youth clubs. Far from creating satisfaction that could build support for the NRM, there is a sense that the allocation of funds generated new forms of resentment and conflict. According to one association chairperson: 'the 10 million that we received is so small for an association of 64 members … expect that this money is going to create chaos and divide us further.'[23]

Similar views and complaints were recorded at Kisekka market in April 2019, on the grounds that funds pledged by the President during a personal visit the previous year had not materialized.[24] According to the Chairperson of Kisekka Vendors, forty new SACCOs were specifically created to receive the money promised by the President in October 2018. By 2019 the anticipation in Kisekka market for the Shs500 million pledged by the President was very high, despite the fact that the money had been delayed, as demonstrated by this comment from the Deputy Chairperson:

> Money will come we are confident of that. Why? Government knows what Kisekka market means—people here we think alike and act as one—you cannot lie to them; they are capable of being very very disruptive. In this market people are very idle and disorderly and need to be kept busy.

This reference to the market's disruptive capacity alludes to the history of violent rioting in the market, and the vendors' confidence is rooted in their history of winning favours due to their capacity to mobilize opposition.[25] Yet there was no indication that the funds would increase NRM support within the market; as the former Chairperson of the Market Vendors' Association pointed out, 'the NRM thinks it is co-opting them but the truth is

---

[21] Meaning 'fresh start'.
[22] Interview with the current Vice Chairman of the Mulago Car Washers SACCO.
[23] Interview with an association chairperson, Kampala.
[24] Chairman of the Kisekka Market Vendors, 18 March 2019.
[25] See Goodfellow (2013) for a discussion of earlier rioting and factional conflicts in Kisekka Market.

[young people] too have learnt to use the system to their advantage'.[26] These findings raise questions about the extent to which those receiving funds see a direct relationship between the money and their political allegiance, or at the very least a change in who they vote for. As the Kisekka Market Vendors' Deputy Chairperson noted, 'Boys here see this as a business—they're disrupters for hire', going on to say that 'When elections come this is an opportunity for them to earn … they'll go elsewhere to act up and it doesn't matter who pays!' This sense that any gains made by Museveni in exchange for payment are extremely short-lived, and would not ultimately lead to NRM support in the context of deep youth disillusionment, was clearly borne out in the 2021 election.

Dominating mobile livelihoods: infiltration and violence in the *boda boda* sector

Another way in which the NRM has sought to gain dominance among urban youth in the city is through specific initiatives to control and gain support in the transport sector. Despite several efforts to expand the formal bus system over the last decade, urban public transport in Uganda remains overwhelmingly dominated by minibus taxis (*matatus)* and motorcycle taxis (*boda bodas*). The *matatu* sector itself has a long history of use by the NRM for political mobilization through a monopolistic organization, the Uganda Taxi Operators and Drivers Association (Goodfellow 2017). Although this organization was dismembered by Musisi in her drive to improve urban transport, *matatu*-based transport remains dominant in the city. Next on Musisi's list was to regain control over *boda bodas*, which had mushroomed in number such that a registration process in 2014 identified 50,000 motorcycle taxis in Kampala alone.[27] However, despite Musisi initially receiving support from the President, the sheer significance of *boda boda* drivers as a (predominantly young) voting bloc meant that she was offered little support for activities to tax or regulate them; indeed, this was one of the issues that dogged her tenure as Executive Director and contributed to her decision to resign.

---

[26] Interview with a former Chairperson of Kisekka Market Vendors' Association.

[27] Interview with a transport police official. This was widely considered an underestimate; the following year KCCA counted 120,000 registered motorcycles, 'most of which' were engaged in commercial activities ('The *boda boda* economy defining the streets of Kampala', *Daily Monitor*, 15 September 2019), available at: https://www.monitor.co.ug/Business/Prosper/boda-boda-economy-defining-streets-Kampala/688616-2869756-d4bwbo/index.html, accessed 18 July 2019.

Even in the early–mid-2000s, repeated efforts by the (then opposition-dominated) KCC to control the burgeoning numbers of *boda bodas* were frustrated by interventions from the President in his efforts to boost support among *boda boda* drivers while also drawing them into the strategy to under-mine the KCC (Goodfellow and Titeca 2012; Goodfellow 2015). In theory, the capacity to control the sector should have improved since 2011 under KCCA. However, the unclear mandates and broken chains of accountability discussed in Section 3.5 have continued to provide incentives for informal political bargaining that have weakened KCCA's enforcement capacity. In fact, the KCCA period ushered in a new dynamic in the politicization of the sector, which saw forms of organization that were both more centralized and more violent. We examine these in the remainder of this section.

Prior to 2010, efforts to organize the sector under the banner of one asso-ciation repeatedly failed. From 2006–7 the police attempted to infiltrate the sector through the creation of an organization called Kuboca, designed to fight crime and monitor the sector's activities from within, but this collapsed after it rapidly became associated with violent extortion. Moreover, its link to the NRM (including through the wearing of yellow T-shirts, a colour strongly associated with the ruling party) was damaging NRM support among rid-ers. During the 'Buganda riots' in 2009 the presence of *boda boda* drivers was widely noted, leading to growing concerns that the sector harboured opposition elements, despite the President's ongoing efforts to win favour by shielding them from regulatory control.

A new opportunity for the ruling elite to gain influence subsequently arose in the form of 'Boda Boda 2010', which was initially a bottom-up organi-zation established by drivers with the intention of helping with emergency response.[28] Realizing that they held a unique position of influence within the sector, some of the organization's leaders capitalized on this by approaching the Inspector General of Police, Kale Kayihura, and other political figures. Through this process an influential local NRM leader by the name of Abdal-lah Kitatta, who was openly critical of the police's previous approach to securitizing the sector through Kuboca, managed to manoeuvre himself into the position of leader of Boda Boda 2010.

Kitatta's rise to prominence coincided with Kizza Besigye's attempt to gal-vanize a street uprising through the 'walk to work' protests.[29] As an NRM mobilizer, Kitatta had created an alternative grassroots network to diffuse the threat of street insurrections. This endeared him to the President and

---

[28] Interview with a *boda boda* coordinator.
[29] See Goodfellow (2013) and Mutyaba (2022) for a discussion of these events.

other senior government officials (Mutaizibwa 2019). Kitatta thus became an increasingly powerful figure, widely feared by police themselves due to his alleged close relationship with Kayihura. After 2011, he issued 'stage cards' to riders to prevent stages (the specified areas in which *boda bodas* wait for customers) from being overrun with new drivers, and to facilitate surveillance within the sector. The sector thus achieved new levels of systematic control under one organization,[30] but this was achieved through violent enforcement and politicization, with Boda Boda 2010 being widely seen as Kayihura's client organization and a quasi-military agent of surveillance. In 2013, its agents blocked an early KCCA effort to register *boda bodas*, allegedly beating up registration officials, while in 2017 its representatives attacked a group of schoolchildren simply on the basis that they were wearing red ribbons—a symbol associated with protest against the lifting of the presidential age limit.[31] Ultimately Boda Boda 2010 was recreating the conditions that had prevailed under Kuboca but on a greater scale, with the organization becoming increasingly armed with weapons and terrorizing its drivers, thereby sowing the seeds for an uprising in the sector.[32] When Kitatta was linked to the murder of an accountant in early 2018, the Minister of National Security, Henry Tumukunde (a long-term rival of Kayihura), initiated an investigation into Boda Boda 2010. This led to Kitatta's arrest and imprisonment, followed by the organization's demise after its offices were stormed by angry drivers.[33]

The NRM's efforts to dominate the sector show how attempts to win over urban constituencies through shielding informal workers from taxation and regulation were ultimately insufficient for sustained support, leading to deepening efforts also to surveil and coerce drivers. These dual strategies have generated conflicting dynamics within the sector: on the one hand, the ruling coalition actively facilitated the growth of a large interest group that it purports to protect, but on the other, it has terrorized the group through a series of proxy organizations. In this sense, the strategy in the sector could be seen as a specific form of 'coercive distribution', in which drivers are offered a form of protection from formal state regulation but through processes that are highly coercive—a strategy that ultimately overreached itself and collapsed.

---

[30] Interview with a *boda boda* coordinator.
[31] 'Uganda: Age limit—one arrested over attack on pupils', *Daily Monitor*, 12 October 2017, available at: https://www.monitor.co.ug/News/National/Age-limit-One-arrested-over-beating-school-children/688334-4136314-8227suz/monitor.co.ug, accessed 18 July 2019.
[32] Interview with a *boda boda* coordinator.
[33] See Goodfellow and Mukwaya 2021a for an extended discussion.

3.7 Conclusion

This chapter has explored how Uganda's ruling coalition used a combination of violent coercion, co-optation, coercive distribution, and legal-institutional manoeuvres to try and enhance its political dominance of the city. From initially neglecting urban constituencies during its early decades of rule, the question of urban opposition became an increasing concern in the first decade of the new millennium. After the split with Besigye and the evidence of growing opposition in Kampala in the 2001 and 2006 elections, Museveni stepped up efforts to gain favour with urban groups in the late 2000s, including through persistent efforts to scupper KCC's attempts to regulate informal trade and transport. This helped the NRM to regain some support in Kampala in 2011. But this was short-lived, with Besigye relentlessly mobilizing opposition on the streets and offering himself as a martyr in front of the media.

In this chapter we have subjected the NRM's strategies for dominance over the subsequent decade to close scrutiny. By the start of the decade, it was clear that the tried-and-tested strategies of repression and elite co-optation were insufficient, necessitating new approaches to urban control. These were pursued both from the 'top down', through legal manoeuvres, and from the 'bottom up' by attempting to build support among urban youth and more deeply to infiltrate organizations in the urban informal economy. The urban modernization project under Jennifer Musisi's KCCA, which put enormous effort into branding and generating civic pride in the hope of bolstering urban middle-class support, initially yielded some rewards. However, the effort to rid the streets of vendors and regulate many urban-dwellers out of existence soon grated against a city population accustomed to a highly permissive urban environment (Young 2017), as evidenced by strong opposition performance in 2016. In consequence, the subsequent electoral cycle saw the ruling elite reinvent its strategy to centralize the governance of the city, alongside continued repression and a host of new street-level strategies to try and win over urban youth—especially since the rise of Robert Kyagulanyi.

A decade of pursuing this suite of both 'generative' and 'repressive' strategies and tactics has only reproduced the situation of contested control in the city. Alongside continuing to exercise highly visible violence against opponents, the ruling elite's overall approach has involved a central contradiction in its attempt to centralize power away from the city population while *simultaneously* championing popular urban groups. This approach fans the flames of opposition even as it binds opposition figures' hands. Fig. 3.3 illustrates

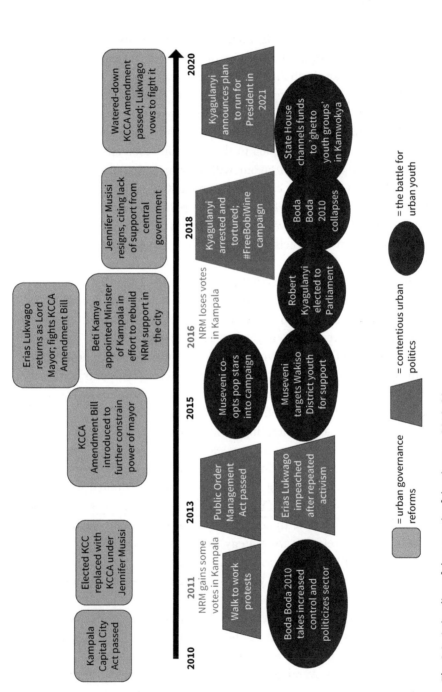

Fig. 3.3 A timeline of the pursuit of dominance, 2010–20

2010 | 2011 | 2013 | 2015 | 2016 | 2018 | 2020

Kampala Capital City Act passed

Elected KCC replaced with KCCA under Jennifer Musisi

NRM gains some votes in Kampala

Walk to work protests

Boda Boda 2010 takes increased control and politicizes sector

Public Order Management Act passed

Erias Lukwago impeached after repeated activism

KCCA Amendment Bill introduced to further constrain power of mayor

Erias Lukwago returns as Lord Mayor; fights KCCA Amendment Bill

Beti Kamya appointed Minister of Kampala in effort to rebuild NRM support in the city

Museveni co-opts pop stars into campaign

Museveni targets Wakiso District youth for support

NRM loses votes in Kampala

Robert Kyagulanyi elected to Parliament

Jennifer Musisi resigns, citing lack of support from central government

Kyagulanyi arrested and tortured; #FreeBobiWine campaign

Boda Boda 2010 collapses

Watered-down KCCA Amendment passed; Lukwago vows to fight it

Kyagulanyi announces plan to run for President in 2021

State House channels funds to 'ghetto youth groups' in Kamwokya

= urban governance reforms

= contentious urban politics

= the battle for urban youth

the interplay of these strategies (and responses to them) across the course of the decade.

The 2021 election results forcefully demonstrated that the suite of strategies deployed was not enough to secure NRM dominance in the city—even following the horrendous violence unleashed on the streets of Kampala in November 2020, in which at least fifty-four people died.[34] Yet these strategies have limited the opposition's capacity to contest dominance in ways that can fundamentally change the balance of power. The result is a continued impasse: the regime is running out of options in its quest to dominate the capital fully, but time and again it has shown it can do enough to prevent urban opposition from becoming transformative or threatening the regime's power and legitimacy nationally. Whether this can change depends on whether the key demographic in the struggle for change—the urban youth—has the numbers, nerve and counter-strategies needed to face off the NRM's overflowing armoury of political weapons in the next political cycle.

References

Abrahamsen, R., and Bareebe, G. (2016). Uganda's 2016 elections: Not even faking it anymore. *African Affairs* 115(461), 751–765.

Amaza, Oondoga O. (1998). *Museveni's Long March: From Guerrilla to Statesman.* Kampala: Fountain.

Batte, B. (2018). Retirement: Museveni stumbles 5 times. *The Observer*, 24 October. Available at: https://observer.ug/news/headlines/59005-retirement-museveni-stumbles-5-times, accessed 24 October 2018.

Beardsworth, N. (2017). Challenging dominance: The opposition, the coalition and the 2016 election in Uganda. *Journal of Eastern African Studies* 10(4), 749–768.

Carbone, G. (2008). *No-Party Democracy? Ugandan Politics in Comparative Perspective.* Boulder, CO: Lynne Reiner Publishers.

City Mayors (2018). The world's fastest growing cities and urban areas from 2006 to 2020. Available at: http://www.citymayors.com/statistics/urban_growth1.html, accessed 28 April 2018.

Daily Monitor (2019). Cabinet endorses Museveni's donation budget. *Daily Monitor*, 29 January. Monitor Publications, Kampala, Uganda.

---

[34] 'Uganda: Bobi Wine suspends election campaign over violence', Al-Jazeera, available at: https://www.aljazeera.com/news/2020/12/2/uganda-bobi-wine-suspends-election-campaign-over-violence, accessed 15 July 2022.

Goodfellow, T. (2010). The bastard child of nobody: Anti-planning and the institutional crisis in contemporary Kampala. Crisis States Research Centre, Working Paper no. 67.2, LSE.

Goodfellow, T. (2013). The institutionalisation of 'noise' and 'silence' in urban politics: Riots and compliance in Uganda and Rwanda. *Oxford Development Studies* 41(4): 436–454.

Goodfellow, T. (2014). Legal manoeuvres and violence: Law making, protest and semi-authoritarianism in Uganda. *Development and Change* 45(4): 753–776.

Goodfellow, T. (2015). Taming the "rogue" sector: Studying state effectiveness in Africa through informal transport politics. *Comparative Politics*, 47(2): 127–147.

Goodfellow, T. (2017). Double Capture'and de-democratisation: interest group politics and Uganda's 'Transport Mafia. *The Journal of Development Studies*, 53(10): 1568–1583.

Goodfellow, T. (2022). *Politics and the urban frontier: Transformation and divergence in late urbanizing east Africa*. Oxford: Oxford University Press.

Goodfellow, T., & Titeca, K. (2012). Presidential intervention and the changing 'politics of survival' in Kampala's informal economy. *Cities*, 29(4): 264–270.

Goodfellow, T., and Mukwaya, P. I. (2021a). *The Political Economy of Public Transport in Greater Kampala: Movers, Spoilers and Prospects for Reform*. Kampala: Frederich Ebert Stiftung.

Goodfellow, T., and Mukwaya, P. I. (2021b). Museveni has failed to win over young, urban Ugandans: Why he's running out of options. The Conversation, 28 January. Available at: https://theconversation.com/museveni-has-failed-to-win-over-young-urban-ugandans-why-hes-running-out-of-options-154081, accessed 7 December 2021.

Golooba-Mutebi, F., & Hickey, S. (2016). The master of institutional multiplicity? The shifting politics of regime survival, state-building and democratisation in Museveni's Uganda. *Journal of Eastern African Studies*, 10(4): 601-618.

Gore, C. (2009). Healthy urban food production and local government. In D. Cole, D. Lee-Smith, and G. Nasinyama (eds), *Healthy City Harvests: Generating Evidence to Guide Policy on Urban Agriculture*. Lima and Kampala: Urban Harvest and Makerere University, pp. 49–65.

Gore, C., and Muwanga, Nansozi K. (2014). Decentralization is dead, long live decentralization! Capital city reform and political rights in Kampala, Uganda. *International Journal of Urban and Regional Research* 38(6): 2201–2216.

Grapevine (2018). The executive is using the army and police to subdue citizens— Nambooze warns after being charged with inciting the public to kill government officials. Available at: https://www.thegrapevine.co.ug/the-executive-is-using-the-army-and-police-to-subdue-citizens-nambooze-warns-after-being-charged-with-inciting-the-public-to-kill-government-officials/, accessed 30 August 2018.

Gyagenda, M. (2018). Kampala MPs move to block 'disenfranchising' KCCA Amendment Bill. *Soft Power Online*. Available at: https://www.softpower.ug/kampala-mps-move-to-block-disenfranchising-kcca-amendment-bill/, accessed 15 August 2018.

Hansen, H. B., and Twaddle, M. eds. (1998). *Developing Uganda*. Oxford: James Currey.

HRW (1999). The movement system and political freedoms in Uganda. Human Rights Watch. Available at: https://www.hrw.org/reports/1999/uganda/Uganweb-07.htm, accessed 28 April 2018.

HRW (2015). *World Report 2015*. New York: Human Rights Watch.

Kaaya, S. K. (2017). FDC alarmed as Museveni buys more of its members. *The Observer*, 10 July. Available at: https://observer.ug/news/headlines/53771-fdc-alarmed-as-museveni-buys-more-of-its-members, accessed 13 February 2019.

Kafeero, S. (2013). Lukwago war. *The Independent*. Available at: https://www.independent.co.ug/lukwago-war/, accessed 2 December 2018.

Kagumire, R. (2013). President Museveni's sack of shame. *Rosebell's blog*, 24 April. Available at: https://rosebellkagumire.com/2013/04/24/president-musevenis-sack-of-shame/, accessed 15 April 2019.

Kagumire, R. (2018). Bobi Wine and the beginning of the end of Museveni's power. *Aljazeera*, 28 August. Available at: https://www.aljazeera.com/indepth/opinion/bobi-wine-beginning-museveni-power-180828111608108.html, accessed 29 August 2018.

Kasfir, N. and Twebaze, S. H. (2009) 'The Rise and Ebb of Uganda's No-Party Parliament', in Barkan, J. D. (ed) *Legislative Power in Emerging African Democracies*. Boulder, Lynne Reinner.

Kasozi, E., and Ssenkabirwa, A.-M. (2011). 'I have defeated President Museveni'—Lukwago. *Daily Monitor*, 15 March. Available at: https://www.monitor.co.ug/News/National/-/688334/1125260/-/c3xl8mz/-/index.html, accessed 20 March 2020.

Kazibwe, K. (2018). Museveni gives out Shs100m to Bobi Wine's Kamwokya ghetto youths. *Nile Post*, 24 September. Available at: http://nilepost.co.ug/2018/09/24/museveni-gives-out-shs100m-to-bobi-wines-kamwokya-ghetto-youths/, accessed 24 September 2018.

Keating, M. F. (2011) 'Can democratization undermine democracy? Economic and political reform in Uganda'. *Democratization* 18(2): 415–442.

Khisa, M. (2018a). The writing has been on the wall for long. *The Observer*, 5 September. Available at: https://observer.ug/viewpoint/58606-the-writing-has-been-on-the-wall-for-long, accessed 7 September 2018.

Khisa. M. (2018b). The limits of renting support. *The Observer*, 10 October. Available at: https://observer.ug/viewpoint/58878-the-limits-of-renting-support, accessed 10 October 2018.

Kiyonga, D. (2013). How Museveni plotted Lukwago's fall. *The Observer*, 24 November. Available at: https://www.observer.ug/index.php?option=com_content& view=article&id=28791:how-museveni-plotted-lukwagos-fall&catid=78: topstories&Itemid=116, accessed 10 December 2018.

Kobusingye, O. (2010). *The Correct Line?: Uganda Under Museveni*. Milton Keynes: AuthorHouse.

Kuteesa, F., Mutebile, E. T., Whitworth, A., and Williamson, T. (2010). *Uganda's Economic Reforms: Insider Accounts*. Oxford: Oxford University Press.

Kyeyune, M. (2017). New KCCA Amendment Bill tabled in Parliament. *Daily Monitor*, 10 May. Available at: http://www.monitor.co.ug/News/National/-KCCA-amendment-Bill-tabled-Parliament-Kadaga-Lukwago-/688334-3921686-hvjg2l/ index.html, accessed 15 August 2018.

Lall, S., Schroeder, E., and Schmidt, E. (2009). Identifying spatial efficiency–equity trade-offs in territorial development policies: Evidence from Uganda. Policy Research Working Paper no. 4966, World Bank.

Lambright, G. M. (2014). Opposition politics and urban service delivery in Kampala, Uganda. *Development Policy Review*, 32(s1): s39–s60.

Leni, X. (2019). Lord Mayor gets back his powers in New KCCA Amendment Bill passed by Parliament. *PML Daily*, 16 August. Available at: https://www.pmldaily. com/news/2019/08/parliament-passes-kcca-amendment-bill.html, accessed 23 March 2020.

Lubowa, F. (2018). Museveni pumps more money into youth projects. *Daily Monitor*, 16 September. Available at: http://www.monitor.co.ug/News/National/Museveni-pumps-money-youth-projects/688334-4760222-l4236s/index.html, accessed 12 October 2018.

Mao, N. (2018). Museveni, Bobi Wine and the law of unintended consequences. *Daily Monitor*, 23 September. Available at: http://www.monitor.co.ug/ OpEd/Commentary/689364-4772984-118pdajz/index.html, accessed 24 September 2018.

Mugabe, F. (2018). How opposition MPs have been tortured since independence. *Daily Monitor*, 29 September. Available at: http://www.monitor.co.ug/Magazines/ PeoplePower/Opposition—MPs-tortured-Independence-Ssebuggwawo/689844-4783338-10vrct4z/index.html, accessed 1 October 2018.

Mugaju, J., and Oloka-Onyango, J. (eds) (2000). *No-Party Democracy in Uganda: Myths and Realities*. Kampala: Fountain.

Muhereza, S., and Hitchen, J. (2022). *Uganda's Sub-national 'Presidents': Understanding the Evolution, Role and Function of Resident District Commissioners.* Kampala: Konrad-Adenauer-Stiftung.

Mutaizibwa, E. (2019). Kitatta: The man who flew too close to the sun. *Daily Monitor*, 11 February. Available at: https://www.monitor.co.ug/SpecialReports/Kitatta-The-man-who-flew-too-close-to-the-sun/688342-4975980-15e5kj6z/index.html, accessed 13 February 2019.

Mutyaba, M. (2022). From voting to walking: The 2011 walk-to-work protest movement in Uganda. In E. Rodrigues Sanches (ed.), *Popular Protest, Political Opportunities, and Change in Africa.* Abingdon: Routledge, pp. 163–180.

Mwenda, A. (2011) 'Why Museveni won and Besigye lost and what can be done for the future', available at: https://www.independent.co.ug/museveni-won-besigye-lost-can-done-future/. Accessed 4 May 2023.

Mwenda, A. and Tangri, R. (2005). Patronage politics, donor reforms and regime consolidation in Uganda. *African Affairs* 104(416): 449–467.

Nantume, G. (2018). How Bobi Wine's trumpet charmed disillusioned masses. *Daily Monitor*, 17 September. Available at: http://www.monitor.co.ug/SpecialReports/Bobi-Wine-trumpet-charmed-disillusioned-masses/688342-4762902-k0pq8ez/index.html, accessed 26 September 2018.

Observer (2016). Mayor-elect Lukwago warns Museveni over Kampala. *The Observer*, 25 February. Available at: https://observer.ug/news-headlines/42799-mayor-elect-lukwago-warns-museveni-over-kampala, accessed 12 December 2018.

Omolo-Okalebo, F., Haas, T., Werner, I. B., & Sengendo, H. (2010). Planning of Kampala city 1903—1962: the planning ideas, values, and their physical expression. *Journal of Planning History* 9(3): 151–169.

Osiebe, G. (2020). The ghetto president and presidential challenger in Uganda. *Africa Spectrum* 55(1): 86–99.

Resnick, D. (2014). Strategies of subversion in vertically-divided contexts: Decentralisation and urban service delivery in Senegal. *Development Policy Review* 32(s1), s61–s80.

Rubongoya, J. B. (2007). *Regime Hegemony in Museveni's Uganda: Pax Musevenica.* New York: Palgrave Macmillan.

Sabiiti, J. (2013). Patience will defeat Museveni schemes. *The Observer*, 28 November. Available at: http://observer.ug/index.php?option=com_content&view=article&id=28864:patience-will-defeat-museveni-schemes&catid=37:guest-writers&Itemid=66, accessed 28 April 2018.

Schneidermann, N. (2015). 'We are with you': Musicians and the 2016 general elections in Uganda. *Mats Utas blog*, 16 November. Available at: https://matsutas. wordpress.com/2015/11/16/we-are-with-you-musicians-and-the-2016-general-elections-in-uganda-by-nanna-schneidermann/, accessed 17 July 2019.

Semakula, J., Wassajja, N., and Mayanja, B. (2017). Does KCCA Bill 2015 leave Lord Mayor empty? *New Vision*, 16 May. Available at: https://www.newvision.co.ug/new_vision/news/1453224/kcca-2015-leave-lord-mayor, accessed 15 August 2018.

Sengoba, N. (2018). Politically, Uganda is moving into a state of 'mental breakdown'. *Daily Monitor*, 4 September. Available at: http://www.monitor.co.ug/OpEd/columnists/NicholasSengooba/Politically-Uganda-moving-into-state-mental-breakdown/1293432-4741958-pf6wtd/index.html, accessed 4 September 2018.

Serunkuma, Y. (2019). Who exactly are these LDUs protecting? *The Observer*, 10 April. Available at: https://observer.ug/viewpoint/60386-who-exactly-are-these-ldus-protecting, accessed 10 April 2019.

Sserunjogi, E. (2018). Battle for the pearl: Bobi Wine, Museveni and the future of Uganda. *The Elephant*, 13 September. Available at: https://www.theelephant.info/features/2018/09/13/battle-for-the-pearl-bobi-wine-museveni-and-the-future-of-uganda/, accessed 28 September 2018.

Tapscott, R. (2016). Where the wild things are not: crime preventers and the 2016 Ugandan elections. *Journal of Eastern African Studies*, 10(4): 693–712.

Taylor, M. (2017). Bit by bit, Uganda is laying the groundwork for future unrest. *African Arguments*, 13 December. Available at: https://africanarguments.org/2017/12/13/bit-by-bit-uganda-is-laying-the-groundwork-for-future-unrest/, accessed 14 September 2018.

The Atlantic (2018). The pop star risking death to bring change. *The Atlantic*, 21 September. Available at: https://www.theatlantic.com/international/archive/2018/09/bobi-wine-uganda/570907/, accessed 24 September 2018.

Tripp, A. M. (2010). *Museveni's Uganda: Paradoxes of Power in a Hybrid Regime.* Boulder, CO: Lynne Rienner Publishers.

Vokes, R., and Wilkins, S. (2016). Party, patronage and coercion in the NRM'S 2016 re-election in Uganda: Imposed or embedded? *Journal of Eastern African Studies* 10(4): 581–600.

Walakira, J. (2018). Beti Kamya's Kampala Ministry adds no value, abolish it now, Kisamba tells Museveni. *Mulengera News*, 27 August. Available at: https://mulengeranews.com/beti-kamyas-kla-ministry-adds-no-value-abolish-it-now-kisamba-tells-m7/, accessed 28 August 2018.

Wandera, D. (2019). Museveni gives Shs3b for skilling youth in 35 districts. *Daily Monitor*, 15 April. Available at: https://www.monitor.co.ug/News/National/

Museveni-gives-Shs3b-skilling-youth-35-districts/688334-5071792-qd5qh7/ index.html, accessed 15 April 2019.

Wilkins, S., Vokes, R., & Khisa, M. (2021). Briefing: Contextualizing the Bobi Wine factor in Uganda's 2021 elections. *African Affairs* 120(481): 629–643.

World Bank (2015). *The Growth Challenge: Can Ugandan Cities Get to Work?* (English). Washington, DC: World Bank Group. Available at: http://documents. worldbank.org/curated/en/145801468306254958/The-growth-challenge-Can-Ugandan-cities-get-to-work.

Young, G. (2017). From protection to repression: The politics of street vending in Kampala. *Journal of Eastern African Studies* 11(4): 714–733.

4

The politics of dominating Addis Ababa, 2005–18

Eyob Balcha Gebremariam

4.1 Introduction

In May 2005, Ethiopia held perhaps the first ever open and competitive election in its recent history. One of the most important consequences of the election was the unprecedented electoral defeat of the ruling party in the capital city, Addis Ababa. The ruling party, the Ethiopian People's Revolutionary Democratic Front (EPRDF),[1] failed to win a single seat on the city council. However, the party remained in power nationally, controlling the federal government. The now-defunct EPRDF responded to the extraordinary political surge of opposition groups by aggressively pursuing a developmental model and revamping its strategy of political mobilization. This chapter argues that the EPRDF succeeded in building and maintaining dominance in Addis Ababa, particularly between 2005 and 2018, because of the politico-legal frameworks and socio-economic policies derived from its developmental aspirations. While a range of repressive measures were certainly used, the case studies in this chapter focus primarily on the provision of socio-economic services through generative interventions and politically driven mobilization of social groups in the city. Effective use of these interventions gave the EPRDF an advanced organizational power to control and dominate Addis Ababa for a considerable time.

---

[1] The EPRDF was a coalition of four ethnically organized political parties: namely, the Tigray People's Liberation Front (TPLF, the founders of the EPRDF); the Oromo People's Democratic Organization (OPDO), which changed its name to the Oromo Democratic Party (ODP) in 2018; the Amhara National Democratic Movement (ANDM), which also changed its name to the Amhara Democratic Party (ADP); and the Southern Ethiopia People's Democratic Movement (SEPDM). Since December 2019, as part of the ongoing political 'reform' in Ethiopia, three of the EPRDF member parties have dissolved themselves and established a new Prosperity Party. The only party that refused to join the Prosperity Party is the TPLF.

Eyob Balcha Gebremariam, *The politics of dominating Addis Ababa, 2005–18*. In: *Controlling the Capital.*
Edited by: Tom Goodfellow and David Jackman, Oxford University Press. © Oxford University Press (2023).
DOI: 10.1093/oso/9780192868329.003.0004

More specifically, three interrelated strategies enabled EPRDF to dominate and govern Addis Ababa during this period. The first, perhaps overarching, strategy was the use of a legitimizing discourse of developmentalism. Legitimizing discourses and narratives buttressed by developmentalism played an instrumental role in generating acquiescence particularly among certain social groups in the city: for example, the urban poor and unemployed young people. The second strategy was legal manoeuvring. Politically inspired legal manoeuvring helped the EPRDF to shape and reshape formal and informal channels of governance and control for the ruling coalition. The simultaneous roles of the formal and informal channels of control helped to constrain the organizational power of rival political coalitions. The third strategy can be broadly categorized as co-optation, which included use of both cooperative empowerment and passive co-optation, though this sometimes tipped into what the editors of this volume term 'coercive distribution'. The urban-specific socio-economic needs of the targeted social groups, such as access to essential food items and employment opportunities, facilitated the use of these strategies by both the EPRDF and the residents of Addis Ababa. Hence, their relations were essentially dynamic and prone to subtle changes but continued to contribute to the EPRDF's meaningful dominance and control in the city.

The empirical section focuses on two case studies: namely, Urban Consumers' Cooperatives (UCCs) and employment creation programmes targeting young people in Addis Ababa. The chapter uses primary data generated through in-depth interviews, focus group discussions, and observations. The primary data were collected in two rounds. The first round was from November 2014 to April 2015, as part of doctoral thesis fieldwork. The second round of data collection, focusing on both case studies, was conducted for twenty days during April and September 2018. In total, thirty-six interviews were carried out to inform the analysis for this chapter. A close reading of government publications, reports, and policy documents, as well as official and internal documents from the EPRDF, also contributed to the analysis of the empirical section.

The remainder of the chapter is divided into five sections. Section 4.2 presents the historical, socio-economic, and political position of Addis Ababa in the Ethiopian political system. Then Section 4.3 briefly presents the ideological orientation of the now-defunct EPRDF, which ruled Ethiopia from 1991 to 2018. Sections 4.4 and 4.5 then present the empirical cases of the chapter, and these are followed by a conclusion in Section 4.6.

4.2 Situating Addis Ababa

Addis Ababa is one of the two semi-autonomous city administrations within the Federal Democratic Republic of Ethiopia. Founded in 1896 during the reign of Emperor Menelik II, Addis Ababa has served as the seat of Ethiopia's successive regimes. According to 2015 data, Addis Ababa is also a prime city and ten times bigger than the next largest city in the country, Adama (Nazreth) (Gebre-Egziabher and Abera 2019). However, recent statistics also show that the primacy of Addis Ababa has been decreasing significantly over the last three decades, with its share of the total population declining from 36 per cent in 1984 to 18 per cent in 2015 (ibid.). Currently, the total population is estimated at around 3.8 million (CSA 2013).

Over the past 125 years, Addis Ababa has played a pivotal role in showcasing the socio-economic and developmental aspirations of ruling elites. Since its emergence as a small village, the city has evolved into an epicentre of the modernization and 'nation-building' political projects pursued by the last two imperial regimes in particular. The capital was the place for the making of the nation and the attainment of certain attributes of modernity (such as clean neighbourhoods, healthy citizenry, an organized and ordered community, and economic development) that were considered the basis of a strong nation and society (Gulema 2013: 172).

The political project of 'nation-building' by successive Ethiopian regimes elevated Addis Ababa as the cultural, economic, and political capital. In a nutshell, the cultural role of Addis Ababa can be seen from two different but not necessarily unrelated critical viewpoints. On the one hand, the city manifests the modernist aspiration of the rulers through its public spaces, buildings, and planning arrangements (Gulema 2013). On the other hand, the city has also witnessed the eviction of the indigenous Oromo community, which led to their sociocultural, political, and economic marginalization under the banner of a 'nation-building' project (Benti 2002; Gulema 2013). As a result, Addis Ababa has been one of the country's hotbeds, in which the lingering fundamental questions of the 1974 revolution—'the land question' and 'the national question'—have remained unanswered.

The approximately central location of Addis Ababa within the geographical jurisdiction of the Ethiopian state plays a vital role in the national political economic structures and power configuration. According to Clapham (2019), one of the fundamental features of the modern Ethiopian state is the degree of divergence in the sources of economic and political power.

The elites that controlled the state were primarily from the northern high-land regions. In contrast, the southern region remained marginal in terms of generating political elites, but continued to provide the economic resources that supported the political elite (Zewde 2002; Gudina 2007). Addis Ababa played a vital role in connecting these two sources of power for the state, by providing a socio-economic and political centre.

Under the current federalist arrangement, Addis Ababa is the seat of both the federal government and the Oromia regional state. Recent political tensions have shown that the EPRDF's ethnolinguistic federal system has barely provided a lasting solution concerning Addis Ababa. A historically rooted claim of ownership is being echoed primarily by Oromo nationalists. There is also an equally valid position which sees belonging in the city as beyond any claim of exclusive ownership by a single ethnolinguistic group. The Ethiopian Constitution (Article 49 (5)) recognizes the 'administrative' links between Addis Ababa and the Oromia region, mainly because the city is an enclave within the Oromia region.[2]

The political sensitivity around the administrative and ownership issues concerning Addis Ababa remained irrelevant in making the city a show-case for the hypermodernist approach to development. Compared with other urban centres in Ethiopia, Addis Ababa has received the highest proportion of infrastructure investment. The capital city also accommodates slightly above 60 per cent of the service sector and nearly 40 per cent of the manufacturing industry of the country (Spaliviero and Cheru 2017). In recent years, the city has benefited from multiple major infrastructure projects, including the Integrated Housing Development Programme (IHDP) as well as private real-estate firms, road complexes, and a light railway system (FDRE 2016). These investments were part of the EPRDF's effort to use a legitimizing discourse of developmentalism as a vital aspect of its dominance in the city.

The symbolic and actual position of Addis Ababa as a centre of political and economic power made the stakes of either winning or losing the capital high during the May 2005 elections. The capital city was the epicentre of opposition political mobilization. Eventually, the opposition succeeded in achieving the ultimate objective of winning all but one of the 138 seats. However, allegations of vote-rigging outside of Addis Ababa by the ruling EPRDF created national-level confrontations and a political crisis. Boosted by its overall victory, albeit contested, in forming a government the EPRDF was

---

[2] https://www.africanews.com/2019/03/09/ethiopia-pm-moves-to-resolve-oromia-addis-ababa-boundary-rift/, accessed 22 March 2019.

determined not to lose its control of Addis Ababa. The then Mayor-elect of the city, Berhanu Nega, recently revealed that the EPRDF government 'refused to hand over' the city administration to the victorious political party.[3]

After violently suppressing the post-election protest in 2005, the EPRDF revamped its approach to governing the city. The party implemented three interrelated strategies that contributed to its eventual recovery from the political and administrative setback of the 2005 elections. The vital first strategy offered an administrative solution by establishing a 'caretaker administration' with a temporary technical mandate and a lifeline until a by-election was held. While this 'caretaker administration' filled the administrative void, the EPRDF mobilized city-dwellers proactively, using its prerogative power as leader of the federal government as a pretext. The historically unprecedented mobilization of different social groups in Addis Ababa came under the banner of establishing a tripartite relationship between the federal government, the caretaker administration, and city-dwellers (Gebremariam 2017b). The implicit political agenda was to establish a social foundation to regain full political and administrative control over Addis Ababa.

The second strategy was purely political, and it introduced new laws of city governance. One of the election-related laws helped the EPRDF to restructure local councils at the national level. The EPRDF enacted legislation to increase the number of local councils exponentially, from fifteen to 300 (Aalen and Tronvoll 2009). As a result, nearly 3.6 million seats became available in local councils across the country.[4] This legislative manoeuvre put massive pressure on opposition political parties to put up several thousands of candidates to win local government administrations. None of the opposition parties were in a position to mobilize such a considerable number of candidates and to win a meaningful majority.

The third strategy was an aggressive mobilization of different social groups (young people, women, inhabitants, traders, etc.). By July 2006, the EPRDF had facilitated the establishment of three forums across the city: the Youth Forum, the Women's Forum, and the Inhabitants' Forum. This mobilization was the third post-election strategy aimed at boosting the EPRDF's membership and thereby its political power. The party was successful in recruiting several new candidates to represent the party during the 2008 by-election (Gebremariam 2017b). As a result, the EPRDF won the local elections across the country by an unprecedented margin and this laid the ground for its 99 per cent control of the federal parliament in the 2010 election.

[3] Birtu Weg, interview on Ethiopian Broadcast Corporation (EBC): https://www.youtube.com/watch?v=b3QgClJNx-Y&t=2s, accessed 16 November 2019.
[4] http://www.ceict.gov.et/web/am/-1, accessed 18 March 2019.

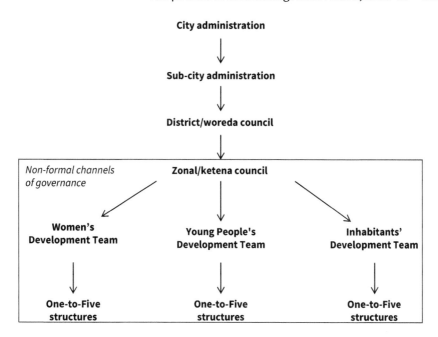

Fig. 4.1 Addis Ababa city administration sub-district level organization, November 2014

In addition to its legal manoeuvring to expand the formal structures of local government, the EPRDF also facilitated the establishment of non-formal channels of governance that fed into the formal structures (see Fig. 4.1). An internal policy document argues that 'developmental good governance' is an essential element in transforming rent-seeking-based socio-economic relations in the city into developmental relations. Hence, the government took proactive measures to mobilize and organize the city population into zones and development teams (AACA 2014: 5). As a result, the city government established 771 zones to facilitate interactions between development teams (of which there were 18,000 across the city) and the districts through public mobilization, participation, monitoring, and evaluation.

4.3 The EPRDF's ideology

The EPRDF's successful dominance of both Addis Ababa and the national government had an ideological basis. Examining its ideological orientation helps to explain how the party related itself to different segments of society based on their social class or cultural identity, and how it deployed different political strategies depending on the context. This section gives a brief background in this regard before the chapter delves into the case studies.

The EPRDF followed an ideology called revolutionary democracy, pioneered by V. I. Lenin, which seeks to establish a proletarian dictatorship that could challenge a bourgeois democracy (Berhe 2009; Bach 2011). Revolutionary democracy advocates for a 'vanguard party' that is committed to the principles of 'democratic centralism'. Democratic centralism is a decision-making process whereby members of the party's core leadership have more freedom to debate and criticize an idea before it is adopted. Once the party adopts a given idea or decision, 'everyone must implement the decision of the [party] no matter what their view' (Angle 2005: 525).

Ideological pragmatism was one of the vital features of the EPRDF, and it enabled the party to remain the dominant political force after its ascent to power in May 1991. The party managed to manoeuvre around a number of internal and external challenges during the last three decades without necessarily abandoning the pillars of its ideology. At the same time, the party remained adaptive and resilient to new challenges and stood its ground to remain the most dominant political force. The pragmatism and resilience of the party were also visible in its capacity to establish a strong organizational power that enabled it to maintain a balance in the wider distribution of power, both horizontally and vertically.

In the first phase of revolutionary democracy (from 1989 to 1995), the EPRDF aspired to build a socialist Ethiopian state. This objective remained intact when the EPRDF toppled the Derg regime in 1991 and formally started spearheading the establishment of democratic institutions in post-Derg Ethiopia. Leaders of the EPRDF were 'reluctant liberals' who were trying to reconcile their Marxism and Leninism-inspired socialist ideology with the practices of facilitating the democratic transition to liberalism (Asrat 2014). While adhering to the influence of the triumphant liberal world order in terms of setting up formal institutions of democracy, the EPRDF also held firm to some of its key ideological bases. This is exemplified by the party's success in resisting a full-scale economic liberalization pushed by the World Bank and the International Monetary Fund (IMF) (Stiglitz 2002; Feyissa 2011). The EPRDF kept the state at the centre of its socio-economic development plan to 'coordinate, shape, and guide' economic forces using fiscal and monetary policies (EPRDF 1993: 43–44).

In the second phase of revolutionary democracy (from 1995 to 2005), the EPRDF attempted to use the formal institutions of democracy as a shield while continuing its project of building the hegemony of revolutionary democracy. Formally speaking, the country adopted a liberal constitution and installed the formal institutions of a democratic government (Yeshanew 2008; Hessebon 2013). Regular elections were also introduced as constitutionally sanctioned ways through which state power was contested and controlled. However, the emergence of a competitive political settlement was limited by the ways in which the EPRDF continued to exercise its political power, derived mainly from its being the leading architect of both the structural and institutional features of the new Ethiopian state. Such a position offered the party a significant advantage vis-à-vis competing political parties.

In the third phase of revolutionary democracy (from 2005 to 2018), the EPRDF adopted a strategy of using state-led developmentalism as a legitimizing discourse to remain dominant. The highly contested election in May 2005 was a watershed moment when the EPRDF's legitimacy was seriously threatened. After suffering a heavy electoral defeat, particularly in Addis Ababa and in many urban areas, the EPRDF needed a set of strategies to address the socio-economic demands of the majority, to broaden the party's social base, and also to constrain the organizational power of rival political actors. The adoption of state-led developmentalism provided the EPRDF with an overarching framework for shaping the post-2005 period and readjusting some of its political principles to the context of urban politics.

The legitimizing discourse of developmentalism also made two of the core principles of the EPRDF less relevant, particularly in the urban environment. These principles were the primacy of ethnically based political mobilization and the EPRDF's aspiration to become a vanguard party. The EPRDF had been very aggressive in preaching ethnolinguistic identity as the most basic unit of political mobilization and organization (Gudina 2011; Berhe 2018). After the shocking results of the 2005 elections, however, its aggressive mobilization strategy focused on different social groups identified primarily by their socio-economic status, rather than by their ethnolinguistic identity. The party's commitment to the role of a vanguard party, derived from its ideology of revolutionary democracy, in which a few enlightened revolutionaries led the majority, also became obsolete as the EPRDF moved towards becoming a mass party. As a result, the party's membership grew exponentially after the 2005 election, from roughly 760,000 to more than 4 million in 2008, and to 6.5 million in 2013 (Aalen and Tronvoll 2009; EPRDF 2013). These political processes played a crucial role in consolidating the EPRDF's dominance, primarily in controlling the vertical distribution of power and expanding the social foundations of the party.

The legitimizing discourse of developmentalism also became effective because of a synergy created between the politico-legal frameworks and socio-economic policies. This synergy enabled the emergence of a 'political set-up' (Zenawi 2012: 170) that facilitated the implementation of both generative and repressive interventions (Gebremariam 2018). The generative interventions enabled the mobilization of different social groups in line with the political orientation of the EPRDF. The repressive interventions, in their turn, contributed to keeping rival political coalitions at bay, preventing them from significantly disrupting the mission of state-led developmentalism. A focus on growth acceleration, which remained a pillar of state-led developmentalism, helped the EPRDF establish a strong alliance with key economic actors who benefited from its economic policies (Gebremariam et al. 2022). As discussed in Section 4.4, the EPRDF also adopted policies that served the immediate needs of low-income urban households.

Key deliverables of developmentalism through generative interventions were socio-economic policies that eventually contributed to society's well-being and welfare. These included the Productive Safety Net Programme (PSNP) (Cochrane and Tamiru 2016; Lavers 2019), industrial policy (Altenburg 2010; Oqubay 2015), agricultural policy (Berhanu and Poulton 2014), micro- and small-scale enterprise schemes (Gebremariam 2017a, 2017b), agricultural and health extension schemes (UNDP 2015; Lenhardt et al. 2015), and infrastructure development (Moller 2015; UNDP 2015; AfDB and OECD 2016; Goodfellow 2018; Weldeghebrael 2020). As a result, the country was praised for achieving rapid economic growth for more than a decade (Moller 2015), for achieving six of the eight targets for gross domestic product on time (World Bank 2016, and, most importantly, for allocating nearly 73 per cent of the national budget to 'pro-poor expenditure' (UNDP 2015; AfDB and OECD 2016). The political outcomes of these socio-economic policies were primarily to keep non-elite groups closer to the ruling coalition and to make the political structures that shaped the vertical distribution of power relevant for the well-being of the majority.

However, it is important to note that the EPRDF's strategy of developmentalism also had winners and losers. For example, the regime's inner-city redevelopment programme had resulted in the displacement of 23,151 households by the end of 2015 to make approximately 392 hectares of 'prime land' available for the market (Weldeghebrael 2020). Some inner-city residents were relocated to the outskirts of the city into new apartments built through the IHDP, whereas those with land deeds were given replacement plots 14–22 kilometres away from their original location with meagre compensation (Planel and Bridonneau 2017; Weldeghebrael 2020). Through the IHDP, the government delivered 175,000 apartments in Addis Ababa between 2005 and 2017, with twenty-year mortgages for city residents who paid a 20 per cent deposit (Keller and Mukudi-Omwami 2017). The entirely new urban lifestyle, socio-economic, and political arrangements that the IHDP facilitated in the peripheries of Addis Ababa can be seen one of the lasting legacies of pursuing developmentalism as a legitimizing discourse. However, this government-led, large-scale 'social engineering' had its drawbacks in squeezing the urban middle class and vulnerable households while facilitating 'accumulation for high-end developers', especially in the city centre (Weldeghebrael 2020: 9).

A legitimizing discourse of developmentalism requires the carrot and stick approach of promoting rapid economic growth and social development while exercising a strong hand to control dissent. In this case, repressive strategies played a paramount role to 'destroy or inhibit' (Goodfellow and Jackman 2020) rival coalitions from mobilizing against the regime. The EPRDF launched three legal frameworks that ultimately gave the ruling coalition the upper hand in relation to competing political forces. These legal frameworks were: the Freedom of Mass Media and Access to Information Proclamation (Proclamation 590/2008); the Civil Society and Charities Proclamation (Proclamation 621/2009); and the Anti-terrorism Proclamation (Proclamation 652/2009). All three proclamations came into force in the wake of the 2005 elections.

The primary purpose of these legal frameworks was to curb rival coalitions' potential for mobilizing their organizational power. Even though they are not the primary focus of this chapter, the cumulative political implications of these three legal frameworks cannot be overemphasized. The EPRDF applied these politico-legal frameworks to criminalize, persecute, silence, and intimidate politically active young people (Gebremariam and Hererra 2016), rival political and social groups (Allo and Tesfaye 2015), journalists, and civil society activists (Human Rights Watch 2013, 2014a, 2013b). By suppressing dissent using these politico-legal documents, the EPRDF aspired to build a dominant-party political settlement. As a result, the political sphere became quite narrow, and the repressive strategies enabled the EPRDF to have almost absolute control over the Ethiopian state after both the 2010 and 2015 elections. In general, it can be argued that the post-2005 political settlement in this way introduced both the repressive interventions that kept rival coalitions at bay and the generative interventions that distributed benefits and services to the non-elites. To examine the role of generative interventions empirically, the next two sections will provide the empirical evidence. The case studies are the Urban Consumers' Cooperatives and the youth employment programmes, which both contributed to the EPRDF's dominance, particularly in Addis Ababa.

4.4 Urban Consumers' Cooperatives

Food prices are a politically contentious issue that affects the relationship between urban dwellers and governments. The most recent price hikes at the global level (in 2007–8 and 2011–12), mainly of agricultural products such as wheat, maize, and rice, affected food prices in many countries. Accordingly, most countries took different policy measures to reduce the impact of price volatility in their respective political economies (Babu 2015; Watson 2015). Protests and food riots are one of the most common consequences of rising food prices in many countries. Studies have shown how different demonstrations and riots related to rising food prices have influenced policy decisions by governments—for example, in Egypt (Ghoneim 2015), Senegal (Resnick 2015), and Zambia (Chapoto 2015).

Low-income families in Ethiopia faced considerable pressure because of the price hikes. For example, national food inflation in Ethiopia was at a record rate of 61.1 per cent in mid-2008. There was also an alarming increase in the retail prices of major grains, such as wheat, teff, and sorghum, by 60, 80, and 90 per cent, respectively, between April and August 2008 (Admassie 2014). However, despite these significant increases in food prices, Ethiopia has never experienced any form of protest or food riot. Indeed, some would argue that the memory of the post-election violence of 2005 has made street protests very unlikely. The absence of any forms of high- or low-level organized protests in urban centres makes the Ethiopian case notable.

Like other governments, the Ethiopian government took various policy measures to address the negative impact of food price hikes. This case study demonstrates how EPRDF's generative intervention towards addressing food price hikes by targeting the urban poor contributed to building and sustaining the party's dominance. The empirical analysis focuses on Urban Consumers' Cooperatives (UCCs). The UCCs were established by pooling financial resources mainly from the economically vulnerable households of Addis Ababa with the primary objective of making essential food items available at affordable prices. By examining the emergence and role of the UCCs, the case study explains how and why they were used by the EPRDF to increase and maintain its dominance in Addis Ababa.

The EPRDF applied a robust political strategy of mobilizing the most affected groups of society in Addis Ababa, hand-in-hand with policy measures to fight the drastic impact of food price hikes. The party built on the momentum it had established in the wake of the post-2005 election to initiate a new mobilization channel, crafting a new player, the UCCs, to join the market and play a key role in facilitating access to and distribution of essential household commodities that the government had subsidized and rationed. In July 2008, at one of his public meetings with thousands of members of the EPRDF's Youth and Women's Forums, the late Prime Minister, Meles Zenawi, gave a specific recommendation on the mounting problem of food prices. He strongly encouraged the participants to establish consumers' cooperatives in their respective districts, to become vital players in the market. One of the respondents, who was a founding member of a UCC, recalls that 'the response from the PM [to the question of price hikes] was that people need to get organized and collectively bring their skills, labour, and capital to play a role in the market'.[5]

The Prime Minister's advice became a de facto policy direction. As a result, the government started to provide all the political, legal, administrative, and technical support necessary to establish UCCs in every city district.[6] Members of the EPRDF forums that were already on the ground as auxiliaries of the party played a crucial role in mobilizing the public to establish the UCCs.[7] Every household in the city was targeted, as bringing everyone on board was one of the EPRDF's strategies for deriving legitimacy. As a result, every district in the city formed its UCC quickly. Founding members bought shares worth a maximum of 100 Ethiopian birr, with a one-off 20 birr registration fee. The government provided office spaces within every local government compound for the UCCs to start operating. Before establishing the UCCs, the government had been rationing subsidized wheat to the residents of the city, using local government structures. Once the UCCs became operational, the government transferred the responsibility for rationing subsidized food items entirely to the UCCs.[8] By doing so, the government empowered and legitimized the UCCs as vital actors in the everyday life of the city-dwellers.

According to a 2015 study by the Federal Trade Competition and Consumers' Protection Agency, there were 150 UCCs in Addis Ababa's ten sub-cities (FTCCPA 2015). Each sub-city has a Union of Cooperatives. The primary purpose of the UCCs was to distribute 'basic goods' to the broader public. According to the Trade Competition and Consumer Protection Proclamation (813/2013), 'basic goods' were items that the government had placed in 'price regulation', as deemed necessary. The government would also control and strictly regulate the distribution, sale, and movement of 'basic goods' to avoid any shortage in the market (FDRE 2013). The underlying rationale of legally protecting these 'basic goods' was to ensure that every

---

[5] UCC leader 03 (April 2018).
[6] UCC leaders 01, 02, 03, 04 (April 2018).
[7] UCC leaders 01, 02, 04 (April 2018).
[8] UCC leaders 01, 02, 03, 04 (April 2018).

(a)   (b)

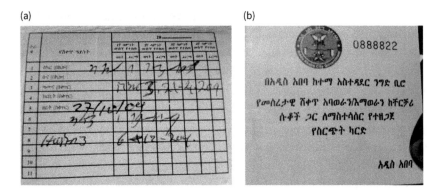

Fig. 4.2 Basic goods rationing card

Note: The cover of the yellow card reads 'Addis Ababa City Administration Trade Bureau: A distribution card prepared to link households (male/female headed) with retailers of basic goods'. The numbered items inside the card from 1 to 5 are sugar, coffee, soap, matches, and cooking oil.
Source: © Eyob Balcha Gebremariam.

citizen had equal access, at least in principle. Until the last round of fieldwork (September 2018), the government had categorized sugar, cooking oil, wheat flour, and petroleum products as 'basic goods', and there was a set price to buy and sell them.

The proclamation also gave the government the responsibility to monitor 'basic goods' production and distribution. For example, to avoid a shortage of bread, every bakery in Addis Ababa was linked with flour mill factories that receive subsidized wheat, primarily imported from the international market. The Addis Ababa trade and industry bureau then conducted rigorous monitoring and control of the size/weight, quality, and price of bread sold by the bakeries that received flour from the designated flour mills.

Likewise, the government subsidized private palm oil imports, and the cooking oil was distributed to the public in the city through UCCs, retail shops, or designated retailers. Similarly, the government used the UCC shops to distribute sugar to every household, at least in principle, in the city. Every household in the city with a yellow rationing card of the 'basic goods' was entitled to 5 kilos of sugar and 5 litres of cooking oil every two weeks (Fig. 4.2).

UCCs and the legitimizing discourse of developmentalism

The authoritarian nature of most developmental states pushes them to derive their legitimacy from their performance in improving people's socio-economic well-being. Because of a direct implication for the welfare of low-income families, increasing food prices had the potential to damage the EPRDF's legitimacy. During the price hike, the government took a swift decision to ration subsidized wheat in the city as a temporary solution until it had aligned its ad hoc response to its developmental orientation. By establishing the UCCs, the EPRDF achieved its developmental objective and political purpose. The developmental objective was to ensure that the urban poor were not severely affected by the price hike. The political purpose was to broaden its social base and improve its legitimacy by mobilizing people at the household level. Hence, instead of facing potential food riots, the EPRDF capitalized on the phenomenon of increasing prices by organizing the urban poor and using the UCCs as an additional channel to build its dominance.

By September 2018, the EPRDF had successfully installed the UCCs as one of the vital players in the market, facilitating access to the 'basic goods' and other essential household items. On top of rationing subsidized 'basic goods' to their membership of more than 400,000 people, the 150 UCCs also provided a retail service. According to the UCC leaders[9], they sell all kinds of groceries, with a maximum profit margin of 15 per cent.

> Initially, we were tied with three 'basic goods': sugar, cooking oil and wheat flour. Now, we sell more than 45 items in our shop, both agricultural and manufactured products. Then a member or a customer coming to buy sugar will also find other essential groceries. This makes us competitive with other privately run shops.[10]

The UCCs have established themselves as vital market players, particularly concerning households of lower socio-economic status. They use different strategies to lure consumers to their shops. The UCCs may add new items to be sold at a competitive price whenever necessary. Usually, during holidays, there is a shortage of household items and an increase in the price of food or non-food items. The UCCs usually add the most wanted items to their shelves. The UCCs also work in close collaboration with each other. They avoid competition by establishing a union that sets commodity prices centrally. The UCC leaders declare that their primary objectives are protecting their members from unfair market competition and stabilizing the market. As one of the respondents stated, the UCCs would prefer to help their members make a saving by selling essential items at a low price.[11]

The UCCs are playing a role that dovetailed into the EPRDF's use of developmentalism as a legitimizing discourse. Politically, the UCCs were primarily

---

[9] UCC leaders 01, 02, 03, 04 (April 2018).
[10] UCC leader 01 (April 2018).
[11] UCC leader 03 (April 2018).

established by initiatives that were either within the ruling party structure (youth and women's leagues) or directly controlled by the party (forums, which preceded the leagues and were co-opted into the latter). Hence, the UCCs added a new force to the EPRDF's organizational power, both to garner grassroots support and to constrain competing political forces. Especially during specific periods that require mass mobilization, such as rallies or elections, the UCCs played a role as important as any other ruling-party-affiliated mobilization platforms within Addis Ababa.

Economically, the UCCs served a vital role in the developmental image of the government as being effective and capable. The UCCs particularly helped the urban poor, who might otherwise not have the economic means to access either the 'basic goods' or other essential household commodities. Indeed, the price difference between UCCs' shops and other privately owned shops is significant. As one UCC leader put it:

> Our price is relatively lower than other retailers because we have very low profit margins. We prefer to let our customers/members keep the money in their pocket than distribute a higher dividend. A kilo of beef meat is, for example, 210/220 birr in the market, but we are selling at 85 birr. By keeping the money in their pocket, we help our members use the money for other essential expenses.[12]

Such service provision to the urban poor at a relatively affordable price vis-à-vis other privately operated retailers helped to build a positive image of the EPRDF-led government. As argued by Wade (2004), 'governing the market' is one of the key features of developmentalism.

Contextualized relations of cooperation and co-optation

While developmentalism set the overarching framework of relations between the UCCs and the EPRDF, the specific features of the strategies that mediated the efforts of building and maintaining dominance varied, depending on the context. Examining the contextual elements of the strategies allows us to identify the specific role that social groups play while a ruling coalition pursues its political goal. It is also imperative to note that, similar to a ruling coalition, social groups also have agency and vested interests. Hence, the political processes for a ruling coalition to build a social foundation by a ruling coalition are far from a one-way project involving passive actors.

---

[12] UCC leader 03 (April 2018).

An overlapping interest between the EPRDF and the urban poor was one of the main reasons why the ruling party succeeded in mobilizing the UCCs as part of its effort to build dominance. By the time the EPRDF was actively encouraging the establishment of the UCCs, the unorganized urban poor were unable to influence market transactions. Instead, the majority of city residents were at the mercy of either the government, which was rationing essential items like wheat, or the market, which was selling essential household items at inflated prices. The ad hoc decision of rationing temporarily addressed the problem. A more systematic approach needed the collaboration of both the urban poor and the government. Vulnerable households needed affordable items in the market, while the government was actively engaged in political strategies to renew its legitimacy. Hence, protecting vulnerable households from market failure was an ideal political opportunity to capitalize on. Eventually, the overlapping interests of the urban poor and the EPRDF-led government became an essential component of establishing a symbiotic relationship.

Cooperation becomes the most reasonable strategy when apparently overlapping interests become the foundation of relations between a ruling coalition and a specific social group. For cooperation to occur, all parties should appreciate the vital role of their counterparts in pursuing their respective interests. For example, the first food price hike from 2008 to 2009 was a period in which the EPRDF was aggressively working to regain its legitimacy in Addis Ababa. It was a period of reclaiming administrative, legal, and political legitimacy in the city while also preparing for the 2010 national election. The political context in the aftermath of the 2005 election forced the EPRDF not to squander any opportunity to maintain the momentum of regaining its legitimacy. Hence, facilitating the emergence of the UCCs was a political endeavour of capitalizing on the overlapping interests of the urban poor and the ruling party. By creating a new grassroots social group, the EPRDF also expanded the social foundation of its coalition.

Social groups that have already empowered themselves through their cooperation with the ruling elites may demand more, by broadening the frontiers of their engagement. In this case, the UCCs successfully lobbied the government to transfer publicly owned businesses into their administration. One respondent involved in the process recalled: 'the UCCs effectively argued that they would become stronger and effective if their economic and financial power is boosted'.[13] The city administration responded positively to the

---

[13] Interview with a former officer at Addis Ababa trade and industry bureau, April 2018.

UCCs' pressure and issued regulation no. 42/2012 to legalize the transfer. At the time of adopting the regulation, there were 1,069 publicly owned businesses (recreation centres, butcher's shops, warehouses, and grain mills) worth 104 million birr (Legesse 2012).[14]

Strategies are context-dependent. While recognizing the vital role of developmentalism and legal manoeuvring, it is equally important to note that the dynamic nature of the context also affects strategies and their efficacy. There were contexts where the EPRDF was more powerful than the UCCs. In the early days of the UCCs, it was relatively easy for the EPRDF to mobilize the UCCs for party-specific activities, such as rallies. 'We were benefiting from the support of the government. Hence, we were also doing our part for their political interest,' noted one UCC leader.[15] One respondent further claimed that, especially during the early years, 'EPRDF used to see UCCs as one of its leagues.'[16] However, as time passed, a power imbalance occurred, and the EPRDF started to force the inclusion of its propaganda messages and agenda items into the general assembly meetings of the UCCs. A former city government official recalled that 'the inclusion of the party's agenda depends on the affiliation and opinion of the government official and UCC leaders'.[17] In a context where the UCCs were effectively infiltrated by EPRDF youth or women's league members, there was a tendency for the general assembly of the cooperative to be co-opted.

To sum up, the forms of co-optation embodied in the UCC strategy were more of the cooperative than the 'passive' variety, though this varied by context. Overlapping interests remained central to the relations. However, the interests and priorities of governments and social groups are dynamic. Hence, there are moments where cooperation was adopted as a tactical option by the UCCs to gain access to certain resources or policy favours, as seen in the transfer of publicly owned businesses. In another context, cooperation can also mean collaborating with the political agenda of the ruling party because members of the UCC find the right political agenda to support. In such contexts, political tactics rather than overlapping interests might be the trigger for cooperation, but the presence of some shared interest in cooperating still provides grounds for symbiotic relations between the UCCs and the government.

---

[14] The newspaper article is at: https://addisfortune.net/articles/addis-abeba-transferring-public-businesses-to-consumers-cooperatives/, accessed 3 July 2020.

[15] Interview with UCC leader 04, April 2018.

[16] Interview with UCC leader 06, April 2018.

[17] Interview with a former officer at Addis Ababa trade and industry bureau, April 2018.

4.5 Youth employment programmes in Addis Ababa

In a context where young people make up a significant proportion of a capital city's demography, addressing their economic needs and expectations is one aspect of building and maintaining dominance. The EPRDF had a positive record in solving the problems of both unemployment and underemployment. For example, between 2003 and 2014, the rate of unemployment in Addis Ababa dropped from 33 to 24 per cent (World Bank 2016). Over the same period, the level of underemployment also fell, much faster, from 52 to 31 per cent in Addis Ababa (ibid.). This section will specifically focus on how the EPRDF's approach to addressing urban youth unemployment contributed to its efforts at building and maintaining dominance in Addis Ababa.

After the 2005 election, the EPRDF-led government produced three policy documents that were directly aimed at addressing youth unemployment in urban areas. The three youth-specific policy frameworks were the Urban Youth Development Package (U-YDP 2006), the Revised Micro and Small-scale Enterprises Development Strategy (2011 MSEs Strategy) and the Revolving Youth Fund (RYF 2016). The EPRDF produced each policy document either as a response to a political threat to its legitimacy or as part of its political dominance project (Gebremariam 2017a).

For example, the U-YDP came into existence after the EPRDF lost its political legitimacy in Addis Ababa in the wake of the 2005 elections. Post-election violence was the main reason why the EPRDF's legitimacy among young people in Addis was ruined. Hence, the U-YDP had both an implicit and an explicit intention of restoring and building the dominance of the ruling coalition (FDRE 2006; Gebremariam 2017a). Then the EPRDF introduced the revised MSEs strategy in 2011 as a vital policy document after securing control over the entire government structure in the 2010 election. The strategy was one way of translating the newly stated objective of building a developmental state into the MSEs sector. Finally, the most recent RYF came into play as a response to the unprecedented wave of violent protest, particularly in Oromia and Amhara regions in 2016 and 2017, while Addis Ababa remained relatively calm.

Youth employment programmes under the EPRDF

All the post-2005 youth employment-focused programmes had both an implicit and an explicit purpose of boosting the legitimacy of the ruling party.

The programmes were part of the EPRDF's generative intervention aimed at providing technical and vocational training for young unemployed people. The programme included financial and administrative support for young people's efforts to 'empower' themselves economically. However, there were also moments where co-optation became the dominant strategy, especially in a context where young people were forced to trade off their civil and political rights in order to access the opportunities in the youth employment programmes.

The political salience of the topic of urban youth unemployment made the government disregard the technocratic processes of producing a new policy framework. The prime minister's office took a bold step of producing the U-YDP and channelled it to the youth ministry for implementation in September 2006. As a result, the U-YDP nullified the existing heavily consulted and formally launched national youth policy and its implementation strategy (Gebremariam 2017a). The urgency of formulating and implementing the U-YDP was justified by the success of the opposition in mobilizing young people effectively in the urban centres, particularly in Addis Ababa during the 2005 election.

The U-YDP had both developmental objectives and political purposes. The developmental objectives sought to address the gaps in the education and skills training of young people vis-à-vis the available job opportunities in the market. It also included the need to boost private-sector engagement to create a vibrant economy with more jobs. In this approach, the leading role of the state remained intact (FDRE 2006; Gebremariam 2017a). The political purpose embedded within the U-YDP emanates from the categorization of young people as 'marginalized social groups' (FDRE 2006: 10). Such labelling became the rationale behind a policy recommendation that proposed the establishment of permanent platforms of youth participation. Informed by the U-YDP, the EPRDF mobilized young people in every district of the city to establish the Addis Ababa Youth Forum—AAYF (Gebremariam 2017b). The AAYF then became one of the multiple channels of public mobilization that the EPRDF established to build and maintain its dominance in the city. At a later stage, the AAYF served as an embryo to create the EPRDF's youth league in Addis Ababa (Gebremariam 2017b). The youth league then played a vital role in the EPRDF's mission of maintaining dominance through repressive interventions. The EPRDF Addis Ababa youth league was one of the channels through which the ruling party carried out its activities of surveillance and intimidation against potential and rival coalitions, and its infiltration of community organizations, particularly before the sweeping reforms of 2018 (Gebremariam 2017b).

The second most important post-2005 youth-employment-focused policy framework that contributed to the EPRDF's dominance in Addis Ababa was the revised MSEs strategy of 2011. The EPRDF-led government revised the strategy fourteen years after its first enactment in 1997. One section in the strategy document reads as follows:

> In rural areas, farmers are the base of our developmental state. In urban areas, a segment of society that is striving to unite its labour and property, [such] as farmers, is a potential actor that will join micro and small enterprises. This segment of society is forced to rely not only on its property but also on its labour; hence, it gets only the leftovers of rent-seeking activities. This segment of society will never become a principal beneficiary [of a rent-seeking dominated economy]. Furthermore, this segment [of society] covers the majority of the urban population … hence, it can become a reliable base for our developmental state. (FDRE 2011: 4)

In another section, the document reiterates that

> So long as they are carefully selected, we need to give recognition and incentives to successful role models [in the MSEs sector]. We also need to create a positive influence by promoting and encouraging role models. [Furthermore] *To attract these vanguards into our party* [emphasis added], we need to empower them to be leaders and mobilise others with their success. (FDRE 2011: 6)

As revealed in the above quotations from the revised MSEs strategy, the EPRDF adopted a plan to use its generative intervention—the MSEs scheme—as one way of mobilizing the socio-economically marginalized segments of society in urban areas. From the perspective of a technocratic approach to development, targeting the urban poor with a generative policy framework is a noble objective. However, the developmental orientation hardly stops at addressing the socio-economic needs of the target group. The political purpose of ensuring dominance is an integral part of the developmental objective.

The mobilization of unemployed youth by the EPRDF's party structure had direct implications in its relations with rival political groups. Having an organized youth group enabled the EPRDF to become a dominant player in the distribution of power, because it controlled access to resources that were key to the livelihoods of unemployed young people. While helping the EPRDF to expand its social foundation, based on the provision of material benefits, the strategy also kept rival coalitions from effectively mobilizing young people against the EPRDF.

The most recent youth employment-focused policy framework, the RYF of 2017, also has an embedded legitimizing discourse, with the aim of maintaining dominance. The government launched the fund with an allocation of 10 billion birr (approximately £360 million). The three interrelated objectives of the fund were supporting young people's entrepreneurial initiatives, providing financial support for organized income-generating activities by young people, and ensuring young people's participation and benefits (FDRE 2017). There are at least two unique features of the RYF. First, the federal government earmarked for the first time a specific amount of money to support young people's entrepreneurial activities. Second, the commercial bank of Ethiopia became the administrator of the fund on behalf of the federal government.

The RYF came into existence as part of the EPRDF's response to a series of protests across the country. The central line of argument from the EPRDF in explaining the causes of these widespread protests was deeply rooted in its developmental discourse. The remedy the government provided similarly echoes the developmental discourse. While announcing the fund in his presidential address, the former President, Mulatu Teshome, reiterated that 'the cause of the recent wave of protests is related to economic interest and benefits' (Teshome 2016). The preamble of the proclamation launching the fund also stated that

> despite benefiting from overall growth and development, young people's interests and demands have not been addressed adequately, mainly because of newly emerging needs and interests induced by recent growth and also because of unresolved problems inherited from the past. (FDRE 2017)

The RYF became operational in a context where political uncertainty was at its peak. The EPRDF coalition was facing challenges both from within and from outside. Hence, the political scene in which the EPRDF was playing a dominant role was quickly vanishing. As a result, there was a narrow window for the EPRDF to use the RYF as another policy instrument for actively mobilizing young people to sustain its dominance. Instead, the EPRDF adopted the more technocratic approach of responding to the immediate demands of young people by creating more job opportunities through training and the provision of finance.

Contextualized relations of co-optation

The contextual strategies of co-optation have direct implications for the distribution of power and thereby for a political settlement. The EPRDF's success in winning the acquiescence of many young people to participate in its developmental programme gave the party a sense of legitimacy and a broader membership base. It also reduced the possibility of rival coalitions mobilizing young people against the EPRDF. Furthermore, the use of multiple formal and non-formal channels of governance also shaped the distribution of power in favour of the EPRDF. This was particularly true of the MSEs scheme. The apex of these structures of governance and mobilization was a 'command post' overseen by the city's Deputy Mayor. The other structures of governance and mobilization included 'village committees', 'zone committees', 'development teams', and the 'development army'. These structures coexisted with the formal layers of governance in Addis Ababa.

These multiple structures of governance and mobilization enabled the EPRDF to reach young people in every neighbourhood. For example, in 2014, the government went door-to-door to register unemployed young people and offer them a promise of opportunities to join the MSEs scheme.[18] This large-scale registration had both symbolic and material significance. It symbolically demonstrated the capacity of the government to reach every doorstep. Furthermore, it revealed the real commitment of the regime to address the challenge of youth employment.

The EPRDF adopted a cooperative empowerment tactic by offering economic opportunities that young people needed to fulfil their aspirations. The revision of the MSEs development strategy and the provision of financial, administrative, and technical support were actual manifestations of seeking acquiescence from young people. Furthermore, by setting political, legal, and administrative requirements, the government also demanded meaningful actions from young people in order to join the MSEs scheme. The political requirements came in different forms, including subtle or open pressure to be a member of the ruling party, and demands to attend training sessions organized by the ruling party on its ideology and the socio-economic policies derived from it, to attend EPRDF-organized demonstrations, and to make financial contributions to such events.

Young people's active role is an essential component of a cooperative empowerment tactic. Their decision to join the MSEs scheme and to fulfil its administrative and legal requirements was a demonstration of their level of commitment. Young people recognized and responded to the economic opportunities that the government was providing. There were minimal opportunities available outside the government's direct control. Establishing a business or joining a government-initiated employment programme within the MSEs scheme thus required conscious effort and decision. As a result, young people responded positively and co-operated with the government

---

[18] Interview with an officer at Addis Ababa Children, Women's and Youth Bureau (February 2015).

in the reinvigoration of the MSEs scheme. While young people were cooperating and pursuing their economic rights, they were simultaneously contributing to the realization of the government's political purposes and developmental objectives. Hence, overlapping interests remained a crucial component of cooperative empowerment.

However, the overlapping interests that led to cooperation between young people and the EPRDF might not necessarily fulfil the expectations of both parties on equal terms. Depending on the context, asymmetrical power relations tended to give the EPRDF the upper hand over the interests and capacity of young people. In this context, the political purpose of maintaining dominance became the primary motive shaping the relationship between young people and the EPRDF. As a result, co-optation became the most visible and effective strategy.

In some contexts, young people already participating in the MSEs scheme were implicitly forced to become members of the EPRDF. For example, when one of the respondents joined the scheme to become a cobblestone producer, he never considered becoming a member of the ruling party. He mentioned that he had no interest in politics at all. When asked how he joined the ruling party, he said, 'A membership form was being circulated, and everyone filled out the form. Only a few refused.'[19] From his point of view, his ability to continue participating in the MSEs scheme was tied to his membership of the ruling party. At the time of the interview, he belonged to the ruling party's cell at his workplace, where he was required to attend meetings every two weeks. He further mentioned that the ruling party mobilized thousands of young people at his production site to get registered for the 2015 election, using the EPRDF party cell structure at his workplace.

While some young people were implicitly forced to join the ruling party, other young people made a calculated decision to join the party as a means of accessing the support in the MSEs scheme. For example, a group of three young people joined OPDO, one of the coalition members of the ruling party, just before they graduated from university. Their main purpose in joining the party was to get a job. As planned, they were all employed in different government offices three months after graduation. A year later, these young people resigned from their respective low-paying and less promising government jobs to establish a poultry and dairy product distribution business using the MSEs scheme. While endeavouring to succeed in their business, they found themselves in the same position again. Through their encounters with district officials, they found out that EPRDF youth league members were favoured in

---

[19] Interview with MSE operator 01 (April 2015).

getting additional services that the government provided for MSEs operators. One member of the group said:

> In one of our several visits to the district MSEs office, we asked why we were not allocated a place in one of the buildings built by the city government as a sell-ing hall. One of the officials replied: 'you guys are not actively participating'. We told them that we attended every training session they organized and also made financial contributions whenever we were asked. Every time the district organizes demonstrations and political rallies, they request MSE operators to contribute to the event financially. Finally, we understood what they meant when they said 'you don't participate'. So we went to the district EPRDF office and filled out a membership form.[20]

After three months, the young people achieved their objective of getting access to the subsidized shop in the selling hall. The district MSEs office offered them a 12 square metre room, which they had been formally request-ing for more than a year and a half. The rent for the subsidized shop was just £5 per month, which was significantly less than the £116 they used to pay to a private landlord. One member of the group said he was happy that they man-aged to get the subsidized shop. However, he also stressed that he was very frustrated. He regretfully mentioned that their business could have thrived if they had been able to invest the money into their business that they had been paying private property owners. He summed up by his feeling by saying: 'I felt that we were betrayed.'[21]

The EPRDF's co-optational strategy of using job creation schemes can also be considered as one aspect of coercive distribution. The strategy allowed the regime to remain in control of young citizens' socio-economic well-being by 'enmeshing [them] in relationships of dependence' (Albertus et al. 2018: 1). The implicit and explicit requirement of party membership in order to benefit from the job creation programme was one way of cultivating the dependence of young people on the government. At the same time, the strategy of co-optation also prevented rival political actors from mobilizing young people because they were far from influencing their lives.

The EPRDF's attempt to seek dominance through co-optation, and even outright coercive distribution, might sometimes create tension among groups of young people who had different interests. A young MSE operator who was leading a group of eighteen young people in an urban agriculture business mentioned several incidents where his group had been approached by local

[20] Interview with MSE operator 02 (March 2015).
[21] Interview with MSE operator 02 (March 2015).

cadres to join the ruling party youth league. The group leader specifically said, 'Our district administrator called me to his office three times to convince me to join the ruling party. But I refused.'[22] Both the leader and other members of the group had to deal with several rounds of pressure from local cadres and district officials to join the ruling party youth league. They were promised individual benefits and also better access to services, such as speedy processing of their requests to use adjacent land for their urban agriculture project. Most of the group members were determined not to join the ruling party; hence the potential progress of their urban farm was compromised. But the group members' refusal to be co-opted lasted only until three of them were recruited at later a stage. This created a tense relationship among the group members, because youth league members are believed to work as spies for the authoritarian developmental state.

It also appears that young people who were already members of the ruling party could use their position as leverage to speed up the process of establishing their business within the MSEs scheme. One young MSE operator, who was also an active member of the EPRDF youth league, shared his experience of setting up his print and advertising business. He highlighted the effectiveness of local government officials in helping him to establish his business in a short period of time. He started running his printing and advertising business at full scale within a six-month period.[23] Registration, renting a subsidized shop, and getting a loan within six months was an extremely speedy process compared to the experiences of other respondents.

As mentioned earlier, the revised MSEs development strategy was in place until the RYF came into force in February 2017. In Addis Ababa, the RYF injected a sense of urgency among government officials who were directly involved in the MSEs scheme to mobilize and organize young people. Indeed, the RYF added new dynamics into the relations between the city government and urban youth. The availability of additional money to support new MSEs created a new sense of responsibility. From the 10 billion birr national fund, 419 million was allocated to Addis Ababa. In the two years from July 2016 to August 2018, the city government disbursed 315 million birr to MSEs run by young people. Within the same period, 65 million birr were also been returned to the fund.[24]

In summary, youth employment-focused programmes in the post-2005 period were embedded into the EPRDF's aspiration of ensuring its dominance, both in Addis Ababa and at the national level. Addressing the problem

[22] Interview with MSE operator 03 (January 2015).
[23] Interview with MSE operator 04 (April 2015).
[24] Interview with Addis Ababa Women, Children and Youth Bureau officer (September 2018).

of youth unemployment in the city is usually seen as a priority. One of the reasons is the potential threat posed by a large number of unemployed and disenfranchised young people and the city's exposure to violence, crime, and political unrest. Ensuring legitimacy in the context of a high rate of youth unemployment can also be quite a challenge. Conversely, effective policy frameworks that reduce the youth unemployment rate can play a substantive role in a ruling coalition's legitimacy. This was the rationale behind the EPRDF's active streamlining of its policy frameworks, as well as financial, technical, and bureaucratic resources, to address the problem of youth unemployment in Addis Ababa.

The youth employment-focused programmes were among the EPRDF's generative interventions, in which the strategies of cooperation and co-optation played a substantive role. Both strategies enabled the EPRDF to generate acquiescence and legitimacy in the eyes of the young people participating in the programmes. The city administration actively mobilized and supported young people seeking employment opportunities. At the same time, young people were also fulfilling expected legal and administrative requirements to benefit from the job creation programme. As discussed previously, there are contexts where overlapping interests sometimes play a major role, or the coercive power of the government becomes more visible in shaping the relationship between young people and government. Understanding the nuanced elements of such relationships contributes to a better appreciation of how generative interventions help in achieving dominance.

4.6 Conclusions

This chapter aimed to answer how the Ethiopian ruling coalition under the EPRDF succeeded in dominating the socio-economic and political spheres in Addis Ababa between 2005 and 2018. The chapter has demonstrated that one possible answer to this question is related to the EPRDF's aggressive and effective mobilization of specific urban social groups. The chapter provided a brief historical and political-economic framework for understanding the Ethiopian context at the national level before delving into the two case studies in Addis Ababa. While the conceptual framework of this book's research initiative highlights the importance of both generative and repressive intervention modalities for dominance, the case studies in this chapter focus specifically on generative interventions.

There are at least three major points of conclusion. First, the empirical case studies illustrate that the EPRDF was highly effective in using both the legitimizing discourse of developmentalism and legal manoeuvring as primary strategies in building and maintaining dominance. The use of legitimizing discourse was a particularly effective way of offsetting the democratic deficit of the regime, particularly after the 2005 election, which resulted in a clean sweep victory for the opposition in Addis Ababa. Similar to other developmental regimes, the EPRDF sought to derive legitimacy from what it delivered to the wider public. Most importantly, the provision of these services went hand in hand with the political mobilization of the target groups. The urban poor were mobilized to establish the Urban Consumers' Cooperatives, and young people were mobilized into Youth Forum and Youth League as well as becoming direct beneficiaries of micro and small-scale job creation schemes.

Second, the EPRDF's successful mobilization of the urban poor, who were hit heavily by food price hikes, can be seen as one of the reasons why Addis Ababa has never seen protests related to food prices. This mobilization, and making the urban poor active players in the market through their cooperatives, were vital interventions, with no less impact than other macroeconomic and social policies. Concerning the tactics that shaped the interplay between the EPRDF and the UCCs, the case study illustrates a contextual use of both cooperative empowerment and passive co-optation.

Third, the youth employment-focused programmes also illustrated the salient role of generative interventions, in both building and maintaining dominance. The case study showed that dominance was maintained through a combination of politically driven policies, the active mobilization of targeted groups, and the deployment of the government's bureaucratic, technical, and financial resources. The MSEs scheme was primarily in line with the strategy of using legitimizing discourse through policy interventions. The actual implementation of the youth-employment-focused programmes also revealed how tactics such as cooperative empowerment, passive co-optation, and coercive distribution occur in various combinations depending on the context. For some young people, passive co-option was a comfortable way of securing access to resources, whereas for others, benefiting from the youth employment programmes only through the fulfilment of formal criteria was less straightforward.

The overall political context in post-2018 Ethiopia is beyond the focus of this chapter. However, it is worth mentioning that certain continuities and discontinuities remain at the centre of how state–society relations are shaped in the urban context. Two issues are worth noting, considering the key arguments of this chapter. The first point is that the newly elected government of the Prosperity Party, led by Prime Minister Abiy Ahmed, has indicated its intention of liberalizing the Ethiopian political economy. The policy decisions towards liberalization certainly affect the legitimizing discourse of developmentalism as a vital strategy in shaping urban citizens' lives. The discourse of prosperity and the creation of business opportunities for local and international businesses might become the new mantra for deriving legitimacy. Especially in Addis Ababa, the creation of open public spaces and the attraction of global capital in hotel, recreation, and real-estate businesses has already become the new government's signature policy (Terrefe 2020). The set of liberalization policies endorsed by the IMF and the World Bank also expects the government to reduce its direct and indirect subsidy of essential consumer goods that directly benefit the urban poor. In the same vein, the Prosperity Party has also adopted a ten-year plan to make the private sector the economy's driving force (FDRE 2021). The combined effect of these policy changes will undoubtedly be to create new spheres of engagement between the urban poor and the unemployed young people of Addis Ababa. Likewise, the role of UCCs, 'basic consumer goods', and the MSEs scheme may also become insignificant in shaping state–society relations in the urban context.

The second issue is the internal strength of the ruling party and its capacity to remain a unified political force. The Prosperity Party inherited the EPRDF structure after removing the TPLF and incorporating parties from peripheral regions. Heightened ethnonationalism and internal political rivalries may prevent the ruling party from achieving levels of dominance similar to those achieved by the EPRDF. The devastating war in the Tigray region will also have a lasting impact on national and city-level politics. Opposition groups are highly energized and mobilized along various socio-economic and ethnicized agendas. Hence, it is very likely that politics in Addis Ababa will become increasingly contentious and less predictable.

References

AACA (2014). *Addis Ababa City Administration (AACA) Sub-District Zonal Administration: Mission and Execution* (Amharic—internal implementation manual). Addis Ababa: AACA.

Aalen, L., and Tronvoll, K. (2009). The 2008 Ethiopian local elections: The return of electoral authoritarianism. *African Affairs* 108(430): 111–120.

Admassie, A. (2014). The political economy of food price policy in Ethiopia. In P. Pinstrup-Anderson (ed.), *Food Price Policy in an Era of Market Instability: A Political Economy Analysis*. Oxford: Oxford University Press, pp. 133–152.

AfDB and OECD (2016). *African Economic Outlook 2016: Sustainable Cities and Structural Transformation*. Tunis.

Albertus, M., Fenner, S., & Slater, D. (2018). *Coercive distribution*. Cambridge University Press.

Allo, A., and Tesfaye, B. (2015). Spectacles of illegality: Mapping Ethiopia's show trials. *African Identities* 13(4): 279–296.

Altenburg, T. (2010). Industrial policy in Ethiopia. German Development Institute Discussion Paper no. 2/2010, Bonn.

Angle, S. C. (2005). Decent democratic centralism. *Political Theory* 33(4): 518–546.

Asrat, G. (2014). *Sovereignty and Democracy in Ethiopia*. Addis Ababa: Signature Book Printing Press.

Babu, S. C. (2015). Policy process and food price crisis: A framework for analysis and lessons from country studies. In P. Pinstrup-Anderson (ed.), *Food Price Policy in an Era of Market Instability: A Political Economy Analysis*. Oxford: Oxford University Press, pp. 76–101.

Bach, J. N. (2011). Abyotawi democracy: Neither revolutionary nor democratic, a critical review of EPRDF's conception of revolutionary democracy in post-1991 Ethiopia. *Journal of Eastern African Studies* 5(4): 641–663.

Benti, S. B. (2002). A nation without a city [a blind person without a cane]: The Oromo struggle for Addis Ababa. *Northeast African Studies* 9(3): 115–132.

Berhanu, K., and Poulton, C. (2014). The political economy of agricultural extension policy in Ethiopia: Economic growth and political control. *Development Policy Review* 32(s2): s197–s213.

Berhe, A. (2009). *A Political History of the Tigray People's Liberation Front (1975–1991): Revolt, Ideology and Mobilisation in Ethiopia*. Los Angeles, CA: Tsehai.

Berhe, M. (2018). From left-wing liberation army into government: The challenges of transition and the case of TPLF/EPRDF. PhD dissertation, University of Victoria, Canada.

Central Statistics Agency (2013). *Population Projection of Ethiopia for All Regions at Wereda Level from 2014–2017*. Addis Ababa: CSA.

Chapoto, A. (2015). The political economy of food price policy in Zambia. In P. Pinstrup-Anderson (ed.), *Food Price Policy in an Era of Market Instability*. Oxford: Oxford University Press, pp. 000–000.

Clapham, C., (2019). The political economy of Ethiopia from the Imperial period to the present. In F. Cheru, C. Cramer, and A. Oqubay (eds), *The Oxford Handbook of the Ethiopian Economy*. Oxford: Oxford University Press, pp. 33–47.

Cochrane, L., and Tamiru, Y. (2016). Ethiopia's productive safety net program: Power, politics and practice. *Journal of International Development* 28(5): 649–665.

EPRDF (1993). Our revolutionary democracy objectives and next practices (in Amharic: *Abyotawi Democraciyawi Alamawochachin ena Qetay Tegbarochachin*), internal party document. Addis Ababa: Ethiopian People's Revolutionary Democratic Front.

EPRDF (2013). EPRDF in brief. Addis Ababa: Ethiopian People's Revolutionary Democratic Front.

FDRE (2006). Youth Development Package. Addis Ababa: Federal Democratic Republic of Ethiopia.

FDRE (2011). Micro and Small Enterprises Development Strategy. Addis Ababa: Federal Democratic Republic of Ethiopia.

FDRE (2013). Trade Competition and Consumer Protection Proclamation No. (813/2013). Addis Ababa: Federal Democratic Republic of Ethiopia.

FDRE (2016). Ethiopia, Annuale Bulletin. Government Communication Affairs Office. Addis Ababa.

FDRE (2017). Ethiopian Youth Revolving Fund Proclamation No. (995/2017). Addis Ababa: Federal Democratic Republic of Ethiopia.

FDRE (2021). 10 Year Development Plan (2020-2030), Plan and Development Commission, Addis Ababa, Ethiopia.

Feyissa, D. (2011). Aid negotiation: The uneasy 'partnership' between EPRDF and the donors. *Journal of Eastern African Studies* 5(4): 788–817.

FTCCPA (2015). *The Role of Consumers' Cooperatives in Market Stabilisation* [baseline study]. Addis Ababa: Trade, Competition and Consumers' Protection Authority.

Gebre-Egziabher, T., and Abera, E. (2019). Urbanisation and industrial development in Ethiopia. In F. Cheru, C. Cramer, and A. Oqubay (eds), *The Oxford Handbook of the Ethiopian Economy*. Oxford: Oxford University Press, pp. 785–803.

Gebremariam, E. B. (2017a). The politics of youth employment and policy processes in Ethiopia. *IDS Bulletin* 48(3): https://doi.org/10.19088/1968-2017.125.

Gebremariam, E. B. (2017b). The politics of developmentalism, citizenship and urban youth in Addis Ababa, Ethiopia. PhD thesis, University of Manchester.

Gebremariam, E. B. (2018). The carrot and stick of Ethiopian 'democratic developmentalism': Ideological, legal, and policy frameworks. In C. Tapscott, T. Halvorsen, and T. Rosario (eds), *The Democratic Developmental State: North–South Perspectives*. Stuttgart: Ibedem Verlag CROP Series in International Poverty Studies, pp. 61–85.

Gebremariam, E. B., and Herrera, L. (2016). On silencing the next generation: Legacies of the 1974 Ethiopian revolution on youth political engagement. *Northeast African Studies* 16(1): 141–66.

Gebremariam, E.B., Isayiyas, D.A. and Weldeghebrael, E.H. (2022). The Political Determinants of Rapid Economic Growth in Ethiopia (2004-2018), Unpublished ESID Working Paper, University of Manchester.

Ghoneim, A. F. (2015). The political economy of food price policy in Egypt. In P. Pinstrup-Anderson (ed.), *Food Price Policy in an Era of Market Instability: A Political Economy Analysis*. Oxford: Oxford University Press, pp. 253–274.

Goodfellow, T. (2018). Seeing political settlements through the city: A framework for comparative analysis of urban transformation. *Development and Change* 49(1): 199–222.

Goodfellow, T., and Jackman, D. (2020). Control the capital: Cities and political dominance. ESID Working Paper no. 135, University of Manchester.

Gudina, M. (2007). Ethnicity, democratisation and decentralisation in Ethiopia: The case of Oromia. *Eastern Africa Social Science Research Review* 23(1): 81–106.

Gudina, M. (2011). Elections and democratisation in Ethiopia, 1991–2010. *Journal of Eastern African Studies* 5(4): 664–680.

Gulema, S. B. (2013). City as nation: Imagining and practicing Addis Ababa as a modern and national space. *Northeast African Studies* 13(1): 167–214.

Hailegebriel, D. (2010). Restrictions on foreign funding of civil society. *International Journal of Not-for-Profit Law* 12(3). Available at: https://www.icnl.org/resources/research/ijnl/ethiopia, accessed 9 July 2020.

Hessebon, G. T. (2013). The precarious future of the Ethiopian constitution. *Journal of African Law* 57(2), 215–233.

Human Rights Watch (2013). *'They Want a Confession': Torture and Ill-treatment in Ethiopia's Maekelawi Police Station*. New York: Human Rights Watch.

Human Rights Watch (2014a). *'They Know Everything We Do': Telecom and Internet Surveillance in Ethiopia*. New York: Human Rights Watch.

Human Rights Watch (2014b). *'Journalism Is Not a Crime': Violations of Media Freedom in Ethiopia*. New York: Human Rights Watch.

Keller, E. J., & Mukudi-Omwami, E. (2017). Rapid urban expansion and the challenge of pro-poor housing in Addis Ababa, Ethiopia. *Africa Review, 9*(2), 173-185.

Lavers, T. (2019). Social protection in an aspiring 'developmental state': The political drivers of Ethiopia's PSNP. *African Affairs* 118(473): 646–671.

Legesse, Y. (2012). Addis Ababa transferring public businesses to consumers' cooperatives. *Addis Fortune Newspaper* 13(654), 11 November.

Lenhardt, A., Rogerson, A., Guadagno, F., Berliner, T., Gebreeyesus, M., and Bayru, A. (2015). *One Foot on the Ground, One Foot in the Air: Ethiopia's Delivery on an Ambitious Development Agenda*. London: Overseas Development Institute.

Moller, L. C. (2015). *Ethiopia's Great Run: The Growth Acceleration and How to Pace It.* Washington, DC: World Bank.

Oqubay, A. (2015). *Made in Africa: Industrial Policy in Ethiopia.* New York: Oxford University Press.

Planel, S., & Bridonneau, M. (2017). (Re) making politics in a new urban Ethiopia: An empirical reading of the right to the city in Addis Ababa's condominiums. *Journal of Eastern African Studies, 11*(1), 24–45.

Resnick, D. (2015). The political economy of food price policy in Senegal. In P. Pinstrup-Anderson (ed.), *Food Price Policy in an Era of Market Instability: A Political Economy Analysis.* Oxford: Oxford University Press, pp. 296–316.

Spaliviero, M., and Cheru, F. (2017). *The State of Addis Ababa 2017: The Addis Ababa We Want.* Nairobi: UN-Habitat.

Stiglitz, J. E. (2002). *Globalisation and Its Discontents.* New York: Norton.

Terrefe, B. (2020). Urban layers of political rupture: The 'new' politics of Addis Ababa's megaprojects. *Journal of Eastern African Studies* 14(3): 375–395.

Teshome, M. (2016). President Mulatu Teshome Annual Opening Speech at the Joint Assembly of the House of Federation and the House of Representatives, 10 October, Addis Ababa.

UNDP (2015). *Accelerating Inclusive Growth for Sustainable Human Development in Ethiopia.* Addis Ababa: United Nations Development Programme.

Wade, R. (2004). *Governing the Market: Economic Theory and the Role of Government in East Asian Industrialization.* Princeton, NJ: Princeton University Press.

Watson, D. D. (2015). Political economy synthesis: The food policy crisis. In P. Pinstrup-Anderson (ed.), *Food Price Policy in an Era of Market Instability: A Political Economy Analysis.* Oxford: Oxford University Press, pp. 102–130.

Weldeghebrael, E. H. (2020). The framing of inner-city slum redevelopment by an aspiring developmental state: The case of Addis Ababa, Ethiopia. *Cities:* https:// doi.org/10.1016/j.cities.2020.102807.

World Bank Group (2016). *Ethiopia: Priorities for Ending Extreme Poverty and Promoting Shared Prosperity.* Washington, DC: World Bank.

Yeshanew, S. A. (2008). The justiciability of human rights in the Federal Democratic Republic of Ethiopia. *African Human Rights Law Journal* 8(2): 273–293.

Zenawi, M. (2012). States and markets: Neoliberal limitations and the case for a developmental state. In A. Noman, K. Botchway, H. Stein, and E. J. Stiglitz (eds), *Good Growth and Governance in Africa: Rethinking Development Strategies.* Oxford: Oxford University Press, pp. 140-174.

Zewde, B. (2002). *A History of Modern Ethiopia, 1855–1991.* Athens, OH: Ohio University Press.

5

Dominating Dhaka

David Jackman

Throughout Bangladesh's history, its capital Dhaka has witnessed intense
political competition, including numerous coups, mass uprisings, and, more
recently, a violent rivalry between the Awami League (AL) and Bangladesh
Nationalist Party (BNP). Over recent decades, rallies, strikes, street fights,
and small bombings have been common, and while undesirable normatively,
these are taken as a sign of lively political competition. It is striking, then,
that since 2015 the opposition has largely failed to disrupt the city, with the
ruling AL achieving a level of dominance previously unseen in the country's
history. These events beg an obvious question: how has this been achieved?
This chapter argues that fundamental to this transition has been a shift in the
character of the coercive organizations available to both ruling and opposition parties, seen starkly in the capital. The AL has strategically empowered
the security agencies, enabling widespread arrests, intimidation, and new
surveillance technologies. This has eroded the organizational strength of the
opposition, who, crucially, are also suffering the legacy of previous decisions,
particularly the killing of gangsters in their last term in office, which today
deprives them of the type of street muscle needed to compete. The BNP is
left overwhelmed, having to negotiate and resist everyday forms of repression.
Dhaka meanwhile is increasingly a site for showcasing the country's development successes, which are now foundational to the legitimacy of the ruling
coalition. The projected image of a prosperous Bangladesh is one with the AL
at its heart.

5.1 Introduction

On the outskirts of Dhaka overlooking a small lake is an obscure bamboo
hut balanced on stilts, kept secure by padlock, and served by a thin, rickety

David Jackman, *Dominating Dhaka*. In: *Controlling the Capital*. Edited by: Tom Goodfellow and David Jackman,
Oxford University Press. © Oxford University Press (2023). DOI: 10.1093/oso/9780192868329.003.0005

walkway. This is the hideout of a politician named Imran,[1] and where we met in early 2018. Imran is one of a small number of locally elected politicians in Dhaka representing the opposition BNP. The BNP was elected to government in 1991 and again in 2001, during decades that saw intense and close-run party-political competition. Since 2008, however, it has dramatically diminished as a political force, with the ruling AL achieving a dominance solidified through three consecutive electoral wins, representing a political continuity unprecedented in Bangladesh's history. The year 2018 was a particularly challenging one for the BNP, beginning with the conviction and imprisonment of the party's leader and former Prime Minister Khaleda Zia on corruption charges, and ending with a massive defeat in the general election. In previous decades, the BNP would have responded to alleged rigging and intimidation through general strike (*hartal*) and a mass movement (*andalon*). In the past, tens of thousands of activists have taken to the streets of Dhaka, bearing weapons and often throwing small bombs, bringing the city and wider country to a standstill. Of late, however, the BNP has only mustered limited street agitations, and become in many people's eyes a 'press club party', organizing sit-downs with journalists and foreign diplomats to voice its frustrations, and left to make requests to the police to hold political events, rather than asserting itself through muscle and public support on the streets.

The lives of BNP supporters such as Imran have become increasingly insecure in the face of arrests, intimidation, and surveillance. To attend the limited street agitation that the BNP managed in 2018, Imran had to take circuitous routes into the city centre and move through inconspicuous areas to avoid detection. Because of his status as one of the few elected local BNP politicians in his area, and his role in protests, he also has a number of police cases against him, and during particularly intense periods has been regularly taken into custody. The hideout was therefore where he would seek refuge to avoid arrest, a place that few knew about, where he could sleep at night on the small bed at the back covered by a mosquito net, and look out calmly at his fish growing in the lake below, fattening lucratively before being taken to market. To meet me that day, he had had to shake off a couple of police informers who were stationed permanently outside his house, and reported on where he went and whom he spoke to, and while we were together he was cautious not to answer calls from unknown numbers or to disclose his location during the calls he did take. As of early 2023, Imran—like many of his

---

[1] All respondents have been anonymized.

fellow BNP activists—has seen spells in jail and continues to fight legal cases against him.

Imran's case illustrates in microcosm the situation and decline of the BNP as a powerful political force, and implicitly the rise of the ruling AL, whose dominance is increasingly being seen as authoritarian in character. This transition can be felt most strikingly in Bangladesh's capital, Dhaka city, which has been the epicentre of political mobilization throughout the country's history. Despite decades of intense party-political competition through the 1990s and 2000s, since 2015 there have not been any significant *hartal* in the capital, and while the city is not without protest, we are witnessing the lowest levels of public violence that it has seen for decades. This observation begs a challenging question: how has this been achieved? And more specifically, what role has Bangladesh's capital played in the consolidation of power felt across society?

This chapter argues that repressive interventions have been foundational to how the AL has consolidated power across Dhaka city. It has politicized and empowered state security agencies, most notably the police and intelligence agencies, to a depth only previously seen during periods of military rule. This has led to the securitization of Dhaka through brute forms of coercion, intense surveillance supported by an investment in street-level informers, as well as a range of new digital technologies to monitor phones and social media. There are, furthermore, signs of a radical vision for how Dhaka could be controlled through technology in the future. Yet, political dominance cannot be understood solely in terms of 'interventions' and has been crucially shaped by earlier shifts in the urban political economy for which the now-ruling party was only marginally responsible. The BNP is organizationally weak in Dhaka in part as a result of historical events from when it was last in office in the early 2000s. The decline of politically aligned gangsters at the BNP's own hands during this period deprives it today of the type of muscle in Dhaka that it could use to try and disrupt the urban political order.

As repressive moves have succeeded in controlling opposition, other more generative interventions have assumed greater importance. Nationally, claims about 'development' are central to the legitimacy and identity of the ruling coalition, and a counterpoint to the lack of political competition. Development is now often the centrepiece of speeches and campaign songs. Declarations of ending poverty and being a 'developed nation' by 2041 are symbolized by large-scale infrastructural developments seen in Dhaka and elsewhere. Yet Dhaka is notoriously unwieldy, and broader grievances that animate the youth have found expression in large scale street movements that are difficult to contain. The staking of political reputations on development highlights the tensions in the ruling coalition, with Dhaka a likely epicentre for both how these achievements are demonstrated as well as how they will be judged on the street through protest.

This chapter is based on research conducted in Dhaka between February and September 2018. This primarily took the form of fifty interviews (lasting between thirty minutes and five hours) as well as informal conversations with activists and leaders within the BNP and AL, auxiliary organizations connected to both parties, and journalists. Many of those interviewed were key individuals mobilizing in Dhaka for the BNP, almost all of whom were on bail or had outstanding police cases against them. Many were staying away from their home to avoid arrest, and by early 2019 a number were in jail. Meetings were arranged in obscure or private locations, such as private homes, restaurants before opening hours, or cafés in inconspicuous areas. All respondents are anonymized; however, a broad indication of status, through terms such as senior, junior, local, and national, is used. Respondents included former ministers, senior leaders in the wings of both parties, as well as junior activists and elected representatives. This chapter also draws for background on urban political-economy research conducted in the city between 2013 and 2015 (Jackman 2018a, 2018b).

5.2 Dhaka as a site of struggle

Following the return to parliamentary democracy in 1990, Bangladeshi politics has been characterized by intense competition between the country's two major political parties, the AL and BNP. In practice, Parliament has been often boycotted by the opposition in attempts to discredit and delegitimize those in power (Khan 2015; Ahmed 2018), with competition instead seen on the streets through violent mobilization and demonstrations of strength. When in office each party has politicized state institutions and directed them against the opposition, while exploiting privileged access to the state and market to support party infrastructure. The intense control held by the party over the state has led to descriptions of Bangladesh's political system as a 'partarchy' (Hassan and Nazneen 2017) and 'party-state' (Suykens 2017), defined by the convergence of these institutions in supporting a political regime. When in opposition, both the AL and BNP have waged protests and violence to undermine the authority of the incumbent and demonstrate their inability to maintain political order. Although parties often deny and condemn violent excesses at the hands of their activists or security forces, such competition became characteristic of a political system where

continued political order and stability depended on each coalition systemati-
cally accessing positions of power, a system Khan (2010) termed 'competitive
clientelism'.

The coercive organizations mobilized by either the BNP or the AL were
through the 1990s and early 2000s built primarily around the deep-rooted
party infrastructure. The character and organization of both parties to a great
extent mirror each other, being at core dynastic, centralized, organized at all
administrative levels, factional, and supported by powerful auxiliary organizations representing particular interest groups, such as students (*chhatra*),
youth (*jubo*), and workers (*sramik*).[2] Viewed as a whole, both parties and their
associated organizations can be seen as pyramids, organized as a myriad of
factions linked through patron–client relations (Khan 2010; Suykens 2017;
Jackman 2018b). While they are often perceived as having weak ideological
foundations, differences do to some extent correspond to the wider political
coalitions they can draw upon. Both parties have formed strong coalitions
incorporating minor parties, and historically this has been important to electoral success. The AL is in alliance with the Jatiya Party, as well as left-leaning
parties such as the Bangladesh Workers Party and National Socialist Party,
while the BNP is aligned to the prominent Islamic party, Jamaat-e-Islami,
which formed an important political ally during its two terms in office during the early 1990s and 2000s.[3] Networks organized around both parties have
dug deep into society, and can be found across all sectors and interest groups,
down to local markets, colleges, and other institutions.

A central repertoire of contentious politics used by the political opposition,
and one which particularly impacts urban areas, is general strikes, or *hartal*.
Prior to Indian partition, *hartal* were associated with the non-cooperation
movement, and part of the Gandhian repertoire of non-violent direct action.
During the liberation struggle and subsequently, however, *hartal* became a
common tool by which interest groups demonstrated their dissatisfaction
and strength, often violently, and thereby attempted to weaken the incumbent, achieve concessions, or ultimately bring about regime change. Even
outside of formal elections or periods of explicit political conflict, *hartal*
are common. The number of *hartal* in the three years following independence was, for example, roughly comparable to those immediately preceding it (UNDP 2005: 17), and the scale and frequency of these intensified

[2] Note that such groups are generally referred to with the term *League* if associated with the AL, and
Dal if associated with the BNP.
[3] During the 2018 election, the BNP formed part of the 'Jatiya Oikya Front' (National Unity Front), led
by the lawyer Kamal Hossain. Since 2013, Jamaat-e-Islami has been de-registered as a political party in
Bangladesh; however, many among its leaders and networks stood as BNP candidates in the 2018 general
election.

considerably with the anti-Ershad movement and competitive clientelism. Typical features of *hartal* through the 1990s and 2000s were shuttered shops, quiet streets, arson, Molotov cocktails, and street fights with the security forces. Such political violence is concentrated in election periods. Data collated by Suykens and Islam from the period 2002–13 suggest that within this time frame, violence peaked nationally in 2006 and 2013, constituting 14.5 and 27.3 per cent, respectively, of all incidents, both years being the final year of a BNP or an AL term in office (Suykens and Islam 2015). On average, violence associated with *hartal* constitutes roughly a quarter of all violent events, rising in key years, most notably 2013, the pivotal year prior to the early 2014 general election (ibid.). It is important, however, to recognize that while *hartal* are a central political tool, they represent only one of the many means of protest that form part of broader political movements (*andalon*). In the democracy movement of the late 1980s and early 1990s, for example, blockades, rallies, meetings, marches, human chains, hunger strikes, sit-ins, sieges, street fights, and vigils were also seen in addition to *hartal* (Uddin 2006).

With party-political networks stretching deep and wide across society, violent competition marks all areas of the country, yet takes on particular significance in the country's capital, Dhaka. According to Suykens and Islam (2015), political violence in major cities constitutes around one-quarter of all incidents in the country, with the levels of lethal violence roughly commensurate across rural and urban areas when considering relative population sizes.[4] The same dataset estimates that 15 per cent of all incidents of political violence occur in Dhaka district, which is considerable, given that there are sixty-four districts in Bangladesh.[5] Dhaka city is the site of most *hartal* violence (17.5 per cent of the total, with the next nearest, Chittagong, at 5.1 per cent).[6] What these data suggest is that, while political violence in Bangladesh is not particular to major cities, Dhaka city and district experience relatively high levels of such incidents.

What such statistics conceal, however, is the symbolic significance of events in Dhaka. Political violence in the city can reflect the machinations

---

[4] This comes with the large caveat that the authors define 'urban' as relating only to city corporations, of which there were eleven at the time of their analysis, and now twelve in Bangladesh.

[5] In the last census from 2011, the population of Dhaka district (of which the city is the vast part) stood at around 12 million, roughly 10 per cent of the country's population at the time of approximately 144 million. Estimates of Dhaka city's population today vary considerably, often between 15 and 21 million.

[6] According to this dataset, however, Dhaka as a district has a lower level of casualties (across the period 2002–13) even than far smaller cities such as Bogra, and comparable to Satkhira. Furthermore, the levels of political violence occurring in Dhaka decreased slightly between 2002 and 2013, with the levels of wounded and lethal casualties decreasing more markedly (ibid.).

of the local political economy, but is often more indicative of national struggles. All major political transitions in the country's history have featured large-scale mass protests and movements on the streets of the capital. Dhaka University (DU) in particular has played a central role in the country's political life (Andersen 2013; Ruud 2014; Suykens 2018; Jackman 2021), such that movements or incidents which occur there and in surrounding areas are often seen as revealing the political pulse of the nation, and inspire similar events around the country. As one student leader from the ruling party put it to me: 'to create instability at Dhaka University means creating instability everywhere' (Jackman 2021: 5). Of particular significance has been the coalescing of student protestors with political parties, as seen during the campaign against dominance by West Pakistan prior to liberation, and the movement against military rule under President Ershad in the late 1980s. Other pressure groups and movements wishing to assert their strength and press their interests on those in power also mobilize in the capital, as seen for example in the 'Shahbag movement' from 2013 onwards and protests by the Islamist group Hefazat-e-Islam (ibid.).

The political importance of events in Dhaka hence means that both the AL and BNP typically draw from their wider networks across the country to mobilize people in the capital. Within the capital itself, students represent a core 'muscular' constituency for the organization of political violence, serving as a motivated and easily mobilized labour force living in the centre of the city. More widely, however, the power of the central parties as well as auxiliary organizations differs between areas, corresponding to the character of the local political economy. For example, in areas with large universities or colleges, the student wing is likely to be dominant, and in areas with a concentration of labourers, such as markets, the workers or youth wing are likely to have power.[7] All such groups are routinely involved in political protest and violence. More brute forms of violent enterprise, in the mould of gangsters and mafia, have also historically sat alongside the parties, wielding significant power at the local level in Dhaka and shaping the character of urban politics, as will be explored more below.

---

[7] Whoever is in office nationally tends to control major public institutions (such as universities) through such networks. When out of power nationally, such affiliates tend to be highly marginalized, except in local strongholds (such as where an opposition MP or Mayor is in office).

5.3 The decline of the BNP

To begin to examine the political control achieved by the ruling coalition in Dhaka, it is important to sketch out the wider events and institutional developments over the past decade which have bolstered the dominance of the AL and appear to have contributed to the BNP's decline as a political force. Central to this history is the removal of the system of caretaker government (Ahmed 2010; Khan 2015; Hassan and Nazneen 2017). Through the 1990s and 2000s, the intense political competition seen between parties was moderated by the role of a non-partisan government administering elections. Within this system, the incumbent stood down prior to the election to make way for a caretaker government, headed by a senior civil servant (most often a Chief Justice), thereby preventing the incumbent from utilizing the tools of the state to skew electoral results. The system was institutionalized in 1996 through the 13th Amendment to the Constitution, following the BNP's attempts to administer the election directly itself, which it did in early 1996, and which led to widespread violent protests in the form of *hartal* led by the AL, alongside pressure from civil society, and the eventual re-running of the election (Khan 2015).

While the system successfully facilitated two further elections, attempts by the BNP to manipulate the system at the end of its term in office in 2006 were followed by a prolonged period of military-backed caretaker government between 2007 and 2009. Moving beyond its mandate, the government introduced reforms in the 'good governance' mould, and targeted the politicians it perceived as a root cause of the country's challenges (Ahmed 2010). The so-called 'minus two solution' attempted to remove both main parties' leaders, contributing to a deep mistrust in the system of caretaker government, and paving the way for the AL government later to repeal the Act with a vague air of legitimacy through the 15th Amendment to the Constitution in 2011, which deemed the system unconstitutional, on the basis that such governments were not elected and therefore were non-democratic. This has been key to the consolidation of power under the AL over the past decade (Ahmed 2010; Hassan and Nazneen 2017; Khan 2017), ending any possibility of cooperation between the parties over the electoral process.

During the AL's first and second terms in office after 2009, a raft of further institutional changes and legal manoeuvrings has had the effect of destabilizing the opposition and bolstering the power of the ruling party. The 'International War Crimes Tribunal' has convicted a number of senior leaders within Jamaat-e-Islami and the BNP, and since 2013 Jamaat-e-Islami has been de-registered by the Election Commission and banned as a political party, preventing it from officially contesting general elections. This by extension has weakened the BNP electorally and on the streets. The media and other 'civil society' actors have been weakened by legislation including the recent Digital Security Act, which rights groups and the 'Editors Council' of senior newspaper editors in Bangladesh claim gives the police arbitrary power to arrest and seize material related to digital platforms, under the threat of severe jail sentences. Meanwhile further key institutions of the state appear to be in alignment with the ruling party. The previous Chief Justice, for example, has claimed he was forced to resign by the government after resisting the 16th Amendment to the Constitution, which gave the government power to remove members of the judiciary. It is important also to note that the past decade of AL government represents the longest stretch in the country's history where the army has not taken an open and significant role in political life—for example, by backing a caretaker government or facilitating a regime change. In mid-2018, General Aziz Ahmed was appointed as the new Chief of Army Staff, two weeks prior to which his younger brother, Joseph (a notorious gangster, who was imprisoned in the late 1990s), had received a rare presidential pardon. It has been widely speculated that, despite the military not taking an overt role in public life, this arrangement reveals the underlying loyalty the military has to the present government.

With the system of caretaker government repealed, the AL government directly administered general elections in 2014 and 2018, the first of which it won uncontested, following the BNP's decision to boycott them, and the second of which it won by a landslide. In terms of political representation, Dhaka and the wider country has therefore been almost completely dominated by the AL or its coalition partners for the past five years. Municipal elections in 2015 brought the AL candidate, Anisul Huq, to power in Dhaka City North Corporation (DNCC)[8] amidst allegations of vote rigging and a last-minute boycott by the BNP. Huq's sudden death in 2017 led to a by-election scheduled for early 2018 being postponed by the Election Commission, in a move seen by some as an attempt to obstruct a risky election in the year prior to a general election, and which was won in early 2019 by the AL, uncontested by the BNP and amid low voter turnout. This decision by the Election Commission came after an order from the High Court following writ petitions from Union Parishad Chairmen in areas to be included within the new boundaries of the DNCC. This was perceived by the opposition as a strategy to deliberately engineer the postponing of the election, fearing an upset in a crucial

---

[8] The city is divided into north and south city corporations.

general election year similar to those seen in municipal elections in Sylhet (won by the BNP) and Rangpur (won by the Jatiya Party).

The BNP's decision to boycott the 2014 election followed the strategy seen during the 1990s and 2000s, where any attempts by the ruling party to manipulate the political system were met with a wave of massive political protest and violence, forcing the party to reconsider. Unlike in previous instances, however, the opposition party was unable to wage a sustained and sufficient political campaign against the incumbent, or to mobilize international pressure, the public, and, ultimately, the military. During 2014–15, the BNP and the coalition it led appeared to resort to increasingly extreme and desperate measures to demonstrate their strength and disrupt Dhaka city, such as petrol bombings (Jackman 2018b), which arguably undermined their image and supported the ruling party's characterizations of the opposition as corrupt and violent.

The decline of the BNP intensified in 2018, with the unprecedented conviction of its leader Khaleda Zia on corruption charges, and her imprisonment in Dhaka Central Jail. This led to a brief escalation in political mobilization, with the BNP announcing *hartal*, street protests, marches, and hunger strikes, most of which were met with a huge number of arrests, violence from AL activists, truncheon charges, water cannons, beatings, and arrests by the police; and all with relatively little impact on daily life in the city compared to previous protests. Even during the December 2018 general election period, the BNP was largely unable to make any mark on Dhaka city, which—similar to much of the country—remained mostly calm. This narrative then presents a significant empirical question crucial for understanding Bangladesh's political transition: why has the opposition been unable to mobilize in sufficient force in Dhaka to oppose the AL's abandonment of the caretaker government system and its increasing dominance over Bangladeshi society?

5.4 The legacy of gangsters

Repressive interventions specifically designed and delivered by a ruling coalition are often crucial in attempts to dominate politically. However, opportunities for dominance are also closely shaped by historical events, and the possibilities these bring. The ruling party is strong in Dhaka in part because the BNP is weak, for historic reasons of its own making. Ruling coalitions in Bangladesh achieve dominance over rivals through drawing together the strength of diverse actors capable of using violence. Throughout Bangladesh's history, ruling and opposition coalitions have mobilized an array of violent entrepreneurs, both within and outside the party and state, enabling them to dominate through different means.[9] The character of these actors, however, shifts over time, enabling new forms of control and contention. To understand the weakness of the BNP in Dhaka, we therefore need to view the current period as shaped by earlier shifts in the urban political economy.

Alongside the intense party-political competition witnessed through the 1990s and early 2000s rose powerful gangsters, often referred to through Bengali terms, such as *santrashi* (terrorist, gangster), *mastan* (thug, gangster, criminal), 'top terror', 'godfather', 'mafia', and 'don' (Jackman 2018a). Nationally, Dhaka was an epicentre for such figures, by virtue of being radically larger and economically more important than other cities in the country. These gangsters were for the most part politically aligned, but organizationally distinct from the parties. Notorious figures rose to power and became almost mythologized in the public imagination, and their names struck fear into the city. They ran extortion rackets and illegal businesses such as drugs, grabbed cuts of tenders, and provided much needed muscle and resources to politicians, often at a very senior level. Their rule, as well as the accompanying competition for territory and supremacy, led to widespread violence and insecurity. Businessmen were regularly kidnapped and extorted, and the security forces were perceived as simultaneously too weak and too collaborative to confront them. During the AL's period in office in the late 1990s, widespread crime and violence became a major source of public discontent, and seriously hindered the party's campaign for re-election (Rashiduzzaman 2002).

The BNP then returned to power in 2001 with a public commitment to rid the country of 'top terror', including many gangsters in Dhaka city. Despite BNP politicians being aligned to, patronizing, or themselves *santrashi* figures, there was a sense that public order had deteriorated to too great a degree, and such a move could enhance the party's legitimacy. This effort eventually found success through the formation of the now much feared Rapid Action Battalion (RAB), which, along with the police, killed many such figures in what have been labelled as 'crossfire encounters', and which are often interpreted as extrajudicial killings (Jackman 2018a). The threat of 'crossfire' scared other figures and groups into hiding abroad, and many were arrested. These events continued under the caretaker regime of 2006–8, and have radically reshaped the urban political economy, as well as directly setting the stage

---

[9] A notable early example in the country's history was the formation of the 'Jatio Rakkhi Bahini' (National Security Force) by Sheikh Mujibur Rahman. This was a paramilitary group drawn from AL ranks, designed to counterbalance the power of the army and to have personal loyalty to him.

for the political transition seen in recent years. Violently wresting control away from violent entrepreneurs, who were operating at one step removed from the party and state, brought new forms of coercive strength to the domestic security apparatus of the state. With this came the capacity to coerce more effectively from the political centre. The popularity of RAB's activities also to some extent normalized extrajudicial practices in the public imagination, giving a tacit legitimacy to extreme forms of state coercion within Bangladeshi political culture. Nationally, one estimate puts the number of people killed extrajudicially between 2001 and mid-2018 at 3,209 (Odhikar 2018a). More generally, according to Suykens and Islam (2015), state enforcement agencies are among the actors most likely to be involved in political violence; between 2002 and 2013 they were responsible for a quarter of all incidents, and 53 per cent of all fatal casualties.[10]

Ironically, these events also directly disempowered the BNP and created the conditions for the AL to solidify power within Dhaka's political economy. The absence of gangsters controlling many aspects to life in the city created a power vacuum, and following the BNP's term in office came the years of the caretaker government and the subsequent election of the AL in 2009. Since then, the AL has then been able to consolidate power at the grassroots, with many of its ward-level leaders and affiliates playing similar roles to the once powerful gangsters. This has meant that, while both parties are organized down to the grassroots, it is the AL that has been able to capitalize on the space left by the decline of gangsters, and expand its organizational strength on the streets. It furthermore means that the BNP is unable to draw upon such gangsters to confront the ruling party. All BNP leaders interviewed acknowledge this as an important dynamic to their weakness in Dhaka. An elected BNP representative in the city put it like this:

> Why does the BNP have such a terrible situation today? I think our madam [Khaleda Zia] made a bad decision ... She was the first one who made RAB, special section, from the police. As she made this new division, she had to give them some tasks, and she gave them the job of cleaning up the BNP-minded criminals, *santrashi*. This was a mistake. These were the first government-employed law enforcement group who started the culture of crossfire, and many of the 'BNP-minded' *cadre-bahini* [militia, group] were killed by RAB ... When the BNP is the ruling party, most

---

[10] While such actors do not figure prominently in contentious politics in Dhaka today, a number of groups beyond the formal political apparatus are drawn upon to wage political violence, including manual labourers (market and transport labourers) (Jackman 2018b), street traders, as well as children and young adults living on the streets who are involved in the implementation of more extreme forms of political violence, such as bombings and arson (Atkinson-Sheppard 2015; Jackman 2018b).

of the *cadre* are on their side, but they killed many of those gang members, they were the victim of crossfire, many left the country, and many joined the AL. This is reflected in the situation now. Now we need to revolt, make a movement, but how can a normal *cadre* lead the movement? We ordinary people cannot participate in the same way. You and me, we have our families, our wives, and we think of them when we take a step in the movement. But when an illegal person approaches the movement, he won't think about anything.

Senior leaders within the party substantiate such a perspective, stating simply that were such gangsters around today, the BNP would be able to utilize them to disrupt the political order in Dhaka. The fact that they are not appears to be a sore point internally within the party. One interpretation of these events, as expressed by a senior party member, is that the BNP inherited a list of the '23 top terror', which had been drawn up during the AL government in the late 1990s, and gave RAB free rein to kill these figures. Because the list had been decided under the AL, it naturally included more 'top terror' who were aligned to the BNP than to the AL. When the BNP came to power, most AL-aligned gangsters went into hiding, and hence those whom the RAB could kill were in general more closely connected to the BNP. Another interpretation is simply that the party knew what it was doing, but decided to make the decision for the good of the nation. Whatever the interpretation, many members across the BNP lamented this decision. For example, as a senior leader described it:

BNP killed its own people, we encouraged it because we wanted to get rid of these *mastan*. A lot of people blame us for killing our own people, but it was in the interest of the people. Sometimes some people say the BNP did the wrong thing by killing their own *mastan*, leaving only the AL *mastan*. But it was a conscious decision, maybe killing was not a good idea, they should have gone through due process, but it was a conscious decision to get some peace and sanity in the country.

During research this was often described by BNP leaders and activists as a 'self-sacrifice' made by the party for the people, meaning that now the BNP is at a double disadvantage—not only did it kill its own political muscle, but the AL has had two terms in office to build its organizational strength at the grassroots, while the BNP has been sidelined. This 'sacrifice', then, forms part of the opposition's present political rhetoric to illustrate the contrast between itself and the AL: while the BNP killed such criminal elements, the AL—the opposition alleges—has allowed black money and criminality in politics. This is not, however, to suggest that, were such gangsters still operating, then the BNP would be able to mobilize successfully against the government. The level of manpower, political empowerment, and technology seen within the security forces today would arguably easily outmatch any such threat. As one college-level president of the *Chhatra dal* described: 'In light of present politics, it was a mistake, but for the betterment of our country, it was not a mistake. With this much ferociousness from the police and RAB, it wouldn't matter if the *santrashi* were here.'

5.5 Security and surveillance

A second process which helps explain how the AL has achieved dominance in Dhaka city lies in how it has strategically empowered the coercive apparatus of the state. While security agencies have always been utilized politically by the incumbent, the extent of investment, degree of dependency, and depth of politicization of the police, all suggest a magnitude of change not seen in Bangladesh since the fall of Ershad's military government (Jackman and Maitrot 2022). At the national level, it is clear that the police have been a budgetary priority in recent years, particularly during the election period. The share allocated in the 2017/18 budget for 'public order and security' increased by over 10 per cent to Tk 22,851 crore,[11] the vast majority of which was allocated to the 'public security division' of the Home Ministry, which includes the Bangladesh police and Ansar (an auxiliary domestic security agency). In the 2018/19 budget, this figure increased again by a further Tk 3,743 crore. Such investments can be seen on the streets of Dhaka, with a visibly greater police presence and new vehicles and equipment. Raw budgetary figures, however, conceal deeper changes in the nature of urban policing. There is a widespread perception—among both the opposition and the wider public—that Dhaka is receiving a disproportionate share of the national resources. BNP leaders frequently described a sense of feeling outnumbered, with the ratio of BNP activists to police inverting, from a typical situation where the BNP activists greatly outnumbered the police, to one where the police outnumber the BNP. One senior leader put it like this: 'The politics of the whole country depends on the capital, and this is why the government are posting people from other districts to Dhaka. More than 50 per cent members of the

---

[11] The increase is in nominal terms. Note that 1 crore is 10 million.

police are just here.' The specifics of this claim are likely to be inaccurate, but the sentiment bears truth.[12]

Not only have the size and resources of the police changed, but allegedly so also has the background profile of the officers stationed in Dhaka. It is widely claimed that the police are increasingly direct AL members, particularly associated, in the case of recruits, with the Chhatra League (student league). One way this has allegedly been achieved is through recruitment processes. As part of the procedure, approval from the local police station (*thana*) where one is registered as residing is required (most often a home district). Known or even suspected affiliation with the BNP or Jamaat-e-Islami is very likely to halt recruitment at this point, and it is claimed that many candidates who have successfully qualified on all other grounds have fallen at this hurdle. A former BNP minister jokingly described the police as inspecting your DNA to see if you, your father, and grandfather all belonged to the AL.

This politicization of the police in Dhaka can also be seen in the home district backgrounds of the police appointed, particularly among senior roles. Not only do the police increasingly come from AL backgrounds, it is alleged, but they are also tied to the Prime Minister through having roots in her home district, Gopalganj, as well as other surrounding AL strongholds, such as Faridpur. Across Dhaka, opposition activists claim that the officers in charge (OC) of the *thana* are 'Gopali' (as people from Gopalganj are derogatorily termed). A mid-ranking police officer who previously worked in intelligence in the capital estimated that 60–70 per cent of OCs in Dhaka are from Gopalganj. An elected BNP leader in Dhaka described the situation:

> Of all the *thana* here in Dhaka more or less 80 per cent of people are from Gopalganj. The local *thana* here is being run by X, who is from Gopalganj. Actually it is not only about Gopalganj, but someone needs to be close to the family of the Prime Minister. They are keeping people not only from Gopalganj, but bringing people close to the family here to Dhaka, and they have a special tie and communication with them. Starting from constable to the higher post, there are many *gopali* in the police, Detective Branch and RAB.

This politicization is symbolized in political discourse by the fact that BNP activists now often refer to the police as the 'Police League', thereby associating them with branches of the AL such as the Chhatra League (the student wing of the AL). Beyond Bangladesh, it has been argued that reorganizing

---

[12] Note that other agencies in addition to the police operate or are regularly deployed in Dhaka, including RAB, border guards, and Ansar.

the 'social composition' of the security forces to better ensure loyalty is a common strategy to guarantee dominance (Greitens 2016: 27).

One reading of these dynamics is that they reflect the dependence of the ruling party on the police to maintain power. A modern, well-trained police force is a normal aspiration for a state; however the police—as well as other security actors, such as the RAB and the intelligence agencies—have played a fundamental role in maintaining the authority of the ruling party over the past decade, a responsibility for which they need to be both empowered and rewarded. In the case of Dhaka, the police have convincingly demonstrated their ability to quell opposition, most critically during the 2013–15 period, when the BNP and opposition appeared to turn to a strategy of petrol bombings to demonstrate the inability of the state to protect its citizens. Other threats controlled by the police and other agencies are numerous, including a real and potent revived threat of terrorism, populist Islamic parties, such as Jamaat-e-Islami, and movements, such as Hefajat-e-Islam, and, most critically, the wide and deeply rooted network of BNP activists.

Through the past decade, and most notably during and since the 2014 election, BNP activists have been arrested, faced criminal charges, and been imprisoned in huge numbers, and in some instances have even disappeared, allegedly at the hands of the state. The scale of this is extraordinary. In January 2018, the BNP claimed that since 2007 over 50,000 cases had been launched against almost 1.2 million BNP activists (Prothom Alo 2018a). In September 2018 alone, the BNP claimed that 3,000 cases had been instigated against 300,000 of its activists, with 3,500 activists and leaders arrested (Daily Star 2018b). Such actions have led to an intense atmosphere of fear and anxiety among BNP activists, knowing that they could be arrested, imprisoned, or worse. BNP activists and human rights groups allege that many activists face torture, in a strategy seemingly designed both to extract information, but also to destroy the morale and motivation of the opposition to contest the ruling party. A college-level *Chhatra dal* leader portrayed the situation:

They are torturing all of the arrested men. They are inserting sticks into their backside, they are clipping your tongue and giving you electric shocks, and pulling out all ten nails. It is a very common practice nowadays, very frequent. Our members have experienced this. This happens in remand. When the court gives one or two days of remand, during this time the police do whatever they want in the *thana* ... Last week one of our members was going to remand and had a stick inserted into his backside, and from that has internal bleeding, and is now admitted into hospital.

More extreme still, human rights groups and activists allege widespread disappearances, with the whereabouts and conditions of BNP members unknown. The human rights organization Odhikar (2018b) estimates that between 2009 and 2018, there have been 505 disappearances, allegedly at the hands of the state, of which the majority were conducted by the RAB, followed by the detective branch of the police and then the police.[13] Such a possibility is reported to be a constant fear for opposition activists, even for student leaders:

> 137 people are missing only from the *Chhatra dal* over the past five years. They have arrested our president. Missing is a new trend for our country. Once you go missing, you will never come back, we don't know where your graveyard is, if you are dead or alive, we just know that you are missing. (College-level *Chhatra dal* leader in Dhaka)

Such dynamics not only represent a political strategy to control the opposition, but appear also to be an opportunity for the police to profit from extortion, an arrangement that police sources suggest has the tacit agreement of political leaders. Following a round of arrests (e.g. during a political protest), activists described first-hand how police divide those arrested into different camps. Some face police cases and possible imprisonment, and others are simply threatened with the plan of extorting them. A large number of activists and leaders arrested are thus routinely released on condition of payment.

With the battle on the streets seemingly won, new forms of repressive intervention have risen in importance to keep threats in check. BNP leaders and activists all portrayed street-level informers as critical for the state to keep tabs on the movements and plans of the opposition. In Bangla, informers are known as 'source', 'former', or, in student circles, *tiktiki* (lizards). In some cases, particularly elected representatives and high-profile leaders, informers literally followed them, while others had their business activities monitored, or when they with other BNP members. A senior *Chhatra dal* leader described the burden this represents:

> The police know where I am going, who I'm speaking to, where I'm sitting, they have their *source* nearby watching. The *Chhatra league* leader has also threatened me. I cannot even sit in my own business, because if the police see me there they will catch me.

---

[13] This figure includes, but is not confined to, the disappearances of people associated with the political opposition.

Crime reporters and opposition activists described the number of informers operating in Dhaka as increasing significantly since around the 2014 election. Unlike in other areas of the police budget, there are no audits for informers, and it is not publicly known how much the state spends on maintaining these networks. Part of the strength of the source networks in Dhaka is the origin of such figures. It is common for sources to have a criminal past, or even present, and therefore to be well integrated into the networks that the police need to monitor. Arrests serve as an opportunity for the police to recruit new informers, offering people arrested for serious crimes a route out, and new opportunities. It is even common for informers to be allowed to continue with petty crimes (such as selling drugs or running a small extortion racket) as a reward for providing information. During the spate of bombings in Dhaka in 2014–15, I witnessed this first-hand. Following the arrest of a local labour leader for orchestrating bombings at the behest of the BNP, the leader managed to be released from prison, but only on the condition that he became an RAB informer.

The AL's three terms in office have also coincided with the proliferation of smartphones and social media supported by a 4G network. Digital surveillance is a new terrain in which coercion is being felt, with widespread fear among the opposition that phones and other devices are being monitored. In reality, the techniques, organization, and extent of digital surveillance are difficult to gauge. Reports indicate that security agencies have purchased extensive surveillance hardware and software from foreign companies. This includes the purchase of 'FinSpy' and 'FinFly USB' from the company Gamma Group, a technology that infects targets through malware, enabling the monitoring of communication devices and reportedly even encrypted information. This was in use at least between 2012 and 2014 (Wikileaks). In 2014, the RAB reportedly attempted to buy the software 'IMSI Catcher', enabling the tracking of mobile phones and potentially also voice interception, from the Swiss company Neosoft (Privacy International 2015); and in 2015, there are reports that the Italian company 'Hacking Team' marketed its technology to the RAB (Prothom Alo 2018b). A key organization supporting the security agencies is the National Telecommunications Monitoring Centre (NTMC) in Dhaka, mandated—according to the objectives outlined on its website—'to establish national-level lawful interception platforms for all kinds of electronic communications as directed by the government'. In 2015, the German company Trovicor was contracted to improve the government of Bangladesh's surveillance systems, focusing on the NTMC (Spohr 2015). As of 2018, there are reports that the NTMC is significantly increasing its surveillance capacities, with social media a priority target (The Independent 2018).

There also appear to be strategies which aim to bring Dhaka city itself under digital surveillance. Attempts to integrate technology into the governance of the city preceded the return of the current ruling party. The late 1990s saw a plan to modernize the Dhaka metropolitan control room, and by 2007 plans for a 'command, control and communications system' (C3S) under the Dhaka Metropolitan Police were being implemented, establishing 155 surveillance cameras at key intersections, priority areas, transport terminals, and other entrances to the city (Daily Star 2007). While this scheme is widely deemed to have failed, it is clear that the government has far greater ambitions. Under the remit of the 'Development of Dhaka City Digital Monitoring System', the government is in the early stages of implementing a plan to install a total of 50,000 CCTV cameras (starting with an initial 16,000), all feeding into a 'Central Command and Control Centre', where 550 officials will monitor the city over sixty monitors (Daily Star 2017a). Speaking at a launch event in 2016. the Prime Minister reportedly described this system as enabling the state 'to instantly monitor any case of accident, fire and criminal activity in any part of Dhaka city using information technology and to take necessary measures accordingly' (Daily Star 2016). Key features of this technology are the ability to track vehicles through their registrations, to detect and pinpoint particular noises (e.g. gunshots), and—perhaps most ambitiously—to recognize faces. If the plans are realized, known 'criminals' will be automatically identified through the technology in a system resembling that recently introduced in many Chinese cities. Indeed, a Chinese company is associated with the contract for the programme, and there are reports of a Memorandum of Understanding for Chinese state funding to support the project under the title of 'Safe Dhaka City'. While it is only at a nascent stage, if feasible such technology could radically transform the means of control available to the ruling party.

To appreciate the diversity of such repressive interventions in action, it is useful briefly to consider the conviction of Khaleda Zia in early February 2018. The imprisonment of the leader of the BNP by an AL government was unprecedented and deprived the BNP of an active figurehead for the 2018 general election. At the time, it also necessitated a show of force and loyalty by BNP members and supporters. When it became clear that Khaleda Zia would be convicted and imprisoned in her final sentencing on 8 February in the court of Bakshibazar in old Dhaka, the government implemented a number of strategies to ensure its grip on the capital. Central to this was the almost entire isolation of the city from the country, which was described in some newspaper reports at the time as 'delinking'. Additional checkpoints were established at all eight entry points into the city.[14] Intense searches were conducted on the railway, waterways, and highways leading to the city, and all terminal junctions reportedly had new CCTV cameras installed to monitor them. Hotels were instructed to collect the identity cards of their guests and submit these to the detective branch on a daily basis. Bus companies reportedly received instructions from police not to rent out buses, and many companies stopped operating altogether during this period. All of this was an effort to reduce the capacity of the opposition to bring in activists from outside to disrupt the capital. A ban on all processions and the carrying of sticks or other weapons was implemented under police instruction. The strategy for arrests also shifted, away from the blanket arrest of opposition members, to the careful targeting of more senior BNP leaders responsible for mobilizing activists (Dhaka Tribune 2018).

On 8 February itself, traffic was almost non-existent, hardly any vehicles entered the city, and any that did had their passengers and luggage searched. Ironically, the level of quiet and yet the anticipation of violence resembled that only seen on *hartal* days. All of the security agencies were deployed, with the RAB guarding entrance points and 10,000 police reportedly positioned on the streets, along with twenty platoons of the Border Guard (forty-nine further platoons were deployed outside of Dhaka). Apps such as Uber and the local equivalent, Pathao, stopped their services and many schools shut for the day. Despite the ban on processions, AL activists paraded around the city. The Chhatra League, for example, occupied key areas of the DU campus to prevent the *Chhatra dal* from mobilizing, including the important Teacher Student Centre at DU. Previously elected officials in Dhaka had talked of the AL in every ward in the city mobilizing to prevent the BNP, and one report indicated the head of a transport union committing 15,000–20,000 transport workers to guard the city's terminals. Khaleda Zia's motorcade came from her residence in Gulshan to old Dhaka surrounded by BNP activists, who described to me seeing small gatherings of loyal supporters waving to the convoy at key intersections, braving the law enforcement and ruling-party muscle. BNP activists fought in small skirmishes with the police and AL, and were met at Bakshibazar itself by a huge number of security forces lining the streets, with a mobile jammer also reportedly installed by the police to prevent news, or more specifically fake news, of events spreading.

---

[14] These were described by the Daily Star (2018c) as 'Postogola Bridge, Sadarghat, Abdullahpur Bridge, Dhaur Bridge in Ashulia, Babubazar Bridge, Gabtoli, Jatrabari and Sultana Kamal Bridge at Demra'.

5.6 Development promises and political risks

The effectiveness of repressive interventions, combined with the fortuity of historical events outlined, has meant that the BNP is dramatically depleted as a political force. Less government attention now appears to be given to the day-to-day efforts to control this threat, while major crises have required considerable resolve, not least managing the world's largest refugee camp and addressing Covid-19. The lack of broadly democratic competition has led to considerable criticism both internationally and at home. It strikes many people as unjust and immoral, particularly when the government has been stung by corruption crises, such as the revelation that certain members of the RAB have been paid to kill politicians extrajudicially in a region close to the capital (Ganguly 2017). The question this raises is: how has the ruling party sustained legitimacy in the face of clear democratic reversal, and what role, if any, does Dhaka play in this story?

Increasingly central to the identity of the ruling coalition are claims about the 'development' seen in the country and the responsibility of the AL for bringing this about. The economic successes that have continued over the AL's past three terms in office are real, important, and a source of pride. Bangladesh is now a 'middle income' (albeit lower-middle income) country, as judged by UN metrics. This appears to be a fulfilment of a key promise made under 'Vision 2021', a centrepiece of the government's agenda for the country's fiftieth anniversary. The wider development achievements seen over the past decade compare favourably to those seen in neighbouring India: poverty has fallen, and infant mortality, literacy rates, and female secondary school enrolment are much improved. Attention has now turned to Bangladesh becoming a 'developed nation' by 2041, a sign also of the longevity aspired to by the ruling party.

Commentators have argued that these successes are showcased as part of an implicit bargain struck with the nation: we may not be democratic, but we are developing (Khalid and Sarker 2018; Mahmud 2021). Campaign songs and slogans during the 2018 election seem to affirm such a message. One new slogan often heard was 'the country floats on development, so we want the boat again', referring to the AL's party symbol of the *nouka*. Even in local elections, development and progress were cast as central to how ruling-party politicians want to be seen. Dhaka plays an interesting role in this vision. On the one hand, it is where key development successes are highlighted, most notably large-scale, eye-catching infrastructure projects. Flyovers now cast shadows across the city, and the country's first Metro Rail is due to open in late 2022 when construction on a Subway will also begin. There is some indication that particular groups may also be induced through state resources.

In the run-up to the 2018 election, for example, the Prime Minister publicly proclaimed that apartment blocks would be built on the city's outskirts to house those currently living in slums, and these would be available for the same price as a shack (Daily Star 2018a). The value of this is less in winning over particular constituencies, however, and more in portraying an image of a compassionate and development-minded leadership. There are signs of even greater and more politically explicit ambitions. Presently a 'model city' is being built at Dhaka's north-east edge, with the centrepiece being three skyscrapers named 'Bangabandhu Tri-Tower'[15] and one set to be the tallest building in South Asia.

On the other hand, however, Dhaka can be a serious weakness in this vision. As a city, it is known as being unlivable, sprawling, with creaking infrastructure, high living costs, and terrible traffic. In many ways, then, the city appears to belie the image of development that the ruling party intends to convey. Infrastructure may address critical transport challenges faced by the city, but other grievances are less amenable to new concrete and foreign engineers. In the crucial election year of 2018, two large-scale student protests closed down much of the city and posed a very serious threat to public order and the stability of the ruling party (Jackman 2021). These were motivated by the lack of good job opportunities, the perception that quotas within the civil service are unfair, and the hazardous and unsafe conditions on roads. The opposition arguably attempted to capitalize on these movements to create moments of crisis in the run-up to the general election, and they were only contained through a mixture of promises of reform combined with direct and severe repression. Attempts to address these challenges also require confronting aspects of the ruling party's coalition. In the 2018 cases, for example, actually meeting such demands would require challenging the interests of powerful party-aligned unions and the families of freedom-fighters.

5.7 Conclusion

The seismic political transition observed in Bangladesh over the past decade has to date been studied primarily in terms of formal institutional developments, exemplified in an amendment to the Constitution abolishing the system of caretaker government which had regulated the intense and violent political competition between the BNP and the AL through the 1990s

---

[15] Bangabandhu ('friend of Bengal') is the name given to Sheikh Mujibur Rahman, Bangladesh's liberation hero, the country's first President and later Prime Minister, renowned AL leader and the father of the present Prime Minister.

and 2000s. Alongside this amendment has been a raft of further developments and legal manoeuvres commented upon widely in the media, which
seem to have enabled the ruling party to consolidate power. These include
the International War Crimes Tribunal, the banning of Jamaat-e-Islami, new
legislation to monitor digital technologies, a repressive approach to domestic
media and other 'civil society' organizations, challenges to the independence
of the judiciary, most notably involving the resignation of the previous Chief
Justice, and the imprisonment of the BNP's leader, Khaleda Zia. By contrast,
this chapter has contributed to our understanding of this transition by drawing attention elsewhere, towards the underlying shifts in coercive capacity
across both ruling and opposition coalitions, which have arguably enabled
many of the dynamics outlined above, and the overarching discourse of development which appears to legitimate it. These are manifest most explicitly in
Dhaka city, which has been argued to be at the heart of how contestation
occurs, and therefore the locus of repressive and generative interventions.

The puzzle presented early in the chapter was how the AL has achieved the
level of dominance it seems to have reached. The story told reveals the disproportionate significance that the political economy of Dhaka plays in national
politics, as well as the role of historical fortuitousness, or lack thereof, in shaping political transitions, alongside deliberate strategy. The roots of the current
transition were argued to lie almost two decades back, when the BNP inad-
vertently undermined its capacity to mobilize muscular cadre through the
formation of the RAB and the subsequent killing of gangsters and other violent entrepreneurs. This period sparked the rise of widespread extrajudicial
practices which have underpinned the threat of violence posed by the regime
today, and begun a journey of increasing domestic state coercive capacity.
It seems plausible that the rapid expansion of this capacity in the early 2000s
empowered future incumbents to better resist the opposition, increasing their
capacity to hold off the opposition's attempts to mobilize, and thereby incentivizing them to deploy this strategy when in power. It was then fortuitous
timing for the AL that it was returned to power when it was.

Control is exercised in particular ways in the capital, as seen through the
alleged favouritism given to police officers and other officials from the Prime
Minister's home district. Although it is at an early stage, there appears to be
serious intent to develop more sophisticated repressive intervention in the
form of surveillance, which may enable more efficient forms of coercion and
greater urban control. Yet the political significance of Dhaka is also about
more than control. It is an arena in which the developmentalist ambitions of
the state can be showcased, ambitions which are foundational to the continued legitimacy of the AL. This exposes a tension which is difficult to reconcile:

the need to demonstrate wide-ranging development outcomes in a context that has deep-rooted and perhaps intractable challenges that are far from easily managed. Continued urbanization, a youthful urban population, a lack of good jobs, and a host of other grievances and governance challenges will require delicate and careful management.

References

Ahmed, N. (2010). Party politics under a non-party caretaker government in Bangladesh: The Fakhruddin interregnum (2007–09). *Commonwealth and Comparative Politics* 48(1): 23–47.

Ahmed, N. (2018). *The Parliament of Bangladesh*. Abingdon: Routledge.

Andersen, M. K. (2013). The politics of politics: Youth mobilization, aspirations and the threat of violence at Dhaka University. PhD dissertation, Roskilde University, Denmark.

Atkinson-Sheppard, S. (2015). The gangs of Bangladesh: Exploring organized crime, street gangs and 'illicit child labourers' in Dhaka. *Criminology and Criminal Justice* 16(2): 1–17.

Daily Star (2007). Entire Dhaka to come under surveillance. 15 August. Available at: https://www.thedailystar.net/news-detail-9, accessed 7 November 2019.

Daily Star (2016). Dhaka being cleared of traffic congestion, violence. 2 June. Available at: https://www.thedailystar.net/city/dhaka-being-cleared-traffic-congestion-violence-1233205, accessed 7 November 2019.

Daily Star (2017). Mega plan for surveillance. 7 October. Available at: https://www.thedailystar.net/frontpage/mega-plan-surveillance-1472680, accessed 7 November 2019.

Daily Star (2018a). There would be no slums in the capital: PM. 20 August. Available at: https://www.thedailystar.net/news/city/multi-storey-buildings-replace-city-slums-pm-sheikh-hasina-1622947, accessed 7 November 2019.

Daily Star (2018b). 3 lakh BNP men implicated in false cases in Sept: Rizvi. 14 September. Available at: https://www.thedailystar.net/politics/news/3-lakh-bnp-men-implicated-false-cases-september-rizvi-1633846, accessed 4 November 2019.

Daily Star (2018c). Dhaka to be delinked. 7 February. Available at: https://www.thedailystar.net/frontpage/dhaka-be-delinked-1531051, accessed 7 November 2019.

Dhaka Tribune (2018). Police focus on controlling BNP organizers ahead of Feb 8. 6 February. Available at: http://www.dhakatribune.com/bangladesh/politics/2018/02/06/police-target-key-bnp-organizers-instead-mass-arrests/, accessed 4 November 2019.

Ganguly, Meenakshi (2017). After Narayanganj verdict, Bangladesh should disband RAB. Human Rights Watch Dispatches. 19 January. Available at: https://www.hrw.org/news/2017/01/19/after-narayanganj-verdict-bangladesh-should-disband-rab#, accessed 4 November 2021.

Greitens, S. C. (2016). *Dictators and Their Secret Police: Coercive Institutions and State Violence.* Cambridge: Cambridge University Press.

Hassan, M., and Nazneen, S. (2017). Violence and the breakdown of the political settlement: An uncertain future for Bangladesh? *Conflict, Security and Development* 17(3): 205–223.

Jackman, D. (2018a). The decline of gangsters and politicisation of violence in urban Bangladesh. *Development and Change* 50(5): 1214–1238.

Jackman, D. (2018b). Violent intermediaries and political order in Bangladesh. *European Journal of Development Research* 31(4): 705–772.

Jackman, D. (2021). Students, movements, and the threat to authoritarianism in Bangladesh. *Contemporary South Asia* 29(2): 181–197.

Jackman, D., and Maitrot, M. (2022). The party–police nexus in Bangladesh. *Journal of Development Studies* 58(8): 1516–1530.

Khalid, Saif, and Sarker, Saqib (2018). Ten years of Sheikh Hasina: Development minus democracy. *Al-Jazeera*, 28 December. Available at: https://www.aljazeera.com/news/2018/12/28/ten-years-of-sheikh-hasina-development-minus-democracy, accessed 29 March 2023.

Khan, A. A. (2015). Electoral institutions in Bangladesh: A study of conflicts between the formal and informal. PhD thesis, SOAS, University of London.

Khan, M. H. (2010). *Political Settlements and the Governance of Growth-Enhancing Institutions.* Mimeo. London: SOAS.

Khan, M. H. (2017). Anti-corruption in Bangladesh: A political settlements analysis. Anti-Corruption Evidence (ACE). Working Paper no. 003, SOAS.

Mahmud, Faisal (2021). 'Development over democracy': Why Bangladesh's foreign affairs advisor has such a difficult job. *Scroll.in*, 19 March. Available at: https://scroll.in/article/987310/development-over-democracy-why-bangladeshs-foreign-affairs-advisor-has-such-a-difficult-job, accessed 29 March 2023.

Odhikar (2018a). Total extra-judicial killings from 2001–2018. Accessed at: http://odhikar.org.

Odhikar (2018b). Enforced disappearances: 2009–2018. Accessed at http://odhikar.org.

Privacy International (2015). Swiss moves to curb surveillance exports an example to the EU. Available at: https://privacyinternational.org/blog/1421/swiss-moves-curb-surveillance-exports-example-eu, accessed 4 November 2019.

Prothom Alo (2018a). 733 BNP activists killed, 1.2m accused in 50,000 cases. Available at: https://en.prothomalo.com/bangladesh/news/170074/%E2%80%98733-BNP-activists-killed-1.2m-accused-in-50-000, accessed 4 November 2019.

Prothom Alo (2018b). RAB denies surveillance equipment purchase from Italy. Available at: https://en.prothomalo.com/bangladesh/news/72109/RAB-denies-surveillance-equipment-purchase-from, accessed 4 November 2019.

Rashiduzzaman, M. (2002). Bangladesh in 2001: The election and a new political reality? *Asian Survey* 42(1): 183–191.

Ruud, A. E. (2014). The political bully in Bangladesh. In A. Piliavsky (ed.), *Patronage as Politics in South Asia*. Cambridge: Cambridge University Press, pp. 303–325.

Spohr, F. (2015). Bangladeshi surveillance: Big brother made in Germany. *Handelsblatt Today*. Available at: https://www.handelsblatt.com/today/politics/bangladeshi-surveillance-big-brother-made-in-germany/23501878.html?ticket=ST-2743072-0GsasGV0z1PkdqwgXcfZ-ap4, accessed 4 November 2019.

Suykens, B. (2017). The Bangladesh party-state: A diachronic comparative analysis of party-political regimes. *Commonwealth and Comparative Politics* 55(2): 187–213.

Suykens, B. (2018). 'A hundred per cent good man cannot do politics': Violent self-sacrifice, student authority, and party–state integration in Bangladesh. *Modern Asian Studies* 52(3): 883–916.

Suykens, B., and Islam, A. (2015). The distribution of political violence in Bangladesh. Ghent: Conflict Research Group.

The Independent (2018). Social media to come under surveillance. 12 June. Available at: http://www.theindependentbd.com/post/153852 (accessed 7 November 2019).

Uddin, A. K. M. J. (2006). The movement for the restoration of democracy in Bangladesh 1982-1990. PhD thesis, University of Leeds.

United Nations Development Programme (UNDP) (2005). *Beyond Hartals: Towards Democratic Dialogue in Bangladesh*. Bangladesh: United Nations Development Programme.

Wikileaks. SpyFiles 4. FinFisher—Customers. Available at: https://wikileaks.org/spyfiles4/customers.html, accessed 7 November 2019.

6

Fragile dominance?

The rise and fall of urban strategies for political
settlement maintenance and change in Zambia

Marja Hinfelaar, Danielle Resnick, and Sishuwa Sishuwa

6.1 Introduction

Zambia's capital, Lusaka, has long been a major site of political contestation, and securing votes from the city's residents is often key for gaining
a foothold on the national political scene. In 1991, support in Lusaka cat-
apulted the Movement for Multiparty Democracy (MMD) to victory and
ended one-party dominance under the United National Independence Party
(UNIP). A decade later, gains by opposition parties in Lusaka gradually
eroded the MMD's dominance until 2011, when the Patriotic Front (PF) won
the city and the presidency. The pattern repeated in 2021 when the opposition United Party for National Development (UPND) defeated the PF and
won 51 per cent of the vote across Lusaka's seven constituencies.[1] Unlike the
UPND, however, which started as a regional party in Southern Province and
gradually expanded its influence (Beardsworth 2015), the PF emerged as an
urban-based party that struggled to retain its core supporters over time. As
such, it provides a useful lens through which to analyse the creation of an
urban political settlement and to examine which strategies can ultimately lead
to its undoing.

In particular, the rise of the PF initially hinged on support specifically
from Lusaka's urban poor and the informal sector. In the run-up to the 2008
elections, the party strategically expanded its support to build alliances also
with urban-based civil society and the middle class, as well as with particular ethnic communities in rural areas. After capturing the presidency, the PF

[1] There are seven constituencies within the district of Lusaka under the mandate of the Lusaka City
Council. However, there are thirteen across the broader province of Lusaka.

Marja Hinfelaar, Danielle Resnick, and Sishuwa Sishuwa, *Fragile dominance?*. In: *Controlling the Capital*.
Edited by: Tom Goodfellow and David Jackman, Oxford University Press. © Oxford University Press (2023).
DOI: 10.1093/oso/9780192868329.003.0006

deliberately relied on co-optation of those groups to prevent their defection to the opposition. However, the party became more vulnerable in the wake of the death of its founder, Michael Sata, in 2014. Intra-party fractionalization, combined with the growing popularity of the UPND, resulted in the PF relying on violence and intimidation of some of its core constituencies to retain its urban dominance.

This chapter first describes the importance of Lusaka in shaping Zambia's political settlement and highlights how the PF became more vulnerable over time. Subsequently, we focus on the three core constituents of the PF—the urban poor, civil society, and the middle classes. By 'urban poor', we are referring to those working in the informal sector or in low-paid work and often living in high-density substandard housing—known as 'shanty compounds' in Zambia. By 'civil society', we mean organizations such as religious bodies and various similar umbrella associations representing women and lawyers that have the capacity to mobilize citizens and check the power of the government. The term 'middle class' refers to those in particular occupations, such as civil servants, managers, senior officials, legislators, professionals, associate professionals, and technicians. We look at PF engagement with these groups over two distinct historical phases. The first phase focuses on the party's attempts to build a solid and populist base ahead of the 2006 and 2011 elections, while the second discusses the co-optation and coercion strategies that it has implemented when in power, from 2011 to date. Throughout, we consider the degree to which these constituencies have been swayed by, or resistant to, such tactics. We contextualize these dynamics vis-à-vis Zambia's broader political landscape, relying on historical processing tracing, in-depth interviews with key elite actors (political leaders, urban planners, business people, civil servants, and civil society actors), and a survey with informal traders. The final section concludes.

6.2 Situating Lusaka

Zambia currently has an estimated 40 per cent of its population living in urban areas.[2] Lusaka, along with cities in the northern Copperbelt region of the country, has long been key to the country's urbanization trends. Originally built for only about 125,000 people (Home 1997), the city currently

[2] In Zambia, the definition of 'urban' is localities of 5,000 inhabitants or more, in which a majority of the labour force is not in agricultural activities.

houses a population of approximately 2.1 million people. By contrast, the next biggest cities of Kitwe and Ndola, which are located in the Copperbelt Province, contain about 590,000 and 500,000 residents, respectively (UN-DESA 2014). The capital's economic base is the country's most diverse, spanning communications, finance, retail trade, manufacturing, and construction services (Resnick and Thurlow 2017).

Successive waves of migration into Lusaka have made it ethnically diverse. In the 1960s and 1970s, most migrants came from Eastern Province, while during the 1990s, in-migration from the Bemba-dominant Copperbelt increased the prevalence of Bemba in the city. Bembas have become the main ethnic group, constituting 22 per cent of the population, with the Chewa (10.8 per cent), Nsenga (10.5 per cent), and Tonga (9.9 per cent) each separately making up the next largest ethnic groups (Central Statistical Office 2014). The rapid population increase means that, in terms of the number of votes, Lusaka's urban constituents are more numerous than the total urban constituents in all of the Copperbelt towns (ECZ 2016). As the seat of government, the capital is also where political coalitions are forged and where political institutions and spaces are fiercely contested.

At the same time, Lusaka is a highly unequal city. Due to colonial town planning principles that continue to persist, about 70 per cent of the city's population live in high-density, poorly serviced areas of the city in informal settlements popularly known as shanty compounds (Mulenga 2013). The array of these compounds around an affluent city centre, with multiple shopping malls and high-end living estates, conveys a clear sense of inequality, underscored by Zambia's urban Gini coefficient stubbornly hovering at 0.61 for the last decade (Central Statistical Office 2016). Services within these informal communities are often substandard, with many relying on pit latrines and lacking solid waste collection or potable water (Kennedy-Walker et al. 2015). Consequently, to win over Lusaka, politicians must often forge cross-class coalitions, through generative interventions, or impede opposition parties from doing the same.

6.3 The urban factor in Zambian history: Dominance and political settlement

Urban areas have always been central to political settlements in Zambia. At the time of independence, the nationalist UNIP had its strongholds in Lusaka, the Copperbelt, and the city of Kabwe, along with Northern and Luapula Provinces (Larmer 2011). Following the inauguration of one-party rule in 1973, the party maintained its dominance by, among other techniques, requiring party membership in order to access market stalls or land plots in urban areas (Fraser 2017). Street protests in Lusaka during the late 1980s, after the removal of maize subsidies, proved the major impetus for democratic transition. When multiparty democracy arrived in 1991, it was a party backed by the country's labour movement, the MMD, and a union leader, Frederick Chiluba, which defeated UNIP at the polls. However, during the course of its twenty-year reign, the MMD gradually became a more rural-oriented party, often buying support through appeals to ethnicity and its massive fertilizer subsidy programme (Mason et al. 2017).

Towards the end of Chiluba's tenure, the MMD began to splinter, and a variety of new opposition parties emerged with the capacity to threaten the MMD's hold on power. The first was the UPND, formed in 1998 by Anderson Mazoka, who left the ruling party after differences with the party leadership. More defections occurred when Chiluba attempted and failed in his bid to change the Constitution to run for a third term. Chiluba subsequently selected Levy Mwanawasa as his successor, a move that aggrieved Michael Sata, who left the MMD to establish the PF.

In the 2001 elections, the PF garnered only 3 per cent of the votes, while the UPND just narrowly lost those elections and won a majority of Lusaka's votes. However, when Mazoka died in 2006, internal fighting within the UPND and the emergence of a political novice, Hakainde Hichilema, caused that party's electoral fortunes to wane. This created a window of opportunity for Sata, who crafted a populist campaign with urban constituents.

During the 2006 electoral campaign, Sata focused heavily on Lusaka and cities on the Copperbelt. He spent most of the campaign mobilizing street vendors, marketeers, and bus and taxi drivers, and held large rallies in shanty compounds. Among other campaign slogans, one of the PF's most notable was 'lower taxes, more jobs, more money in your pockets'. Sata often attacked the MMD's poor record on employment creation and promised to upgrade, rather than demolish, shanty housing, provide a clean water supply, and end harassment of street vendors. The PF, in turn, won large numbers of votes in these cities in those elections, particularly in the high-density settlements and among the urban poor (Cheeseman and Hinfelaar 2009; Resnick 2014). After the 2006 elections, the PF won control of the city councils in Lusaka, Kitwe, and Ndola.

Subsequently, Sata tried to expand his support base to include middle-class voters, while adapting his campaign message to maintain his urban poor constituents. He also engaged civil society leaders by actively supporting their causes, most notably demands to revise the Constitution (Sishuwa 2020a).

This tactic, combined with overtures to particular ethnic groups in rural areas, enabled Sata to increase his vote share in the 2008 elections that followed when Mwanawasa died in office, and which ultimately resulted in the PF's capture of the presidency in the 2011 elections.

6.4 Intra-PF fragmentation increases party vulnerability

As noted by Mudde and Kaltwasser (2013), populist parties' emphasis on direct linkages between leaders and the masses can result in intolerance of independent institutions and civil liberties if such parties gain the opportunity to govern. This proved equally true under Sata's presidency. A culture of paranoia and sycophancy emerged within the party (Sardanis 2014), which resulted in political chaos when he unexpectedly died in office in October 2014. After a fractious period that led to many defections from the PF, Edgar Lungu, the party's General Secretary at the time, was selected as the party's flagbearer for the January 2015 by-election.[3] Lungu went on to win Zambia's election, after narrowly defeating Hakainde Hichilema, who had broadened the UPND's appeal after almost a decade as its leader. The PF leadership at that point recognized its vulnerability and sought to consolidate its hold on power ahead of the elections, through a mix of government programmes and increased control of state institutions (the Electoral Commission of Zambia, judiciary, police, etc.).

In the 2016 general elections, Lungu won 50.3 per cent of the votes and therefore only marginally passed the $50 + 1$ threshold needed to defeat Hichilema. As a liberal, business-minded party, the UPND did not gain the same traction among the urban poor as the PF did in its heyday, but it still attracted 30 per cent of the votes in 2016, both in high-density, low-income areas and in low-density, more affluent neighbourhoods (ECZ 2016). This momentum was achieved despite limited opportunities to campaign in Lusaka due to severe restrictions being placed on the party's campaign activities and high levels of electoral violence in the city (Wahman and Goldring 2020).[4]

---

[3] Before the Constitution was amended in 2016, the death of the President in office caused a 'presidential by-election' within three months.

[4] In Kanyama, the UPND polled slightly over 50 per cent in local government elections, and just missed the National Assembly vote (36,674 for the PF versus 31,934 for the UPND). Indeed, originally 14,049 UPND votes were missing, but these were added after they were found dumped into bins (see Mukela 2018).

Lacking Sata's charisma and everyman appeal, Lungu struggled to gain legitimacy as the PF leader. Many founding members and 'ideologues' of the PF defected under his presidency, and the party no longer has the same appeal to the urban poor. As the political settlements framework suggests, a shift in the distribution of power among the ruling coalition, caused by threats both within the party and outside, increases contestation and, in turn, the vulnerability of the elite coalition's dominance (Whitfield et al. 2015). Confronted by an increasingly popular opposition leader, Lungu resorted to more overt ethnic nationalism to discredit the UPND. Since the UPND is largely seen as a party of the Tonga and Lozi ethnic groups, many of Lungu's political appointments revolved around Bemba and Nyanja politicians (Fraser 2017).

In addition, Zambia's relationship with the international donor community shifted, affecting the prevailing political settlement. For instance, Western donor support dropped from over 35 per cent of the national budget in the late 1990s to less than 3 per cent in 2016 (Republic of Zambia 1996–2019).

In 2011, the year of political turnover in Zambia, the World Bank reclassified Zambia as a lower-middle-income country, which meant that it could no longer access concessional donor financing and precipitated a turn towards commercial loans from private creditors and China. In recent years, Zambia has obtained $3 billion by issuing three Eurobonds. Money for patronage was now widely available and fully utilized (see the annual reports of Auditor General and the Financial Intelligence Centre). In addition, and despite Sata's initial xenophobic rhetoric towards the Chinese, China has become heavily involved in the economy.

The Chinese state and companies have a strong presence in mining industry and infrastructure projects, but also provide security systems (CCTV) to public institutions and ministries. Chinese concessional loans supported Zambia's police force, the Zambian Air Force, and the army in terms of providing housing, uniforms, and equipment. Recent estimates suggest that China holds almost 30 per cent of Zambia's external debt, with eighteen separate Chinese creditors holding liabilities totalling $6.6 billion (Brautigam and Wang 2021). Collectively, these external shifts meant that traditional bilateral donors and international financial institutions had less leverage with the Zambian government, and declining funding for civil society affected the ability of the latter to serve as a countervailing force.

These dynamics had key implications for the PF's engagement with three key critical constituencies: the urban poor, the middle class, and civil society. While Sata's initial electoral gains depended on mobilizing the urban poor by promising radical pro-poor policies, combined with a broader ethnic mobilization in rural areas (e.g. Cheeseman and Hinfelaar 2009), he subsequently saw Lusaka's middle class as an important political ally. He tried to gain their support by siding with civil society over necessary constitutional reforms (Sishuwa 2020a), promising civil servants better working conditions, and combatting corruption. His cross-class appeal was borne out by the 2011 election results: all Lusaka's constituencies, both those in the poor, high-density areas and those in the affluent, low-density neighbourhoods, went to the PF, while the surrounding (rural) areas still supported the MMD. To better understand these trends, the following section details the contours of these relationships during the period of Sata's rise and tenure.

6.5 PF's erstwhile urban constituents: Vendors and marketeers

As in other African countries, markets and street trade play a critical role in providing both food security and employment in Zambia. In urban Zambia, approximately 81 per cent of the labour force works in the informal sector (Central Statistical Office 2015). Within Lusaka, many of those in the informal economy labour as merchandise and food sellers within the city's more than sixty open-air markets, or they hawk their goods along the capital's streets. The numerical importance of informal workers in Lusaka makes them a constituency that is vulnerable to both co-optation and harassment, depending on whether the ruling regime views them as a source of political support or a threat to its dominance.

The simultaneous processes of economic and political liberalization that Zambia encountered in the early 1990s temporarily shifted the balance of power in favour of informal traders. Price controls were lifted and traders became a critical source of votes in the new democratic environment. Under Chiluba's tenure, Zambia began a structural adjustment programme that reduced the number of jobs in the formal sector, as state-owned enterprises were disbanded, and removed controls on imports and prices, which reduced barriers to entry into the informal sector (Hansen 2007). The MMD Minister of Local Government (MLG) in the early 1990s—who was, in fact, Michael Sata—also instructed the Lusaka City Council (LCC) to leave vendors alone, causing a further growth in *tuntembas*, or wooden shacks, on the streets and pavements (Nchito 2006).

As the decade progressed, however, conflicts between the LCC and the national government that had existed under UNIP resurfaced, creating alternate periods of alienation and co-optation of traders. A violent crackdown by the LCC in 1993 resulted in large-scale riots, ultimately convincing Chiluba to intervene on their behalf. In 1996, an election year, he established a vendor's desk at State House and appointed a deputy minister in charge of street and market vendors' affairs. Because of the protections they were afforded, vendors collectively were referred to as the 'Office of the President'. By 1998, however, Hansen (2004: 62) notes that street vending had reached 'anarchic proportions', with the whole city centre becoming an outdoor market. When the LCC pursued a massive sweep across the city in 1999, destroying hundreds of *tuntembas*, Chiluba deviated from past behaviour and decided not to intervene (Hansen 2007).

When his successor, Levy Mwanawasa, took office in 2001, the MMD was already beginning to lose its popularity in urban areas. A large-scale fertilizer subsidy programme initiated during Mwanawasa's first year as President enabled the MMD to consolidate a greater hold in rural areas. Under his New Deal government, Mwanawasa sought to attract the private sector, generate growth, and combat corruption, and by the mid-2000s, growth rates had rebounded and inflation had fallen to single digits. However, urban inequality became more pronounced, and formal sector employment declined by 24 per cent between 1992 and 2004 (Larmer and Fraser 2007). As part of the 'Keep Zambia Clean and Healthy' campaign launched in 2007 by Mwanawasa and his MLG, Sylvia Masebo, more stringent provisions were added to the Street Vending and Nuisances Act (1992) and many hawkers and *tuntembas* were removed, often with the use of bulldozers and paramilitary officers (Times of Zambia 2007).

By this time, the PF had already grown in popularity among Zambia's urban poor and had taken over control of the LCC, as well as cities on the Copperbelt. Sata vocally decried crackdowns on vendors. In fact, members of the PF-dominated LCC admitted trying to sabotage the MLG's attempts to remove vendors as much as possible, even obtaining temporary court injunctions against planned MLG evictions of traders (Resnick 2014).

6.6　PF inroads into Lusaka's middle class

Despite the lack of jobs that has pushed many into the informal economy, there is a small middle class that benefited from Zambia's economic boom from 2003 to 2014, during which there was growth in gross domestic product of around 6–7 per cent (Resnick 2015). Lusaka is the seat of a highly centralized government system. All ministries, state-owned enterprises (SOEs), such as the Industrial Development Corporation (IDC) and ZCCM-IH, and statutory bodies (pension funds, revenue authority, etc.) have their headquarters in Lusaka. As a result, most (senior) civil servants live in Lusaka, and they make up a good part of Lusaka's middle class. The same applies to international organizations, such as the Common Market for Eastern and Southern Africa, the United Nations, WaterAid, donor agencies, foreign embassies, and local organizations. Consequently, the middle class, though proportionally small, not only occupy a privileged spatial position in Lusaka in terms of access to land and services, but also form an important political constituency.

This relatively affluent segment of the population is less vulnerable to economic shocks, as compared to the lower middle class, and has earnings above the tax credit threshold (Nalishebo 2013). Szeftel found in the 1970s that Zambia's middle class had a strong material ethic, in which an overlap of public positions and private business interests was very common (Szeftel, quoted in Tordoff 1980 110). This still holds today and explains the dominance of 'tenderpreneurs' in the political settlement. These are simultaneously civil servants and business people, who vie for and profit from government contracts. Defending the individual interests of this affluent middle class tends to undermine social spending (ZIPAR-UNICEF 2019).

Wragg and Lim (2013) show how the liberalization policies of the 1990s affected space making in Lusaka, highlighting how foreign-global-capital spaces are increasingly taking over Lusaka, at the expense of its informal sector population. The new visions of space increasingly exclude the poor, and have allowed for their dispossession. Although there have been a couple of state-sponsored housing projects in recent years, these have all targeted civil servants, many of whom are already known to have built houses (Embassy of the Republic of Zambia 2018). Although the Housing Act (1996) required 15 per cent of the national budget to be allocated to housing, the actual figure has never surpassed half of that amount (Mbati-Mwengwe 2001). The highest planned allocation to housing as a percentage of the total national budget between 2006 and 2017 was 6.5 per cent, and the highest actual expenditure was 5.4 per cent. Since then, housing expenditure has plummeted to below 1 per cent, of which a minimal amount goes to low-income housing projects and initiatives. Civil servants have been the beneficiaries of these housing allocation decisions, which are largely viewed as an entitlement that accompanies their job position. Nevertheless, they overwhelmingly supported the PF in the run-up to 2011. They were not only disgruntled with corruption under Mwanawasa's successor, Rupiah Banda, but also mobilized by the PF's promises of increased wages for workers and civil servants, and a fairer distribution of wealth.

6.7 The PF and civil society

Concurrent to these interactions with informal workers and the middle class from Chiluba onwards, Zambia was also experiencing an opening of civic space. Countries that feature a strong 'civil society' are often assumed to have the best prospects for democratic consolidation in Africa. Indeed, the literature on this subject is characterized by a remarkable consensus on the capacity of trade unions and religious organizations to force presidents to compromise, whether under authoritarian or democratic rule (Von Doepp 2005; Gould 2009; Sishuwa 2020b). Zambia is often held up as an example of the democratic gains that can result from a robust non-state sector capable of checking government power. During the 1990s, and in the absence of a viable and effective political opposition, it was civil society organizations, represented by the three Christian church mother bodies, the Law Association of Zambia (LAZ), and the disparate women's organizations in the Non-Governmental Organizations Coordinating Committee (NGOCC), that largely held power to account (Gould 2009).

One of the peculiar features of Zambian civil society organizations is that they are largely concentrated in Lusaka alone, although the churches retain a broader geographic membership. This meant that opposition forces were much stronger and, indeed, more regularly found a united voice in Lusaka than in any other part of the country. The democratic political environment that thrived under the MMD administrations of Chiluba and Mwanawasa provided the incentive necessary for the growth of non-state actors with the capacity to affect public opinion. In fact, it was civil society organizations grouped around the Oasis Forum, a coalition of civic associations formed by the three broad institutions mentioned above, that defended term-limits against the attempts of former President Chiluba to secure an unconstitutional third term in 2001 (Gould 2011).

The legal climate of civil society organizations changed markedly following the passage of the Non-Governmental Organization (NGO) Registration Act in 2009. The Act represented an early attempt by the governing MMD and President Banda, following his narrow victory in late 2008, to control the activities of civil society organizations, many of which were generally seen to be aligned to the main opposition, ahead of the 2011 elections. As argued by Ndulo (2010), this legislation gives broad discretion to the government to deny registration to NGOs, gives powers to dictate NGOs' thematic and geographical areas of work, and imposes mandatory re-registration every five years.

Nonetheless, in 2011, the resilience of Zambia's civil society movement was apparent when several organizations campaigned against the enactment of an MMD-sponsored Constitution that was widely unpopular. The PF courted civil society organizations using constitutional reform to position itself as the political ally that non-state actors needed. The opposition party had previously been mistrusted on the subject, owing to the close association that its leader, Michael Sata, had with former President Frederick Chiluba at the height of the latter's third-term bid. Furthermore, the working relationship on constitutional reform between civil society and the governing MMD, led by President Mwanawasa, who succeeded Chiluba in 2001, was initially close. It was the split between Mwanawasa and non-state actors in 2007, which persisted under President Banda, who succeeded Mwanawasa after the latter died in office, that gave Sata his opportunity. The PF seized this opening to develop a threefold strategy. First, to secure the trust of non-state actors, the then main opposition party refused to send representatives to the National Constitutional Conference (NCC), a broad-based body created by Mwanawasa to rewrite the constitution. The PF's move came after civil society organizations had earlier boycotted the NCC in protest against its composition, which they argued was tilted towards the government. Second, when the MMD took to Parliament a constitutional amendment bill that did not contain the popular clauses demanded by civil society, such as the requirement that a winning candidate in a presidential election should secure more than 50 per cent of the votes cast and that the Vice-President should be elected alongside the President, PF lawmakers shot down the bill (Sishuwa 2020a). This consolidated the party's relationship with civil society. Third, having successfully frustrated the political programme of the MMD, the PF made its own promises on constitutional reform, promising to enact 'within 90 days of assuming power' a Constitution supported by civil society and containing the rejected clauses.[5] The main opposition later moved to reflect this promise in its 2011 manifesto, which was released a few weeks after the defeat of the MMD-sponsored constitutional bill.

In addition to NGOs, the democratic transition in the early 1990s led to the expansion of the private media. More specifically, one of the pre-election pledges that swept the MMD to power in 1991 was the liberalization of the media after nearly two decades of one-party state censorship. Following their victory, Chiluba and the MMD moved to implement this campaign promise, partly in response to demands by donors for media freedom as a precondition for accountability, transparency, and good governance. Over the course

[5] Interview with Suzanne Matale, 2 October 2015.

of the next decade, hundreds of independent radio stations and newspapers were established. *Radio Phoenix* and *The Post* newspapers, both headquartered in Lusaka, were emblematic of this new independent media that held power to account and provided an important platform for civil society organizations and opposition parties. Phoenix's *Let the People Talk*, a weekly broadcast programme that hosted prominent personalities to discuss different national issues, became a household name for many Lusakans. Thanks to *The Post*, state-driven corruption was exposed throughout the 1990s, civil society organizations found their voice on important national topics, and many Zambians became increasingly critical of the ruling MMD. When Chiluba attempted to seek an unconstitutional third term of office in 2001, it was *The Post* and *Phoenix* that successfully galvanized opposition forces against the move, demonstrating the power and influence of the independent media in post-1991 Zambia.

The next MMD administration, led by Mwanawasa, generally remained committed to the promotion of media freedom, notwithstanding the constant frictions that occasionally arose mainly between the state and *The Post* throughout the early 2000s. Under Mwanawasa, a number of private television and radio stations were opened in Lusaka and even the public media, long disparaged by the public as a mouthpiece for the ruling party, gained some semblance of credibility by giving coverage to the opposition. Opposition forces, and especially Sata's PF, thrived under this political environment.

Following Mwanawasa's death in August 2008, the space for media freedom began to shrink. The administration of Rupiah Banda, the MMD leader who succeeded Mwanawasa, in an attempt to cripple their revenue base, threatened to shut down critical media institutions and banned government ministries from advertising in publications that were deemed hostile to the ruling party. This response reflected attempts by the MMD to tighten its grip on power in response to a narrow electoral mandate and in the face of mounting opposition from the PF ahead of the 2011 general election.

6.8 Consolidating dominance while in power: The PF's control of Lusaka, 2011 to date

The above sections indicate that Sata's PF benefited from the open political environment provided by the country's democratic transition and mobilized a cross-class urban coalition of voters who were aggrieved by the growing inequality and corruption that prevailed under the MMD. In the early years of his tenure, Sata attempted to maintain this coalition, but he slowly began to undermine any sources of opposition to his rule. This pattern became more pronounced under Edgar Lungu, who took over as President after Sata died in 2014, and who employed various modes of repression and co-optation vis-à-vis the PF's three sets of core urban constituents.

6.9 Empowered or extorted? Traders navigate the PF's waning urban dominance

After Sata won the presidential election in 2011, he issued a letter to all the councils in Zambia ordering them to cease harassment of street vendors. The PF General Secretary at the time even claimed that, as a policy of the 'PF Caring Government', vending should be legalized. In 2012, Sata demoted his MLG when she planned to sign a new statutory instrument against vending. PF cadres were even allowed to have their own market, known as Donchi Kubeba, on a flyover bridge in Lusaka.[6]

After Sata's death, the PF policy of co-opting marketeers and street traders continued. The most obvious attempt to do this was Lungu's announcement in 2015 of a Presidential Empowerment Initiative Fund (PEIF), which would be funded by 10 per cent of his own salary. The terms were extremely generous; the only qualification was that an applicant should hold a National Registration Card and operate from an established market.[7]

Besides PEIF, Lungu continued Sata's policy of benign neglect of street vendors. They were generally left unmolested and protected by the national government, even as they were not necessarily provided with better trading conditions. An analysis of media events shows that episodes of crackdowns on traders in Lusaka were non-existent between 2011 and 2016, when the PF finally controlled both the national government and the LCC (Resnick 2019).

In addition, many of the markets, especially in the central business district, came increasingly under PF control. Just like UNIP and the MMD when they were in office, the PF established offices in most of the central markets. Although PF party members claim that this allows politicians to get first-hand information on marketeers' needs,[8] such offices facilitate surveillance of marketeers' activities. In addition, the PF benefited from using lower-level party cadres within both the markets and bus stations (Beardsworth et al. 2022).

---

[6] 'Donchi Kubeba', or 'don't tell', was the PF's 2011 campaign song. In it, voters were encouraged to take gifts from all political parties, but not tell them that they were ultimately going to vote for the PF.
[7] Interview with the national coordinator and fund manager of the PEIF, July 2018.
[8] Interview with the Hon. Elizabeth Phiri, Kanyama constituency, July 2018.

These were typically young men who mobilized votes and finance for the PF, often through the use of violence or extortion (Hansen and Nchito 2013). The attraction of markets for cadres is that they are not just a concentrated source of information and votes, but also a major source of revenue, with some of the major ones generating more than a million Kwacha a month.[9]

As Hichilema's influence grew over time and he lost to Lungu by only 100,000 votes in the 2016 general elections, conflicts between PF and UPND cadres in markets within Lusaka and cities on the Copperbelt became more pronounced. Most dramatically, a series of arson attacks spread through-out markets in mid-2017 as political tensions escalated following Lungu's arrest of Hichilema in April of that year on charges of high treason, when the latter refused to stop his car when the President's motorcade passed. After a fire outbreak in July 2017 within City Market, one of Lusaka's largest, Lungu responded by blaming the UPND and invoked emergency powers for three months to prevent what he claimed was further 'sabotage' by the UPND. With Hichilema still in jail at the time, these emergency powers enabled the police to prohibit public meetings, search without a warrant, close roads, impose curfews, restrict movements, and detain suspects for longer than usual. Lungu insisted that such actions were needed to allow a thorough investigation of the market blaze and other market fires (Cotterill 2017). Yet, the fires also provided Lungu with an excuse to consolidate power and suppress civil liberties.

Shortly thereafter, in late 2017 and early 2018, a large-scale outbreak of cholera prompted a sharp deviation from the PF's strategy of accommoda-tion and benign neglect of street vendors. Despite having come to power through the support of traders, the PF issued Statutory Instrument (SI) No. 10 in February 2018, known as an amendment to the Local Government Street Vending and Nuisances Regulations. The SI updated the fines for contraven-ing any of fifty-five potential restrictions, including working as a hawker in the same area for more than five days in a calendar month, selling food in any street or public place besides a market, and failing to provide adequate clean and safe water on one's business premises (GRZ 2018). In sharp contrast to Sata's calls a few years earlier to legalize street vending, the new SI essentially penalized the practice again.

To implement the SI, the government razed a number of *tuntembas*, removed traders from the streets, and closed down thirty markets in Lusaka for several weeks (Kasonde 2018). To enforce the restrictions, the government

---

[9] Interview with the Department of Housing and Infrastructure Development, Ministry of Local Government, July 2017.

brought in the national military (Blomfield 2018). While this decision was most likely made because of the low levels of capacity among LCC police to enforce regulations, the tactic created the impression that traders were miscreants who needed to be controlled to protect other citizens of Lusaka. The presence of soldiers on the street further symbolized efforts by the state to intimidate the broader citizenry and control any resistance to the regime. These actions limited the ability of traders, both street hawkers and marketeers, to pursue their livelihoods. More importantly, it failed to address the root of the epidemic, which was the substandard water, sanitation, and garbage collection facilities, both in the shanty compounds where most traders lived and in the markets where they worked.

How did traders react to the government placing restrictions on their livelihoods? There were some signs of outright resistance. Most notably, when a seven-day curfew was placed on the compound of Kanyama, which is one of Lusaka's most densely populated townships and considered the centre of the cholera outbreak, residents rioted (Mitimingi 2018).

Such reactions, and the recognition that so many of the poor depend on trade for their livelihoods, likely prompted the PF's more accommodative approach towards traders when the Covid-19 pandemic arrived in the country in 2020. An early plan by Lusaka's PF Mayor to remove street vendors for health reasons was quickly aborted in recognition of the fact that this was not viable from both an enforcement and an economic perspective.

Yet, while repressive tactics became less common, the entrenchment of PF cadres within the markets continued. In some sense, this reflected the unwillingness of the PF leadership to alienate their rank and file, whose mobilization tactics would be essential as the 2021 general elections neared. Given that cadres are typically more motivated by access to patronage than by party affinity, they can be difficult for political parties to control; this explains why the PF repeatedly ignored LCC requests over the years to rein in the cadres, who were essentially siphoning off revenue from the markets and bus stations that were legally under the LCC's control. In fact, one study found that 14 per cent of market traders in Lusaka admitting paying a fee to the cadres on a regular basis (Resnick 2018).

The consequence, however, was that the PF increasingly lost the support of its original base, the urban poor. Indeed, as the 2021 elections neared, and Lungu placed the military on the streets, ostensibly to deter electoral violence, few were deterred. As one Lusaka resident noted, 'Soldiers on the street don't scare me to vote—I am more comfortable to see soldiers because then I know that party cadres will not harass or intimidate me' (cited in Sinyangwe 2021). At the same time, Hichilema had learned over the years from the populist tactics of Sata. Having been viewed as distant and elitist in the past, he cultivated a more approachable persona, abandoning technocratic jargon and business suits for more direct language and casual attire, often singing and dancing at rallies (Beardsworth 2015). These combined dynamics— growing resentment by many of the urban poor and the growing appeal of Hichilema—certainly go a long way to explaining the UPND's unprecedented vote share in 2021 in some of Lusaka's highest-density constituencies.

6.10 The middle-class shift from incorporation to disunity

After Sata's rise to power, the government's close relation between the political elite and the middle class continued, and with it the deeply rooted urban-elite bias in policy making. Indeed, as with the 1991 electoral turnover, regime change never brought fundamental changes. Sata's cabinet consisted of many 'recycled' politicians who came from UNIP and MMD-Chiluba days and belonged to the same economic elite as Lusaka's middle class, and, equally, were beneficiaries of these policies. With the Lungu faction gaining the upper hand within the PF, and the incorporation of a more 'neoliberal' section of the MMD, there has been a move away from the PF's affinity with the urban poor and a preferential treatment of the middle class.

For instance, Lusaka's civil servants profited from a boom in public expenditure, most notably in terms of wage increases and enhanced emoluments, which included utility vehicles and out-of-town allowances of up to $500 a day when travelling abroad for work.[10] Sitting allowances in statutory bodies became another means of clientelism that benefited senior civil servants and politicians. The pledge to improve the living conditions of the informal and working class was partially undermined by wage increases initiated by the PF administration. In the Medium Term Expenditure Framework (2018–20), the government disclosed that the public service wage bill consumed over 51 per cent of domestically generated revenues, crowding out domestically financed operational capital expenditure (Budget 2018).

The close-knit networks of Lusaka ensured that loyalists were given government positions or contracts. The PF incorporated those who had been strong advocates of media freedom when the PF was in opposition. For example, the former Vice-President of the Press Association of Zambia and a journalist who worked for *The Post* newspaper—Amos Chanda—became the State

---

[10] Interviews with senior civil servants in the Ministry of Finance, 2018.

House spokesperson, while the former Director of Transparency International Zambia (TIZ), Goodwell Lungu, became Deputy High Commissioner to Botswana after the 2016 elections.[11]

Due to the disorderly transition from Sata to Lungu, which left many politicians on the sidelines, disunity began to undermine the party. Internal disagreements and the overruling of technocrats' decisions by the PF resulted in ad hoc policy making, and many reversals, which undermined the overall functioning of the government. Moreover, quiet resistance emerged from within the civil service. While ministers, permanent secretaries, and even directors of departments are political appointments, the civil service as a whole was not entirely loyal to the PF. This led to high-level leaks to foreign media, most notably *Africa Confidential*, resulting in the uncovering of hidden debts and high-level corruption cases. The Auditor General's office also remained steadfast in reporting corruption within the ministries. The emergence of a strong Financial Intelligence Centre (FIC) within the Ministry of Finance revealed high-level political involvement in financial crimes such as corruption and tax evasion, among others (in 2017 this amounted to a record-breaking K4.5 billion). Their case studies revealed the direct involvement of politicians and their business networks (companies, accountants, and lawyers). The FIC demonstrated how institutions that should provide oversight (e.g. the Patents and Companies Registration Agency and the Zambia Revenue Authority) are not fulfilling their role, or, as they put it privately,[12] are prevented from fulfilling their role. While it was constantly under attack, the FIC's particular status within the ministry, combined with international support and a seemingly incorruptible board, made it relatively autonomous from the usual political pressures.

In addition to quiet resistance, middle-class voters in Lusaka demonstrated growing opposition to the PF through their voting behaviour. For instance, the 2016 elections saw Lusaka more divided among the total main parties than in the previous general elections in 2011, though in the end the PF took all the seats in the city. It must be noted that two constituencies, Lusaka Central and Munali, which contain middle-class areas, were contested in the High Court on account of violence and intimidation. While the election results were overturned within the stated three months of the election petition, an appeal was launched in the Constitutional Court, which in 2018 ruled in favour of the PF candidates.

---

[11] See https://www.lusakatimes.com/2018/01/22/former-tiz-director-appointed-zambia-deputy-high-commissioner-botswana/, accessed 10 February 2020.

[12] Interview with the FIC, November 2017.

But while the largest opposition party, the UPND, had made inroads in Lusaka, until 2021 it was unable to gain a majority. UPND supporters could not freely express their support on the streets of Lusaka without risking being beaten by PF cadres. Intimidation of voters by a show of weapons (pangas, sometimes guns) contributed to low voter turnout in 2016. As a result of its loss of support, the PF moved from co-optation and clientelism to more coercive means of maintaining dominance in Lusaka, aided by the courts, which lost their neutral position in political cases. However, despite the challenges of campaigning in Lusaka in the 2021 elections, the UPND won four out of the seven parliamentary seats in the capital.[13]

6.11 Co-opting and controlling civic space

The space for civil society engagement as a means of keeping the government accountable also became extremely circumscribed over time, precipitated soon before the 2016 elections as Lungu tried to consolidate his legitimacy within the PF. In June of that year, *The Post* newspaper, whose editor was an erstwhile PF supporter-turned-critic, was forcibly shut down, ostensibly over a tax dispute. Another leading media outlet, the popular Prime Television, was closed in early 2020 on account of unspecified 'security and national interest' considerations. The closure of critical media outlets had a chilling effect on other private media organizations, which sought to avoid the same fate by moderating their coverage. In 2016, state security forces also briefly shut down a private television station, Muvi, after it broadcast what the authorities deemed as subversive content. In addition, the government co-opted compliant private media by offering incentives for them to remain silent on controversial political matters—or, indeed, support the ruling authorities. Between 2016 and the 2021 elections, the Lusaka-based *Daily Nation* private newspaper assumed notoriety for discrediting opposition forces and defending government as well as ruling-party positions. In return, the government advertised in the *Nation*, boosting the newspaper's revenue base, and helped transport its newspapers to areas beyond Lusaka.

The urban character of the established private media in Zambia drove much of the PF's media strategy of co-optation and control. Of the country's four major private daily newspapers—*News Diggers*, *The Mast*, *Daily Nation*, and *New Vision*—only one (*Daily Nation*) is distributed throughout the country. *The Mast* and *News Diggers* have their highest circulation and readership

---

[13] The other three constituencies are being petitioned in court.

in Lusaka, where the two publications are produced and concentrated. The remaining paper, *New Vision*, is sold in Lusaka alone. Similarly, the broadcast media—that is, both radio and television private stations—is predominantly concentrated in Lusaka. Official figures from the Independent Broadcasting Authority (IBA), the state-run licensing body and regulator of broadcasting in the country, show that the capital city alone has thirty-two radio stations, more than four times the average number (seven) in the remaining nine provinces.[14] Zambia's two major private television stations, Prime (before its shutdown in 2020) and Muvi, only cover Lusaka, though both also offer digital services.[15]

The net result of this increased media presence is that the consumption of information, especially among middle-class urbanites, is very high. Attempts by the PF to control and suppress the flow of information, and to placate the middle class with other incentives, should be understood in this context: as a response to the potential political consequences of the capacity of these private media to shape and influence the thinking of urban voters. Worried that the private media stations, and publications that the PF had relied upon to ascend to power, might serve as organizing platforms for its political opponents, the PF employed over the course of 2016–21 a strategy of co-optation and control. The IBA, despite its name, has largely served at the behest of the state. Under the PF, the body ignored repeated opposition complaints of blackouts and imbalanced coverage in the public media, but was quick to threaten to withdraw the licences of media institutions that were overly critical of the ruling party.

Besides the media, the civil society movement has also encountered repressive interventions by the PF. As noted earlier, the MMD introduced the Non-Governmental Organization Registration Act in 2009. Although the PF opposed its enactment at the time, ironically it was the PF that took significant steps to implement the law fully after ascending to power. The introduction of the NGO Act represented part of official state efforts to limit the freedom of civil society organizations to operate independently and effectively. Prior to the introduction of this law, some 10,000 NGOs were estimated to be operational in Zambia. Only 550 were registered under the Act as of September 2019.[16]

[14] IBA, 'Breakdown by province for radio and television stations', email correspondence, Lusaka, 17 January 2019.
[15] As of January 2019, Zambia had a total of forty private television stations, but many of these are community based, limited to one province, and focused largely on religious and non-political content (ibid.).
[16] 'Government revises the NGO Act', *Lusaka Times*, available at: https://www.lusakatimes.com/2016/05/05/government-revises-ngo-act/, accessed 1 November 2018.

In more recent years, more heavy-handed and arbitrary methods have been used to control the operations of non-state actors. Prominent civil society activists who questioned the government about sensitive areas such as corruption were harassed by police, arrested on trumped-up charges, or denounced as opposition sympathizers or Western agents.[17] Arrests and court cases have a demonstrative effect on even those activists who are not caught up in them, showing the costs of participating in political activities deemed inappropriate by the government. Activists are made aware that at any time they could have their lives upended and spend months or even years in protracted legal cases, as a result of challenging the government. Where repression has not been employed, civil society organizations have been muted through co-optation with government funds, effectively restricting their independence by making them dependent on the state.[18] As noted earlier, prominent figures from civil society have themselves been the beneficiaries of what look like generous gestures on the part of the government, such as appointments to the diplomatic service or to public bodies.[19] The collective impact of such actions is to remove significant numbers of influential leaders from the opposition forces. The knowledge that these opportunities are available also secures the silence of others, who, as one informant put it, reason that even if they are not in receipt of such a reward at the time, they might be in the future and would not wish to undermine their chances by upsetting the government.[20]

Finally, the government has also sought to undermine the effectiveness of critical civil society organizations by advancing its supporters to lead such bodies. In April 2018, for instance, the influential LAZ held its elective conference, during which several key individuals who support the PF and hold positions in the ruling party were elected to the body's leadership. As Sishuwa (2018) argued, placing partisan supporters within such critical civic organizations advances the interests of the ruling elites and undermines potential criticism of the government.

---

[17] A case in point is that of Laura Miti, arguably Zambia's foremost civic activist and leader of the Alliance for Community Action, who rallied Zambians to protest against suspected government corruption in September 2017. Police quickly arrested her alongside five other leading civil society activists, and charged them with conduct likely to cause a breach of peace. Their case has dragged on since then after several adjournments.

[18] Interview with Linda Kasonde (prominent lawyer and former President of the LAZ, in which capacity she played an important public role), September 2018.

[19] For instance, a prominent civil society activist who served as executive director of an anticorruption organisation prior to the PF's election in 2016, was subsequently appointed Zambia's deputy high commissioner to Botswana,[to be inserted].

[20] Interview with Linda Kasonde, September 2018.

6.12 Resistance to domination and control: The response of civil society

Opposition forces refused to be complacent or passive in response to the restrictions placed upon them by the PF. Instead, civil society organizations and the media managed to create and maintain some level of autonomy. First, individuals who had previously been associated with *The Post* were, in the wake of its closure, involved in forming two new independent newspapers, *The Mast* and *News Diggers*. Both publications have a frequently updated web presence. This scenario points to a more significant development in terms of media: the widespread adoption of social media and their use for communicating news events quickly and exposing the excesses of government. This move represents in some ways a response to the restrictions imposed on traditional media. At the same time, it invited further restrictions in the form of the Cyber Security and Cybercrime Act, which the PF enacted in the run-up to the 2021 elections. This Act gives the police the power to confiscate electronic devices of individuals and organizations suspected to be promoting interests that are inimical to those of the state.

Second, civil society groups refused to register under the NGO Act, and the number of courageous individuals willing to brave arrest and harassment to draw attention to official corruption and other abuses of power rose considerably ahead of the 2021 elections. In addition to more recently established civil society organizations (CSOs) like the Alliance for Community Action and the Chapter One Foundation, which maintained the high ground, institutions that make up the Oasis Forum have, in recent years, also voiced their positions on a significant number of national issues, such as the shrinking democratic space. Although the space for opposition forces has indeed been significantly curtailed, it has not been eliminated and the government's measures of control continue to be heavily contested.

Third, CSOs such as the Chapter One Foundation and prominent activists like John Sangwa initiated a series of court actions that challenged some of the PF's strategies of dominance. These included the attempt in 2020 to pass a constitutional amendment bill that would have effectively made it impossible to dislodge the party from power. Though the CSOs did not always win, the cases raised awareness among urban voters and helped galvanize the political opposition.

The net result was that civil society, even in its diminished form, was able to work with the new media outlets and use social media platforms such as Twitter and Facebook to push through significant changes that countered dominance. As argued by Pruce et al. (2021), 'linkages between progressive

CSOs, intellectuals, lawyers and artists, and the innovative use of social media amidst media repression and COVID-19 restrictions, meant that civic awareness messages still managed to reach a broad audience'. This contributed to an empowered electorate that voted for the opposition UPND and its leader Hakainde Hichilema, who decisively defeated Lungu and the PF both in Lusaka and in the overall national elections in 2021. 'While Lungu's bid for dominance was clear from the outset of his tenure, the election outcome demonstrates that there can be limits to incumbent advantages and authoritarian strategies in the face of weakening institutions, a failing economy and poor service delivery' (ibid.: 000).

6.13 Conclusion

Due to its population density, concentration of wealth, and position as the seat of power, the dominance of Lusaka is just as critical to Zambia's political settlement now as it was in the past. Lusaka's residents were at the forefront of democratization efforts in the early 1990s under the MMD, and the urban poor, the middle class, the private media, and NGOs were fundamental to the PF's victory in 2011. Their gradual disaffection with the PF during Lungu's tenure coincided with growing support for the UPND in Lusaka, which saw its vote share increase from 9 to 32 per cent between the 2011 and 2016 elections before the party received more than 50 per cent in the 2021 elections.[21] The threats to the PF's hold in Lusaka coincided with a sharp rise in political violence and repression in the city.

Unlike its predecessors, the PF encountered this gradual erosion of its traditional urban base without having been in office long enough to establish a stronghold in rural areas. Under Sata, the PF garnered ethno-regional support in the Muchinga, Luapula, and Northern Provinces. Under Lungu, the PF's ruling coalition shifted more towards Eastern Province and had less affinity with the urban poor. Social programmes like farmers' inputs and social cash transfers were no longer supported as an ideological cause, but were ringfenced to award patronage in the rural areas, albeit with limited effects in the UPND's strongholds of Southern and Western Provinces. The PF has shifted towards liberal policies, favouring foreign capital over local entrepreneurship, and prioritizing middle-class interests over those of the poorer population in regard to infrastructure, housing, and land. Yet, the

---

[21] Calculated from results from the Electoral Commission of Zambia, available at: https://www.elections.org.zm (accessed 27 October 2021).

PF's corruption and mishandling of the economy augmented middle-class discontent. Zambia's debt crisis—it defaulted on its Eurobond repayments in November 2020—resulted in the delayed payment of civil servants' salaries, a spike in inflation, and an increase in the cost of living.

The PF's estrangement from its original social foundations undermined its attempt to achieve dominance. This was precipitated by: the flawed internal PF transition process in the wake of Sata's death in 2014, which created rifts in the elite; the rise in the UPND's popularity, which was facilitated by that flawed transition process and also threatened the PF's hold; and the decline in the macroeconomic situation that began under Sata, but worsened under Lungu, making the dispensing of patronage to maintain both elite and popular support increasingly less viable. As a result, the PF relied on more legally repressive or explicitly violent tactics to maintain its dominance. This occurred most markedly with respect to civil society and the independent media, whose support for political liberalization and competition was key to the PF's rise when in opposition but seemed inconvenient once in power. These constituents, however, showed some capacity to repel such tactics, by taking advantage of social media, ignoring legal restrictions, and working together to push changes even within the constrained political environment. Another key support base for the party—marketeers and vendors—endured simultaneous tactics of co-optation, intimidation, extortion, and surveillance. Such tactics were often unevenly enforced across the city and justified on public health grounds (e.g. preventing cholera). When combined with the highly heterogeneous interests of informal workers, the party's tactics generated very little overt resistance.

Due to its size and influence, the PF's hold on Lusaka needed to be maintained if the party was to retain the presidency in the 2021 elections. Ultimately, however, Lungu's presidential bid in 2021 failed. Despite the Covid-19 pandemic and the PF's placement of the military on the streets of Lusaka, voter turnout exceeded 70 per cent, and Hichilema won the presidency with a larger vote margin than any previous candidate. Indeed, just as the PF rose to power by creating alliances across classes and education levels, its decline in popularity coincided with simultaneously alienating the urban poor, the middle classes, and civil society. For the UPND, which gained more votes in Lusaka in 2021 than ever through a similar cross-class alliance, the lessons are clear: urban dominance strategies that rely on repression, co-optation, and extortion—without the concurrent provision of services and respect for the rule of law—can be short-lived.

References

Beardsworth, N. (2015). 'Zambia elections: The Lungu succession and rise of the UPND'. *African Arguments*, 29 January. Available online: https://africanarguments.org/2015/01/29/zambia-elections-the-lungusuccession-and-rise-of-the-upnd-by-nicole-beardsworth/ (accessed 17 February 2020).

Beardsworth, N., Cheelo, C., Hinfelaar, M. with Mutuna, K. and Shicilenge, B. (2022). Study on political cadres and the financial sustainability of local authorities. Discussion Paper no. 6, Southern African Institution for Policy and Research, Lusaka.

Blomfield, A. (2018). 'We are facing a sanitation crisis': Zambia's uphill struggle against the deadly scourge of cholera'. *The Telegraph*, 22 May. Available at: https://www.bloomberg.com/news/articles/2018-01-12/zambia-cholera-deaths-infections-rise-as-riot-erupts-in-slum, accessed 10 February 2020.

Brautigam, Deborah, and Yinxuan Wang (2021). Zambia's Chinese debt in the pandemic era. China Africa Research Initiative Briefing Paper no. 5, Johns Hopkins School of Advanced International Studies, Washington, DC.

Central Statistical Office (2014). *2010 Census of Population and Housing: Lusaka Province Analytical Report*. Lusaka.

Central Statistical Office (2015). *2014 Zambian Labour Force Survey Report*. Lusaka, Zambia.

Central Statistical Office (2016). *Zambia: 2015 Living Conditions Monitoring Survey Key Findings*. Lusaka.

Cheeseman, N., and Hinfelaar, M. (2009). Parties, platforms, and political mobilization: The Zambian presidential election of 2008. *African Affairs* 109(434): 51–76.

Cotterill, J. (2017). Arson attacks stoke political crisis in Zambia. Financial Times, 25 July. Available at: https://www.ft.com/content/1720af3a-6e32-11e7-bfeb-33fe0c5b7eaa, accessed 30 March 2023.

Electoral Commission of Zambia (ECZ) (2016). 'General election 2016'. Online resource: https://results.elections.org.zm/general_election_2016.php (accessesd 17 February 2020).

Embassy of the Republic of Zambia (2018). Government to construct 5,000 houses for civil servants in Zambia. Embassy of the Republic of Zambia, Washington, DC, 16 January. Available at: http://www.zambiaembassy.org/article/government-to-construct-5000-houses-for-civil-servants-in-zambia-0, accessed 10 February 2020.

Fraser, A. (2017). Post-populism in Zambia: Michael Sata's rise, demise and legacy. *International Political Science Review* 38(4): 456–472.

Gould, J. (2009). Subsidiary sovereignty and the constitution of political space in Zambia. In J. Gewald, M. Hinfelaar, and G. Macola (eds), *One Zambia, Many Histories*. Lusaka: Lembani Trust, pp. 275–293.

Gould, J. (2011). Postcolonial liberalism and the legal complex in Zambia: Elegy or triumph? In T. Halliday and L. Karpik (eds), *Colonialism's Legacies: Variations on the Theme of Political Liberalism in the British Post-colony*. Cambridge: Cambridge University Press, pp. 412–454.

GRZ (2018). Statutory Instrument No. 10 of 2018: The Local Government (Street Vending and Nuisances) (Amendment) Regulations. Lusaka: Ministry of Local Government, Government of the Republic of Zambia.

Hansen, K. T. (2004). Who rules the streets? The politics of vending space in Lusaka. In K. Tranberg Hansen and M. Vaa (eds), *Reconsidering Urban Informality: Perspectives from Urban Africa*. Uppsala, Sweden: Nordic Africa Institute, pp. 62–80.

Hansen, K. T.(2007). The informalization of Lusaka's economy: Regime change, ultra modern markets, and street vending, 1972–2004. In J.-B. Gewalt, M. Hinfelaar, and G. Macola (eds), *One Zambia, Many Histories: Towards a Post-colonial History of Zambia*. Leiden: J. Brill, pp. 213–242.

Hansen, K. T., and Nchito, W. S. (2013). Where have all the vendors gone? Redrawing boundaries in Lusaka's street economy. In K. T. Hansen, W. Little, and B. L. Milgram (eds), *Street Economies in the Global South*. Santa Fe, NM: SAR Press, pp. 49–70.

Home, R. (1997). *Of Planting and Planning: The Making of British Colonial Cities*. London: Chapman & Hall.

Kasonde, K. (2018). Zambia: Displaced street vendors to move into city market tomorrow. Times of Zambia, 15 January. Available at: https://allafrica.com/stories/201801150490.html, accessed 13 February 2020.

Kennedy-Walker, R., Amezaga, J. M., and Paterson, C. A. (2015). The role of power, politics and history in achieving sanitation service provision in informal urban environments: A case study of Lusaka, Zambia. *Environment and Urbanization* 27(2): 489–504.

Larmer, M. (2011). *Rethinking African Politics: A History of Opposition in Zambia*. London: Routledge.

Larmer, M., and Fraser, A. (2007). Of cabbages and King Cobra: Populist politics and Zambia's 2006 election. *African Affairs* 106: 611–627.

Mason, N. M., Jayne, T. S., and Van De Walle, N. (2017). The political economy of fertilizer subsidy programs in Africa: Evidence from Zambia. *American Journal of Agricultural Economics* 99(3): 705–731.

Mbati-Mwengwe, C. (2001) 'Implementation of the Zambian housing policy: Empowerment through home ownership'. Available online: https://vdocuments.

net/implementation-of-the-zambian-housing-policyspecial-reference-to-the-sale-of.html (accessed 17 February 2020).

Mitimingi, T. C. (2018). Zambia cholera deaths rise as police arrest 55 after riots. *Bloomberg*, 12 January. Available at: https://www.bloomberg.com/news/articles/2018-01-12/zambia-cholera-deaths-infections-rise-as-riot-erupts-in-slum, accessed 10 February 2020.

Mudde, C., and Kaltwasser, C. R. (2013). Exclusionary vs. inclusionary populism: Comparing contemporary Europe and Latin America. *Government and Opposition* 48(2): 147–174.

Mukela, J. (2018). Zambia's disputed elections: On claims of binned ballots and 'systematic bias'. *African Arguments*, 17 August. Available at: https://africanarguments.org/2016/08/17/zambias-disputed-elections-on-binned-ballots-and-systematic-bias/, accessed 10 February 2020.

Mulenga, C. (2003). Urban slums reports: The case of Lusaka, Zambia. In *Understanding Slums: Case Studies for the Global Report on Human Settlements*. London: Earthscan Publications, p. 16.

Mulenga, C. (2013). *The State of Food Insecurity in Lusaka, Zambia*. Cape Town: African Food Security Urban Network (AFSUN), University of Cape Town.

Nalishebo, S. (2013). Distribution of household income and the middle class in Zambia. ZIPAR Policy Brief no. 12, Zambia Institute for Policy Analysis and Research, Lusaka.

Nchito, W. (2006). A city of divided shopping: An analysis of the location of markets in Lusaka, Zambia. Paper presented at 42nd ISoCaRP Congress, Istanbul, 14–18 September.

Ndulo, M. (2010). Freedom of Association and NGO Law: The constitutionality of the 2009 NGO Act. *The Post*, 14 December, p. 12.

Pruce, K., Siachiwena, H., and Hinfelaar, M. (2021). Against the odds? Democracy counters dominance in Zambia's 2021 election. Blog piece, 26 October 2021. Available at: http://blog.gdi.manchester.ac.uk/against-the-odds-democracy-counters-dominance-in-zambias-2021-election/, accessed 27 October 2021.

Republic of Zambia (1996–2019). National budget speeches. Available at: http://www.parliament.gov.zm.

Resnick, D. (2014). *Urban Poverty and Party Populism in African Democracies*. Cambridge: Cambridge University Press.

Resnick, D. (2015). The middle class and democratic consolidation in Zambia. *Journal of International Development* 27: 693–715.

Resnick, D. (2018). Tax compliance and representation in Zambia's informal economy. Policy Brief no. 41418, International Growth Centre, London.

Resnick, D. (2019). The politics of crackdowns on Africa's informal traders. *Comparative Politics* 52(1): 21–51.

Resnick, D., and Thurlow, J. (2017). The political economy of Zambia's recovery: Structural change without transformation? In M. McMillan, D. Rodrik, and C. Sepulveda (eds), *Structural Change, Fundamentals, and Growth*. Washington, DC: International Food Policy Research Institute (IFPRI), pp. 235–266.

Sardanis, A. (2014). *Zambia: The First 50 Years*. London: Bloomsbury Academic.

Sinyangwe, C. (2021). Zambia election: Lungu fights to retain strongholds as young voters push for change. *The Africa Report*, 11 August.

Sishuwa, S. (2018). Has the Law Association of Zambia finally been captured? *News Diggers*, 4 June, p. 7. Available at: https://diggers.news/guest-diggers/2018/06/04/has-the-law-association-of-zambia-finally-been-captured/, accessed 1 November 2018.

Sishuwa, S. (2019). Why the Copperbelt remains Zambia's factory of political change. Blog piece, *Comparing the Copperbelt: Political Culture and Knowledge Production in Central Africa*, 26 September. Available at: https://copperbelt.history.ox.ac.uk/2019/09/26/why-the-copperbelt-remains-zambias-factory-of-political-change-sishuwa-sishuwa/, accessed 6 February 2020.

Sishuwa, S. (2020a). 'Join me to get rid of this President': The opposition, civil society and Zambia's 2011 election. In T. Banda, O'B. Kaaba, M. Hinfelaar, and M. Ndulo (eds), *Democracy and Electoral Politics in Zambia*. Leiden: Brill, pp. 11–33.

Sishuwa, S. (2020b). Surviving off borrowed power: Rethinking the role of civil society in the third-term debate and the defence of democracy in Zambia. *Journal of Southern African Studies* 45: 3. 471–490.

Times of Zambia (2007). Mwanawasa to launch Keep Zambia Clean Campaign. 22 June.

UN-DESA (2014). *12 United Nations World Urbanization Prospects*. New York: United Nations, Department of Economic and Social Affairs, Population Department.

Tordoff, W. (1980). *Administration in Zambia*. Manchester: Manchester University Press

Von Doepp, P. (2005). Party cohesion and fractionalization in new African democracies: Lessons from struggles over third-term amendments. *Studies in Comparative International Development* 40(3): 65–87.

Wahman, M., and Goldring, E. (2020). Pre-election violence and territorial control: Political dominance and subnational election violence in polarized African electoral systems. *Journal of Peace Research* 57(1): 93–110.

Whitfield, L., Therkildsen, O., Buur, L., and Kjaer, A. M. (2015). *The Politics of African Industrial Policy*. Cambridge: Cambridge University Press.

Wragg, E. and Lim, R. (2013). 'Urban visions of the excluded: Experiences of globalization in Lusaka, Zambia'. N-AERUS 14th Conference, 12-14 September,

Enschede. Available online: http://naerus.net/web/sat/workshops/2013/PDF/N-AERUS14_Wragg_Lim_FINAL.pdf (accessed 17 February 2020).

ZIPAR-UNICEF (2019). *Analytical Brief on the 2020 Social Sector Budget in Zambia: Safeguarding and Sustaining Social Sector Gains.* Available online: https://www.unicef.org/zambia/reports/analytical-brief-2020-social-sector-budgetzambia (accessed 17 February 2002).

7

Geographies of urban dominance

The politics of Harare's periphery

JoAnn McGregor and Kudzai Chatiza

7.1 Introduction

Harare has been a solidly opposition-supporting city since the year 2000. The ruling ZANU(PF) party's quest for dominance over the past two decades has thus failed in the capital overall, as voters have repeatedly returned opposition MPs and councillors. Yet in some urban spaces ZANU(PF) has continued to dominate—in new settlements on the periphery, which are the focus here, as well as the city's central markets. The ruling party's capacity to dominate city-edge settlements needs to be situated in ZANU(PF)'s broader nation-wide repression and shift into patronage politics, which had a significant populist redistributive element through land reform and land occupations. In the context of a huge unmet housing demand, the homeless and others mobilized themselves through the party structures to take advantage of politicized opportunities for land access, and to push for recognition and regularization.

In elaborating this case, the chapter contributes two arguments to debates over how urban dominance should be conceptualized. First, it calls for a geographical approach to capital cities that treats urban spaces as differentiated in terms of their politics, rather than presenting urban terrain as monolithic. This draws attention to how, in opposition-supporting cities, where the ruling party has failed to dominate overall, it can nonetheless control certain spaces—in the Harare case, peripheral lands, new settlements, and central markets. Thinking spatially about urban dominance demands attention to how centralized ruling-party/state institutions relate to authority and contestation within these specific sites. This can also add new dimensions to understandings of urban informality in Zimbabwe (Kamete 2007, 2009a, 2012, 2013, 2018; Chirisa et al. 2014, 2015; Muchadenyika 2015, 2020; Mbiba 2017a, 2017b; Muchadenyika and Williams 2017). As urban scholars beyond this specific context have noted, claim-making and practices of authority

JoAnn McGregor and Kudzai Chatiza, *Geographies of urban dominance*. In: *Controlling the Capital*.
Edited by: Tom Goodfellow and David Jackman, Oxford University Press. © Oxford University Press (2023).
DOI: 10.1093/oso/9780192868329.003.0007

within quasi-legal settlements are enmeshed in messy legal and bureaucratic formalities, which matter even when honoured only in their breach (Lund 2006; Sawyer 2014). The dominance of new settlements by ZANU(PF) 'land barons' and local-level ruling-party committees was enabled by land reform, permissive legislation, and conflicting political interests on the part of the Ministry responsible for Local Government[1] and the opposition-run city. These party authorities filled a regulatory gap that endured because of partisan interests, which delayed settlements' bureaucratic incorporation into the city's governance. Yet ZANU(PF) dominance of these spaces has been contested and has changed over time, as settlements have grown and densified. Their sheer scale increasingly mitigated against the likelihood of wholescale demolition, and residents' unrelenting pressure for recognition and services not only raised the prospects of greater tenure security and bureaucratic incorporation, but also undermined one of the key levers for reproducing political dominance.

Second, and related to the above, the chapter calls for attention to the quality of party-political domination, lest the term itself imply undue fixity, solidity, or stability. In Harare, even in those spaces where ZANU(PF) can be said to dominate, this domination is far from total. Performances of ZANU(PF) support were often hollow, and the party has faced overt challenges as well as being riven by internal factional struggles that also affect the grassroots. While overt protest has been the main way in which the literature on dominance has conceptualized contestation, here we draw attention to the role of clientelist engagement as a tactic to undermine as well as support dominance. Political dominance can be slowly chipped away from the bottom up by ordinary residents living in these spaces, who resort to using clientelist tactics of party support for survival and a route to home-owning. Greater security of tenure, when achieved, undermines strategies of political dominance that rely on manipulating insecurity. Further, local processes of seeking tenure security involve serious contestations and leadership changes that can disrupt the control of external elites.

We argue, therefore, that approaches to political dominance should look beyond top-down elite and institutional strategies, to examine their interaction with grassroots manoeuvres. Thus, rather than working with the concepts of co-option or coercive distribution, we explore local-level authority and political tactics within party-dominated locales to conceptualize these

---

[1] We use this formulation as a shorthand. The ministry responsible for local government has undergone repeated name changes, reflecting shifting functions. After independence it also took on public works and construction before shedding these and taking on rural development and resettlement. Rural responsibilities, housing, and public works have moved in and out of its portfolio.

spaces as co-constituted, albeit in the context of deeply lopsided power relations. This grants some agency and autonomy to the residents of these spaces, even within repressive contexts. The convergent interests of patron and client, which work to co-constitute dominance, mask important differences in outlook that can create political change. In the cases we discuss, most residents opted for clientelist tactics simply to live and gain homes, which Caldeira casts as 'transversal' interests in property (Caldeira 2017). Elsewhere, we have argued that these tactics can be conceptualized as offering a path out of dependency towards citizenship and rights (McGregor and Chatiza 2020). Indeed, such manoeuvres are well documented in literatures on urban citizenship, occupations and building (Bayat 2000; Chaterjee 2004; Holston 2008, 2009; Mitlin 2014; Banks et al. 2020). Understanding how urban dominance hinges on interactions with residents shows the limits of an authoritarian 'toolkit' approach (Cheeseman and Klaas 2018), as the latter does not provide insight into politics and historical change. These interactions reveal urban politics to be more than simply a dialectic between control and protest. They shed light on manoeuvres that are dispersed through the practices of everyday living and building, which influence the capacity for political dominance to be reproduced or lost over time.

We draw on findings from research conducted in 2016–17, and ongoing observations in these settlements.[2] In our previous work, we examined the role of central party/state policies and political calculations, which produced what we characterized as a form of urban frontier politics (McGregor and Chatiza 2019). We also examined how grassroots party committees and urban residents sought to navigate ZANU(PF) authority in these spaces, not only by articulating but also by contesting and undermining the 'partisan citizenship' promoted by the ruling party (McGregor and Chatiza 2020). Here we bring these insights into dialogue by exploring ZANU(PF)'s strategies for dominance, and the quality of dominance in contested spaces, taking the cases of Hatcliffe Extension, Epworth Ward 7, and New Park. The three locales show how party-political dominance over new settlements emerged variously: through state land allocations and land occupations. In our first case, political dominance was produced through layers of top-down central state interventions—via resettlement schemes and formal allocations to cooperatives. The other two cases originated in land occupations without formal

---

[2] The research included interviews with officials, councillors, grassroots ruling party committees, and residents' organizations. We focused on three informal settlements (Hopley, Hatcliffe Extension, and Epworth Ward 7), conducting focus groups, oral histories, and a survey of 500 residents, but also did interviews in other places, including New Park. The survey and oral histories were conducted by a team of researchers from DEGI and Dialogue on Shelter/The Federation.

bureaucratic involvement: Epworth Ward 7 was the largest single occupation in the Harare region, sometimes seen as a successful case of 'bottom-up' regularization, while New Park was a failed occupation, whose inhabitants were evicted. While bureaucratic incorporation promised a potential end to the insecurity on which political dominance was initially built, the process was uneven and tended to further differentiate residents (e.g. rich versus poor; leaseholders versus lodgers and new occupiers). Trajectories of formalization are incomplete at the time of writing and thus reversible, particularly for the urban poor.

Before exploring the strategies and qualities of ZANU(PF)'s post-2000 dominance any further, it is important to revisit early independence, when the ruling party dominated the city more broadly and very differently.

7.2 Historical trajectories: Harare and Zimbabwe politics, 1980–2020

Harare after independence: State planning and adjustment, 1980–97

After winning Zimbabwe's first democratic elections in 1980, ZANU(PF) enjoyed mass popular support in Harare and much of the country, with the notable exception of Matabeleland, which supported the opposition party, ZAPU. ZANU(PF)'s political dominance was expressed through the institutions of a strong technocratic state, the party's own structures, and its capacity to monopolize the liberation legacy. Strategies for urban dominance hinged on policies to dismantle racial segregation and a commitment to redistribute to the black majority, relying on the strength of the inherited legal-bureaucratic architecture of urban planning control to achieve this.

Indeed, Zimbabwe is renowned among scholars for having one of the continent's most stringent and well-institutionalized urban planning bureaucracies, which was a Rhodesian inheritance. In the first decade of independence, the challenges of providing urban housing for the city's workers and new rural migrants were met by significant redistributive initiatives, including house purchase schemes for African civil servants, upgrading in the high-density suburbs, new building programmes, site and service schemes, and legal changes to benefit tenants (Mutwiza-Mangiza 1991; Rakodi 1995; Potts 2011; Muchadenyika 2020). Standards for new housing were too high for the poor, and new investment in housing was insufficient to meet demand. Overcrowding, lodging, and the building of illegal backyard structures that commenced towards the end of the liberation war continued thereafter (Patel and Adams 1981). Unusually, however, the capital had no substantial unregulated settlements: most that did form were demolished (Auret 1995). There was a strong sense of Zimbabwean exceptionalism among officials, planners, scholars, and the middle classes, who all felt that wider debates over slums, informality, and patron-clientelism were largely irrelevant to Harare. Although the slum-free tag was inaccurate, the scale was nonetheless minor in the first decade after independence, and very small compared to other African cities (Chatiza and Mpofu 2014).

Beyond state institutions and planned initiatives, the ruling party also dominated urban arenas of association and mobilization. ZANU(PF)'s nationalist alliance initially incorporated and subsumed the trade unions, student and women's movements, churches, and residents' organizations (Raftopoulos and Phimister 1997; Raftopoulos and Sachikonye 2001; Raftopoulos 2006). ZANU(PF)'s popularity in the capital helped to mask the party/state's repressive capacity, the full force of which was felt from the outset in Matabeleland and the Midlands where the military campaign against a small number of 'dissidents' provided the justification for the Fifth Brigade of the army, police, and the Central Intelligence Organization (CIO) to ruthlessly crush ZAPU through abductions and massacres of civilians. This state violence ended only when ZAPU signed a Unity deal in 1987 and was incorporated into ZANU(PF) (CCJP and LRF 1997; Alexander et al. 2000). Yet nationwide there were other forms of rights violations, including repeated urban removals. In all these violations, Zimbabwe's CIO was important to ZANU(PF)'s hold on power from the outset.

By the end of the 1980s, this nationalist alliance and the commitment to state-led development frayed in a context of economic decline and the enforced adoption of structural adjustment. The 1990s were shaped by the devastating effects of adjustment (Mlambo 1997; Bond 1998; Bond and Manyanya 2003). Housing waiting lists grew, as did the number of backyard urban dwellers. Demolition and denial continued to mark city planners' approach to informality. New informal settlements that emerged were repeatedly bulldozed and their inhabitants relocated to securitized camps on the city edge. Non-governmental organizations (NGOs) grew in influence, and an urban cooperative movement flourished to fill the ever-growing gaps in state provision of housing and services (Chitekwe-Biti and Mitlin 2001; Chitekwe-Biti 2009). Over the course of the 1990s, the party lost its hegemony over the city's wider sociopolitical movements—trade unions, students, and war veterans emerged as stringent critics of neoliberalism and of the ruling party's authoritarian tendencies, corruption, and lack of accountability.

Urban politics came to be marked by strikes and protest (Raftopoulos and Phimister 1997; Dorman 2016a).

Economic decline was becoming freefall by the end of the 1990s. The social movements that had been mobilizing outside the ruling party coalesced around constitutional reforms. Activist urban residents' associations expanded in Harare in both elite and high-density suburbs, making connections between 'urban' and 'national' politics (Pasirayi 2021). They pushed for accountable urban governance in the light of gross corruption on the part of the ZANU(PF)-dominated Harare Council, failing services and inadequate housing (Kamete 2009b). In 1999, these political movements combined to form a new opposition party—the Movement for Democratic Change (MDC), which had its roots in the capital but also had nationwide reach, and hence posed a serious threat to ZANU(PF) (Raftopoulos 2009; Dorman 2016a, 2016b). The MDC's formation and grounding in movements with mass popular support marked the end of ZANU(PF)'s dominance of the capital. It heralded an era of political polarization, including within state ministries and local authorities, as well as among civil society organizations. As ZANU(PF) invested in its own counterparts, so urban residents typically developed rival ZANU(PF)- and MDC-aligned residents' associations (Musekiwa and Chatiza 2015).

Zimbabwe's 'crisis' decade, 1998–2008

The interlinked national and urban crises deepened as ZANU(PF)'s political dominance was challenged by the MDC, provoking far-reaching changes to the state, and to the mix of 'repressive' and 'generative' strategies. The shift into patronage politics is often said to have begun with ZANU(PF)'s deal with war veterans for pension payouts in 1997 (Hammar et al. 2003, 2013; Kriger 2003; Raftopoulos 2009). This co-opted a potent, hitherto critical interest group, turning them into powerful allies, but did so at the cost of economic freefall. War veterans were symbolically important in ZANU(PF)'s return to liberation rhetoric. The main veterans' organization—the Zimbabwe National Liberation War Veterans Association—became a key player in the Fast-Track Land Reform Programme, formalized in 2000 to redistribute prime agricultural land from white commercial farmers to black Africans. Land redistribution became the ruling party's key 'generative' strategy, alongside indigenization and increasing use of patronage. Nonetheless, the MDC demonstrated its electoral clout by defeating ZANU(PF) in a constitutional referendum in early 2000. The hotly contested parliamentary and local elections in 2000 and presidential elections in 2002 took place amidst intense state violence. Strategies against the MDC and its allies involved a barrage of repressive legislation and detention, increased surveillance and torture by the CIO and party-aligned militia. ZANU(PF)'s support shrank dramatically and its heartland became rural (Raftopoulos 2009; Hammar et al. 2013).

Harare thus became an embattled MDC stronghold, with an MDC council. City politics were shaped by ZANU(PF)'s strategy to subvert the municipality—not unlike other cases detailed in Resnick (2014a, 2014b) and Muwanga et al. (2020). To regain urban control, ZANU(PF) recentralized through the Ministry responsible for Local Government, taking powers away from elected mayors and councils (Chatiza 2010; McGregor 2013). Ministries and municipalities were securitized as the CIO ousted officials and council-lors who were actively MDC. From 2002 to 2008 the city of Harare was run through an appointed Commission (Kamete 2009b, 2013). This recentraliza-tion hinged on legislation from the Rhodesian era—in particular, the Urban Councils Act—which gave the Minister responsible for Local Government overweening powers (Kamete 2009a; Chatiza 2010; McGregor 2013; Pasirayi 2021). At the same time, the ruling party also developed parallel structures of control in the periphery and central markets, supported by state security.

The ruling party's strategy towards urban opposition voters (i.e. most of the city) was characterized by a politics of neglect and punishment—infrastructure decayed, overcrowding in backyard shacks increased, home-lessness grew, and housing lists grew longer. This neglect was moralized as Mugabe elevated the countryside to the patriotic heartland and labelled urban residents 'totemless' (Raftopoulos 2004). Demolitions and evictions had long been a central tool of planning, and in 2005 Operation Muram-batsvina ('Clean the Filth') took forward this tradition but on an extraor-dinary and unprecedented scale. Housing deemed to break planning law was demolished—including markets and backyard shacks, but also concrete buildings that were a lifetime's investment, including some where residents had valid leases (Potts 2006; Kamete 2009a). Nationwide, 700,000 people lost their livelihoods and/or homes; many lifelong Harare residents were dumped in rural areas, where they had never lived and had no means of support, and large camps of homeless and destitute emerged on the city edge (UN 2005; Potts 2006). Planners were commandeered into legitimizing the operation (Kamete 2007, 2009a).

Although some planners continued to cleave to authoritarian modernist planning ideals, subsequent years have been characterized by a moratorium on large-scale demolitions, and a shift towards *in situ* slum upgrading and

regularization. It was no longer possible to maintain that the city lacked informal settlements. They had burgeoned in a policy context which had lowered
standards to make housing affordable for the poor, and which had allowed
'parallel development', so that people could inhabit stands before servicing.[3]
Bulldozing them *en masse* through Operation 'Clean the Filth' provoked
an international outcry that dented the ruling party's international reputa-
tion, while its devastating afterlife endures in the politics of the periphery
today. The losses people sustained, and the state's willingness to use force
on such a scale, were central to residents' decisions to engage in clientelist
tactics and displays of support for ZANU(PF). This shift to clientelist support reflected ZANU(PF)'s control over peripheral land and new settlements
where displaced people sought to rebuild their lives and create new homes.
The disorderliness of land reform (sometimes referred to as *jambanja* or
'chaos') created flimsy rights in urban peripheries that are reversible through
the courts. As such, *jambanja* and 'lawfare' disempowered the victims of
Operation 'Clean the Filth' who were trying to rebuild their lives in the
urban periphery, forcing them into clientelism (Mbiba 2022). In the wake
of this policy, there was some state investment in military-led resettlement
and building programmes, most notably Operation 'Stay Well' in 2006–7. But
this was totally inadequate and, as hyperinflation spiralled, everything informalized and the city's health and water infrastructure collapsed (Jones 2010a
2010b; Chigudu 2020). The peak of this crisis was marked by the extreme violence of the 2008 parliamentary and presidential elections and a devastating
cholera epidemic. ZANU(PF) lost to the MDC parties[4] in both the parliamentary and presidential elections, and the subsequent presidential run-off
was so marred by party/state violence against the MDC that legitimacy could
only be restored through a power-sharing arrangement.

Power-sharing, factionalism, and renewed crisis, 2009–20

Under the lopsided Inclusive Government (2009–13), power remained
skewed in ZANU(PF)'s favour. This was because it retained control over
the security arms of the state and other key ministries, including those
responsible for Lands and Local Government (Chatiza 2010; IDAZIM 2010).
ZANU(PF) used the Ministry of Local Government's powers to continue

---

[3] These included Circular No. 70 of 2004, which aimed to make housing affordable (Government of
Zimbabwe 2005).
[4] The MDC party split in 2005. Harare supported the bigger of the two groups, known as MDC-T,
headed by Morgan Tsvangirai. After Tsvangirai's death, the party splintered, with the biggest grouping for
the 2018 elections being the MDC-Alliance (MDC-A).

to control and subvert the city. Over this period, peri-urban land occupations in Harare escalated, particularly in the run-up to the 2013 elections, as both parties sought to win urban votes through offers of land and housing (Muchadenyika 2015, 2020; Muchadenyika and Williams 2017). But ZANU(PF) had the clear advantage, as it controlled more land—particularly on the city edge, due to land reform.

Within the established core of Harare, ZANU(PF) continued to undermine the authority of the MDC-led municipality and treated civil society organizations as extensions of the political opposition (EU 2014; Dorman 2016a). Urban residents' associations lost their social movement character in a context of ongoing repression (Pasirayi 2021). There were many ways in which the MDC-run city's authority was subverted by both the Minister responsible for Local Government and other ruling-party-controlled forces. ZANU(PF) continued to invest in parallel structures to control key spaces and resources—for example, the city's central markets in Mbare were controlled via the militia known as Chipangano, which had policed vending from the early 2000s (McGregor 2013; Mutongwizo 2014; Maringira and Gukurume 2020). This diverted revenue from the markets to ZANU(PF) and leveraged clients by establishing partisan terms of access. Municipal finances were further undermined by the minister writing off ratepayers' debt, contributing to its inability to provide services and to ratepayer resistance (Chatiza et al. 2013; City of Harare 2018).

New peri-urban settlements were subject to surveillance by the party structures and youth. ZANU(PF)'s interests in controlling these spaces were both political and financial, as revenue streams from land sales and rents were redirected into party coffers and politicians' pockets. Some settlements remained 'no go' areas for the MDC and opposition-aligned civics as well as city officials.

The relative stability of the power-sharing period ended with ZANU(PF)'s electoral victory in 2013. Harare remained overwhelmingly opposition supporting, but the significant inroads that ZANU(PF) made were linked to constituencies of *de facto* ruling-party dominance—the central market area and new peripheral settlements. ZANU(PF) thus increased its number of councillors in Harare from one to five (out of forty-six), and its MPs from one to three.

After 2013, with ZANU(PF) back in sole control of the state, urban policy was marked by a drive to regularize informal settlements to regain legitimacy (McGregor and Chatiza 2019).[5] This was not about ending patronage;

---

[5] A new 2013 Constitution promised profound devolutionary changes to local government but these have not been implemented (Chatiza 2016).

rather it was about bringing it back under state control, and was embroiled in the party's internal disputes. The drive to formalize occurred when factionalism within ZANU(PF) over succession after President Mugabe became increasingly all-encompassing. Internal rivalry had already led to the assassination in 2011 of Colonel Mujuru, an important figure in Harare whose influence reached downwards via Harare MPs to the urban grassroots in peripheral settlements and the militia Chipangano. But from 2013, the two main factions were those loyal to the then First Lady, Grace Mugabe, known as 'G40', versus Emerson Mnangagwa's grouping, known as 'Lacoste'.[6] G40-linked ZANU(PF) MPs in Harare came to dominate the urban periphery, and Chipangano's leaders were publicly beaten up.

This factionalism mattered for urban policy and politics, as the new Minister responsible for Local Government, Saviour Kasukuwere, was a key player in G40. The peri-urban land audits he commissioned during this period legitimized a new role for the central state in regularizing settlements through the Urban Development Corporation (UDCORP). They also laid the basis for prosecuting individual 'barons' aligned to other factions. G40's influence was, however, brought to an abrupt end by the army-led coup in 2017 that installed President Emerson Mnangagwa.

Immediately following the coup, leading G40 figures were arrested on treason and corruption charges, and some fled into exile, including Kasukuwere, while the preceding Minister for Local Government, Ignatius Chombo, was detained and tortured. President Mnangagwa's victory in the 2018 elections was facilitated by the fragmentation of the MDC opposition parties, the largest grouping of which fought the elections as the MDC-Alliance (MDC-A) and won Harare. This reversed some of the previous ZANU(PF) electoral gains in the capital, but also blurred the past political polarization somewhat, as the MDC-A allied with the remnants of the G40 faction in Harare. The election was remarkable in the light of previous campaigns, in that surveillance of Harare's new peripheral settlements was relaxed and the opposition campaigned therein openly. ZANU(PF)'s election campaign had promised moves to address corruption, particularly accumulation through illegal urban land sales.

The 2019 national Commission of Inquiry into the sale of state land in and around urban areas since 2005 (Fig. 7.1) showed the scale of benefits to ZANU(PF) 'barons'—and the commensurate loss of revenue to the state and local authorities. This was particularly pronounced in Harare and environs:

---

[6] G40 or Generation 40 included many younger politicians who were too young to have liberation war credentials; Mnangagwa's faction gained the nickname 'Lacoste' from the sportswear's crocodile insignia, because Mnangagwa's nickname was 'crocodile'.

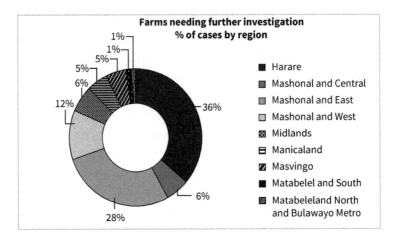

Fig. 7.1 Commission of Inquiry into sale of state land in and around urban areas

Source: computed from Uchena Commission (Government of Zimbabwe 2019).

the state had not collected US$3 billion, or 90 per cent of the intrinsic land value (Government of Zimbabwe, 2019). Indeed, 36 per cent of the farms 'needing further investigation' were concentrated in Harare (i.e. 156 farms or 36 per cent of the total number of farms redistributed). This concentration showed the politicization of land and housing around the capital city, where land values are exceptionally high.

President Emmerson Mnangagwa's regime has been marked by strong continuities in repression and patronage from the Mugabe era. The militarization of the state has become more apparent than ever, populist redistributive policies have been de-emphasized, and pronouncements on devolution have not altered central ministerial powers. At the time of writing, ZANU (PF) legitimacy was once again at an all-time low, while opposition fragmentation persisted, with abductions and torture of MDC MPs and youth leaders continuing in both central and peripheral parts of the city.

It is already clear that ZANU(PF)'s use of land reform was its key 'generative' strategy from 1998 to 2020. In the next section, we turn to its implications for how authority was co-constituted in peri-urban spaces specifically.

7.3 Land reform and dominance of the Harare periphery

The dual processes of land reform—land occupations from the late 1990s plus state allocations from 2000—reshaped authority to produce ZANU(PF) dominance of the city periphery. This overtook formal processes of 'orderly' city expansion, which had been too slow to accommodate demand (Marongwe et al. 2011). The state allocations to 'barons' and cooperatives from 2000 onwards were overseen by new land committees that were ZANU(PF)-dominated (on Harare's committee, which comprised senior state officials, army, police, CIO, and veterans, see Marongwe (2009: 280)). In peri-urban contexts, high land values and the pressure from homelessness created particular opportunities for huge profits from subdivisions, sales, and renting.

Occupiers in peri-urban locations (as in rural areas) comprised mixed interest groups, however, including the homeless and victims of the demolitions, who were told by politicians that the land was a conditional 'gift' of the ruling party (on rural areas, see Zamchiya (2013); Chamunogwa (2019, 2020)). Some occupations were spearheaded by war veterans, including the largest in Harare's vicinity (discussed below). Others were led by party youth and encouraged by ZANU(PF) MPs, councillors, or other members of the ZANU(PF) provincial and district structures. In all contexts, occupiers legitimized their claims by forming party structures plus grassroots 'development committees' to seek recognition from the state (Chaumba et al. 2003; Scoones et al. 2010; Cliffe et al. 2011; Chamunogwa 2019, 2020).

Cooperative policies for housing and servicing were particularly important in shaping the form that ZANU(PF) authorities took in peri-urban areas. ZANU(PF) 'land barons' based their claims to legitimate authority on their formal status as leaders of the cooperatives charged with developing these lands, not only their party credentials. Some received land from the Ministry responsible for Local Government way beyond that warranted by their membership. The law was permissive towards predatory rent collection on the part of cooperative leaders, subdivisions, and illegal sales (Muchadenyika 2020). 'Barons' encouraged occupations with promises of land and housing development, and charged membership fees and development levies, often delivering no improvement (Chirisa et al. 2014, 2015; Muchadenyika 2015; Muchadenyika and Williams 2017; McGregor and Chatiza 2019).

New settlements needed to be incorporated into MDC-run municipalities, through a cumbersome process marked by protracted delays exacerbated by partisan interests (Chaeruka and Munzwa 2009). Unlike rural areas, where new resettlement lands were relatively quickly absorbed within rural district administrations and the period of 'partisan authority' was brief (Chamunogwa 2019, 2020), in peri-urban Harare, this process was long-drawn-out and subject to an institutional stand-off and resistance from the 'barons'. As a result, 'barons' and party structures continued to act as *de facto* authorities for long periods (McGregor and Chatiza 2019).

Through these processes ZANU(PF) dominated the periphery for a protracted period. Partisan interests prevented bureaucratic resolution of the problems of protracted insecurity, exploitation, and lack of servicing that the policy produced. Technocrats stressed how 'political interference' was key to understanding the dysfunctional relations among state institutions, the powers of the 'barons', and the irresolvability of regulatory and servicing gaps. A senior official described many barons as 'untouchable'.[7] The Ministry responsible for Local Government tried but failed to prosecute notorious 'barons': one alone—Nelson Mandizvidza—had made US$3 million, through his positions as Chairperson of the Union of Cooperatives and Chairman of Caledonia and Eastview Development Consortium. The barons' powers hinged on the permissive legal framework, a compromised judiciary, and party-political standing, as well as on their capacity to mobilize grassroots support and votes.[8]

Activist residents' organizations, such as the Combined Harare Residents Association (CHRA) and the Harare Residents Trust (HRT), were physically banned from all these new peripheral settlements, and residents were subjected to surveillance and political victimization.[9] Even organizations that had opted for engagement rather than protest against the ruling party were sidelined, such as Dialogue on Shelter and the Homeless People's Federation.[10] In Kamete's (2018) analysis, the ZANU(PF) structures controlling informal settlements acted as 'petty sovereigns', with powers to evict and punish, supported by the CIO.

Notwithstanding ZANU(PF) dominance and the political and economic benefits to the party of perpetuating insecure settlements, there has nonetheless been a trajectory towards consolidation and bureaucratic incorporation in some. The Ministry responsible for Local Government's top-down drive to survey and re-register land holdings through UDCORP pushed some settlements towards greater security, while others achieved recognition through 'bottom-up' processes. There is thus more to the political history of these settlements than a simple story of elite accumulation and exploitation of the urban poor for rent and votes. In the next section, we look at these processes of consolidation, discussing the insights they provide into the qualities of political dominance in these spaces.

[7] Ministry for Local Government official, 7 April 2017, cited in McGregor and Chatiza (2019).
[8] CEO, CHRA, 12 April 2017.
[9] Director, HRT, 12 April 2017.
[10] Interview with Dialogue/Federation, 13 April 2017.

7.4 Qualities of dominance: The politics of clientelism and consolidation

The notion of 'dominance' can imply a misleading solidity or fixity. We argue it is necessary to understand the qualities of political dominance, by analysing relations of power, authority, and life within dominated spaces and trajectories of change. This necessitates attention to the views and practices of residents and the local structures of authority they support, as well as the top-down calculations prioritized in the concepts of 'co-option' and 'coercive distribution' (Goodfellow and Jackman 2020: 22–23). It also means showing how political dominance is created and contested, either won or lost in relation to any given settlement's consolidation (or not).

Key sources of political dominance change over time and space: from the initial 'generative' opportunity for access to land/housing and promises of regularization, to the 'repressive' strategies of demolitions and threats of eviction. One state official remarked: 'it is easier to evict when a settlement first appears, not ten or fifteen years later when people have built homes and it has grown—then the logic is to regularize'.[11] The notion that time and size alone consolidate settlements is, however, somewhat misleading. It does capture how everyday life can create a momentum for change and grants residents some role in this shift. But it masks the reality of contested histories in which residents have participated by manoeuvring actively both to shore up and undermine political dominance through clientelist engagement. The co-constituted nature of political dominance is evident in the initial coalition of interests involved in peri-urban land occupations, in residents' 'choice' of clientelist strategies for lobbying for recognition via party committees, and naming settlements after liberation war heroes. Yet this latter can also be route to undermine dominance. There is not one fixed or predetermined outcome.

Below we take three specific examples of settlements on the periphery to illustrate diverse pathways to consolidation or displacement and its relationship to the perpetuation or undermining of ZANU(PF) dominance. We compare: first, a former resettlement scheme and cooperative area regularized from the top down (Hatcliffe Extension); second, the city's largest single land occupation, formalized in a 'bottom-up' manner through a ZANU(PF)-aligned development committee (Epworth Ward 7); and third, the case of a failed land occupation, moved to make way for elite housing and army and

---

[11] Interview with the former CEO, Epworth Local Board, April 2017.

government buildings (New Park).[12] Together these cases provide insight into the varied, shifting, and contested qualities of ZANU(PF) dominance of the urban periphery. We argue that there is nothing automatic, linear, or universal about processes of regularization, and any lessening of political dominance in these settlements has so far been partial and uneven for reasons we explain.

It is important to stress how the city's history of evictions and violence lingers across new informal settlements.[13] Yet this has not rendered residents pure victims and they have actively shaped the forms that local authority has taken. 'Survival' underpins many decisions to demonstrate party support and uphold ZANU(PF) political dominance. Occupations have also been infused with an opportunistic moralizing logic through the notion of *garawadya* (literally, 'better to stay/live having eaten'), implying that it is foolish not to seize an opportunity. But residents have also found means to undermine partisan privilege by invoking the party's own history of developmentalism and collective grassroots interests in land rights, recognition, and services. Support for party dominance was hollow: the civic mobilizations of the 1990s have left their mark in residents' ideas and understandings of themselves as rights-bearing citizens, which have been suppressed rather than eliminated in these settlements (McGregor and Chatiza 2020). Moreover, ZANU(PF) internal factionalism, the renewed hyperinflationary spiral, and a heightened army and police presence have also been grounds for disillusion at the grassroots. Bureaucratic incorporation and tenure security may thus undermine the party's capacity to continue to dominate the city's periphery, and in some places there are indications that this has begun to happen, albeit unevenly.

Layers of central state intervention: Hatcliffe Extension, Harare North

The case of Hatcliffe Extension shows how ZANU(PF) political dominance has been achieved through successive layers of central state land allocations (rather than by the party directly, as in our other two cases). Residents have, however, both contributed to and contested dominance directly as well as seeking to manoeuvre out of insecurity and dependency by using the party to lobby for regularization and services. The settlement's history is messy because of the layers of formal allocation and reallocation

---

[12] For other cases, see McGregor and Chatiza (2019, 2020), and for detailed planning history, Muchadenyika (2020).
[13] Detailed in McGregor and Chatiza (2020).

through resettlement projects and cooperatives, in addition to occupations, and because it spans the boundary between the city and two different rural councils (Goromonzi and Mazowe). But it has similarities to other large, new peripheral settlements on Harare's borders shaped by 'top-down' interventions by the Ministry responsible for Local Government.[14]

The settlement began in 1993 as a temporary holding camp for evictees (those moved from other camps),[15] which became a flagship site for NGOs working with the homeless, such as Dialogue on Shelter and the Federation of Homeless People.[16] In 2000, the Ministry responsible for Local Government allocated plots and individual leases to those in the camp, responding to residents' self-organized efforts through Dialogue and the Federation. Residents decided to occupy their stands in 2001–2 before servicing, due to rumours of the land being double-allocated to soldiers who had served in the Congo. They organized through the ZANU(PF) District Coordinating Committee (DCC) for further protection, despite the MDC having a significant history of support among them. Residents decided to build and invest because they had leases.

Yet, Hatcliffe Extension was flattened in Operation 'Clean the Filth' in 2005: 3,200 homes were destroyed by the army, rendering more than 12,000 people homeless, including members of the DCC: Tondori, a district-level party official, lost a lifetime's savings that he had poured into a brick, cement, and asbestos home.[17] The residents were scattered: some were taken to holding camps in other parts of the city periphery or dumped in rural areas. Those with leases contested their eviction through the High Court, assisted by Dialogue and Zimbabwe Lawyers for Human Rights. But they lost. The High Court ruled that the government, as issuer of the leases, had the right to remove them at any time. Among the displaced, the demolitions were widely understood as an act of punishment by the defeated Harare North ZANU(PF) MP, Nyasha Chikwinya, who lost to the MDC's Trudy Stevenson in the 2005 elections.[18]

The next phase of the settlement's history was shaped by a new layer of state land allocations through Operation 'Live Well' in 2006–7. Some of the original lease-holding families were included, but sections were also distributed to ZANU(PF) clients, including members of the police, soldiers, and property

---

[14] E.g. Caledonia Farm (McGregor and Chatiza 2019; Muchadenyika 2020).
[15] Including Churu Farm, Porta Farm, and Dzivarawekwa Extension.
[16] Interview with Dialogue/Federation, 13 April 2017.
[17] Tondori, 17 and 18 September 2017.
[18] Focus group, Hatcliffe Extension, 17 November 2016.

developers. Some parts of Hatcliffe Extension were allocated to cooperatives and Hon. Chikwinya herself secured a farm.

During the 2008 elections, Hatcliffe Extension experienced severe violence linked to ZANU(PF) militia bases that were used to try to coerce votes through abductions, beatings, and torture. ZANU(PF) won in the rural constituencies (which incorporate part of the settlement), but lost again in Harare North. In 2010 the Hatcliffe Extension militia bases were used to abduct and murder the wife of the MDC's acting Mayor of Harare, Chiroto.

The settlement then informalized during the power-sharing period, as cooperative leaders and ZANU(PF) politicians and councillors sold and subdivided land and led occupations within both the resettlement and cooperative sections. Tondori described renewing his activism with ZANU(PF) in 2010 'for survival—not because we love them', and because lobbying via a non-aligned development committee had failed and ended in detention.[19] ZANU(PF)'s victory in Harare North in 2013 was widely attributed to the party's powers to allocate land and housing.

The cooperative sections of Hatcliffe Extension (Acorn Farm, Glen Forest, and St Augustine's) were wracked by internal ZANU(PF) in-fighting, typical of the 'frontier' politics of other parts of the Harare periphery (McGregor and Chatiza 2019). An audit of Harare North cooperatives in 2015 detailed a long list of illegal practices. In Glen Forest, Hon. Chikwinya was in dispute with Mafuyana cooperative, and throughout the cooperative sections there had been double allocations, illegal sales, repossessions, evictions, 'political interference, violence and intimidation'. No cooperatives had undertaken meaningful development (Government of Zimbabwe 2015). Disputes among some cooperatives were still with the courts at the time of writing, and Minister Chikwinya faced losing her land through corruption charges after the coup, as she was part of the G40 faction.

The regularization of Hatcliffe Extension in 2016 by the Ministry responsible for Local Government through UDCORP entailed resurveying and reallocating plots and leases. This encouraged residents to invest and some sections of the settlement now have bigger homes than many older high-density suburbs, while services have also improved. Yet many poorer residents still felt insecure: they had been told repeatedly 'this area is not for the likes of you'.[20] Those who had personal experience of homes being bull-dozed notwithstanding valid leases doubted whether their new documents conferred security; others violated the terms of the new leases by having

---

[19] Ibid.
[20] Ibid.

lodgers or failing to pay rates. Nonetheless, UDCORP's reordering, despite its lack of transparency and concerns of partisan favouritism, plus building and servicing, gave the settlement a very different feel from the earlier informal 'camp', and ended at least some of the battles in the cooperative areas. This recognition undermined party-political leverage over votes, and in 2018 Harare North voters returned an MDC-A MP, although rural constituencies incorporating part of the settlement remained ZANU(PF).

The messy trajectory of this settlement, where ZANU(PF) dominance was shaped by repeated layers of central state intervention through resettlement schemes, cooperatives, and top-down regularization, is typical of many new, informal settlements on the former farms of the Harare periphery. Bureaucratic incorporation undermined political dominance by removing a key lever (tenure insecurity), but did so unevenly and partially. Processes remain incomplete, and the poor, in particular, remain insecure. Our next two cases are different because the settlements were more clearly co-constituted from the outset, as they originated in large-scale land occupations.

'Bottom-up' regularization: Epworth Ward 7

The recognition of Epworth Ward 7 occurred through a different process and with little bureaucratic involvement. For around twenty years, this settlement remained under the control of district-level ZANU(PF) structures and an interlinked development committee. The settlement is the largest single land occupation in the Harare region, and at the time of writing was home to circa 80,000 people and 20,000 leaseholders on surveyed plots, registered at Epworth Local Board. Although ZANU(PF) politicians have been heavily involved as patrons, the grassroots party structures held out against allocations to cooperatives. At the time of the research, this settlement was upheld by officials and planners as a 'successful grassroots regularization' and possible model for other peri-urban areas (Muchadenyika 2020: 183). Here we explore the qualities of ZANU(PF) political dominance, conflict, and change as the settlement consolidated. In contrast to the previous case, however, regularization had not produced a shift in voting away from the ruling party.

Epworth is Harare's oldest informal settlement. It originated during the liberation war as the war-displaced sought sanctuary on land belonging to the Methodist church (Chitekwe-Biti et al. 2012; Chirisa and Muhomba 2013; Muchadenyika 2020). After independence, the land was ceded to the state and it continued to grow, notwithstanding demolitions and evictions. Despite its being close to the city centre, the City of Harare refused to accept responsibility, so it gained its own local board in 1986, and wards 1–6 were regularized *in situ* over the 1990s, with World Bank assistance (Chitekwe-Biti et al. 2012). Ward 7 is the newest section of Epworth, located on what was the grazing land of 'original' Epworth residents. It is also known as '*magada*' or squatted (literally, 'those who have sat'): the occupiers were former tenants and outsiders who bought plots illegally from 'originals'. In the context of the politicization of land in the late 1990s, the *magada* organized themselves into ZANU(PF) grassroots structures, including a group of war veterans among them. They were supported by heavyweight ZANU(PF) patrons, including Amos Midzi, a Politburo member who was in Colonel Mujuru's network with strong connections to Chipangano. Another patron was retired Lieutenant Nyanhongo, a ZANU(PF) Central Committee member, who was elected MP for Harare South in 2008.

The Epworth Local Board (ELB) tried repeatedly and unsuccessfully to evict the *magada*, even appealing directly to ZANU(PF) to allow this.[21] But the ELB 'could not evict even with a court order' because of the combination of political interests: MPs who needed supporters to build their careers, and occupiers who benefited from MPs' lobbying.[22]

During Operation 'Clean the Filth' in 2005, Ward 7 was spared. Local ZANU(PF) members claim that this was because President Mugabe intervened personally, though it may have escaped simply by virtue of size and being last on the list to be demolished, by which time the operation had been halted amidst international outcry.[23] Whatever the reason, the settlement was allowed to persist and it mushroomed, as victims of the demolitions elsewhere sought refuge and land from the Epworth Ward 7 ZANU(PF) structures. Dialogue and the Federation began to work with the ELB, University of Zimbabwe planning students, and the Department of Physical Planning to regularize this *magada* section (Chitetwe-Biti et al. 2012; Muchadenyika 2020: 183).

In 2008, Epworth was wracked with violence, as the main—secure—part of Epworth had a history of MDC support, and it was only in Ward 7 *magada* that residents supported ZANU(PF). ZANU(PF) established militia bases, both in Epworth itself and in neighbouring Harare South, which were used for abductions, beatings, and torture to try to coerce ZANU(PF) support. The bases were said to be controlled by Midzi and Nyanhongo (Anatomy of Terror, cited in Kriger 2012: 18–20). This violence persisted in Epworth during the Inclusive Government, with these politicians reputedly being motivated

---

[21] Interview with the former CEO, ELB, 4 April 2017.
[22] Ibid.
[23] Ibid.

by their defeat by the MDC as well as needing to show grassroots support in their (rivalrous) bids for the post of Governor of Harare in 2011 (Kriger 2012).

The local ZANU(PF) party structures continued to allocate land to new-comers during the Inclusive Government, acting as *de facto* authorities. Dialogue and the Federation found it increasingly difficult to maintain their own grassroots structure in Ward 7, and by the time of our research, the ZANU(PF)-aligned development committee had captured the process of grassroots regularization. The party-aligned committee was in sole charge of resolving disputes over plots, leading to accusations of partisan 'tyranny' and violence.[24] The effects of grassroots ZANU(PF) demonstrations at the local board offices and interventions by senior politicians were, however, beneficial to residents collectively, as they lowered surveyors' fees. More-over, MDC supporters were far from totally expelled from the settlement: the Epworth Ward 7 MDC district and youth executive members echoed accusa-tions of partisanship and violence, but also secured stands for themselves and a broader network of covert supporters.[25] We witnessed people celebrating as they received their new home numbers from the local board. The develop-ment committee was proud of its achievement and of the improved services, including a school.

Though local party officials continued to express gratitude to ZANU(PF) in public, however, many admitted they were disillusioned when interviewed anonymously. The ZANU(PF) elite's factional politics and grassroots history of violence contributed to this disillusionment. The factionalism led to suc-cessive changes in the MPs with whom local party activists worked most closely as patrons, and many feared reprisals for links to MPs and councillors now out of favour. Several ZANU(PF) district officials in Epworth described politics as 'dirty', dangerous, and contemptuous of those at the grassroots. They emphasized their disengagement from politics, other than in the quest for development and services.[26]

The trajectory of Epworth Ward 7 towards regularization can undoubt-edly show the agency and manoeuvres of grassroots settlers. In this instance (unlike the previous case), regularization did not lead to increased opposition votes, notwithstanding a much less violent campaign, perhaps because of the greater sense of grassroots control, or perhaps because of lingering insecu-rity. The relationship between regularization and the reproduction or loss of political dominance is thus not straightforward, and many factors are at play.

---

[24] Interview with Epworth Residents Development Association, 11 April 2017.
[25] Interview with Epworth Ward 7 MDC officers and youth, 22 November 2016.
[26] Interview 3, Epworth Ward 7, 10 October 2017.

A failed occupation: New Park

It is important to end with a failed occupation, to make the point that there is no guaranteed trajectory towards regularization and recognition for all settlers in the ZANU(PF)-dominated periphery, including active grass-roots clients. Occupations have been a risky strategy, particularly on the edge of elite neighbourhoods of Harare that are attractive sites for new up-market developments. In such locations, the urban poor who participated in occupations have been displaced by a new round of property owners and treated as disposable by former patrons. Clientelism did not protect them or enable a trajectory towards landowning. Their vulnerability highlighted the profoundly lopsided nature of relations between patron and client that it is important to bear in mind when conceptualizing party dominance as co-constituted at local level.

The case of the remnants of a land occupation camped in shacks in New Park, while the infrastructure for elite housing was laid out around them, captures so strongly the sense of being used that we heard across the city periphery, not only from 'ordinary' families, but also among grassroots party structures. The occupation had been encouraged in 2000–1 by the former ZANU(PF) politician Patrick Zhuwao, and others, including the late David Karimanzira. Zhuwao was MP for Zvimba East, held various ministerial positions, and was a Politburo member and G40 kingpin expelled after the coup. Karimanzira had a long career in the party, and from 2005 to 2011 served as resident minister and Governor of Harare Province.

The occupiers we interviewed were grassroots party activists and saw Zhuwao as their patron: they felt they had 'helped him climb' through their support in the land occupations, before being discarded.[27] Some had been among the first group of occupiers, involved in the process of helping to evict a former white farm-owner. The area more broadly had become populated by retrenched local brickfield-workers staking plots alongside rural people. The occupiers formed themselves into a ZANU(PF) district committee and coop-erative, through which they claimed to have leases. The land was, however, later earmarked for an elite suburb close to the New City, where new build-ings are planned for national government and state institutions, including Parliament.

During Operation 'Clean the Filth' in 2005, occupiers' homes were demol-ished. Five thousand families were rendered homeless in this section of the north-west Harare periphery, our group claimed, their number having been

[27] Group interview, New Park, 21 November 2016.

enumerated in United Nations investigations in the aftermath of the operation. Some of the homeless were resettled in other parts of the periphery as part of Operation 'Stay Well', and others had gone back to rural homes, but our interlocutors were among those left out of the resettlement with nowhere to go. They were living in homes built from the rubble of housing destroyed in 2005, knowing they clearly had no future in the location. They had survived initially with blankets from the International Organization for Migration and food from Christian Care, and over the subsequent twelve years had been working for a neighbouring group of war veterans, whose land claims seemed more secure. Across the lands being developed in this section of the city's borderlands, there were other clusters of poor families trying to survive on piecework and vending (see also Dialogue on Shelter 2014).

The three groups of private developers putting in infrastructure around them were working for the City of Harare and Zvimba Rural District Council: at the time of our visit, roads had been tarmacked and plots for up-market housing marked out, with cement foundations laid. Family groups were being evicted gradually—our group said that during the previous week, their neighbours in an adjacent plot had been thrown out and were now living on a nearby riverbank. They recounted their long history of lobbying offices: when they visited Zvimba district offices for help, they were referred to Harare, and in Harare they were referred back to Zvimba. At one point, they had been offered land in Zvimba to move to, but they could not afford the charges for the leases, which were US$2,000 per plot. They had pleaded in vain to be able to pay in instalments, but were not deemed suitable. They had also tried to seek out their former ZANU(PF) patrons, hoping for assistance as recompense for their work for the party, but their capacity to make any contact had been drastically eroded after the death of their former ZANU(PF) district chair and cooperative leader, as well as his deputy. Their most recent attempt had been with the Harare provincial administrator, who had referred them to the Minister responsible for Home Affairs/ZANU(PF) Secretary for Administration. But they felt they had 'exhausted all avenues of negotiation'; indeed, they were desperate. Given the extent of building, eviction was likely to be a matter of weeks away. One explained:

If you are choked for a long time you will end up saying 'let him do whatever he wants'. That's the position we are in now, for us to overcome this person using power—we can't because there is need for money and we don't have the money.[28]

---

[28] Ibid.

Our own attempt to follow up with City of Harare regarding their plight showed that the officials knew about their case, but they reiterated the view that they were not responsible and referred us to Zvimba. These grassroots occupiers had been abandoned so starkly by politicians partly because they occupied such a strategic location. Spatial context and their own poverty mattered in this history of their displacement and the failure of their clientelism to deliver a trajectory towards secure homes. They had proved disposable in the reproduction of political dominance in this part of the city periphery.

7.5 Conclusion

What do these settlements' twenty-year trajectories towards consolidation or continued precariousness and displacement tell us about the history, practices, and qualities of ZANU(PF) dominance of Harare's periphery? How can they add to debates over how to conceptualize political dominance in relation to capital cities?

The mechanisms of ZANU(PF) domination of land and new settlements on Harare's periphery since the late 1990s differ substantially from those of early independence, when the ruling party can be said to have dominated the capital more broadly and enjoyed popular support in the city. The qualities of its political dominance of the capital have altered over time. Then, the party/state worked to deliver on its redistributive promises through a professional state planning and local government apparatus that was authoritarian and centralized, but was not notably corrupt; planners were not compromised by overwhelming securitized political pressures and the accompanying threats and enticements. Planning processes were slow and standards of housing were too high, but the urban poor in new settlements did not fall into an institutional stand-off that was irresolvable, due to partisan interests or factional politics. The state's repressive, militarized capacities were experienced mostly elsewhere than in the capital. But the interlinked national and urban 'crises' marked an important shift as city politics was polarized between MDC-aligned civic and political movements, and the ruling party's counter-mobilizations. State institutions themselves transformed to become part of a patronage politics enmeshed in complex ways with the party's own centralized structures. ZANU(PF)'s strategies have been shaped by a politics of state institutional control and elite accumulation, as well as by opportunism, including at the grassroots. Land reform has been a key 'generative' strategy, enabling its political dominance of the periphery. But the party has also treated the urban majority, including its own lower echelons, as usable and disposable, reducing people to desperate, survivalist calculations. Attempts to coerce or entice the city's voters back have failed, other than in specific spaces that the party controls, through land reform allocations, resettlement, and party-led occupations, where dominance was co-constituted through grassroots party structures.

Most components of the authoritarian 'toolkit' have been applied in the city as a whole over the last two decades, as within the periphery, but the 'generative' politics of land and the party's partisan patriotism have marked the city's borderlands in distinctive ways. We have argued, however, that the party's top-down co-optive and coercive-distributive measures do not fully capture local political dynamics in these city-edge spaces. This is because residents themselves have been more active in trying to shape processes and local authorities than top-down formulations convey, notwithstanding highly skewed power relations. In some instances, the sheer scale of life accommodated in the settlements itself became a factor in their recognition, though regularization was only achieved through a history of continual and active lobbying. We have shown the grassroots tactical or 'tangential' manoeuvres involved in clientelist strategies, which have in some cases delivered greater security and recognition for land holdings and undermined one of the key means of achieving dominance through threats of eviction. But we have also shown the limits of this strategy, as trajectories towards recognition and bureaucratic incorporation were patchy and context dependent, and the poor were particularly vulnerable to further displacement.

This discussion of the politics of the Harare periphery can evidence two broader conceptual arguments. First, it supports the case for a spatial approach to cities and political dominance. Rather than following the usual approach of focusing primarily on deal-making between politicians and interest groups, such as young people, vendors, or informal transport operatives, we have instead examined the ruling party's capacity to achieve dominance through control of specific city spaces and related resources—notably land on the periphery. This capacity hinged both on controlling state institutions responsible for formal land allocations, and on the parallel structures of the party itself, down to the grassroots and party-aligned militia and CIO. Second, we have shown why it is important to understand the qualities of political dominance in these spaces—particularly its contested qualities—and the nature of change over time. This means understanding how power and authority works at the grassroots and discussing contours of struggle that can be overlooked if the focus is on overt verbal dissent and protest. Clientelist manoeuvres through which residents have organized themselves into local party authorities have been encouraged and used by politicians as part of a partisan architecture of surveillance, coercion, and reward to co-constitute authority in these spaces. But residents were motivated to mobilize themselves and demonstrate support simply for survival or through tactical calculations as to how best to secure homes, services, and recognition. Locally constituted party dominance has been a means through which ZANU(PF) has achieved political support in an otherwise opposition-supporting city. But, as residents sought to use the party as a route towards home-owning, their tactics to consolidate rights in the settlements may also be a path through which the ruling party's leverage for domination is undermined.

Although trajectories towards regularization undermine the main leverage of political dominance in irregular settlements, the Harare case currently shows how patchy, risky, and long-drawn-out this process can be because of the political and economic interests vested in maintaining insecurity. The urban poor, in particular, have proved vulnerable and disposable. There is nothing automatic, linear, or universal about processes of regularization, and any lessening of political dominance in these settlements has so far been partial and uneven. What is notable in Harare's ruling-party-dominated peripheral settlements is the protracted nature, incompleteness, and unevenness of bureaucratic incorporation, as well as the levels of contestation involved.

Acknowledgements

This research was funded through the Royal Geographical Society Research Programme 'Migrants on the Margins', ESRC ES/N004140/1 and AHRC ES/P005128/1. We would like to thank the Ministry responsible for Local Government for research clearance. We are also indebted to Dialogue on Shelter and the Federation of Homeless People, Zimbabwe, and to the officials, councillors, and urban residents who participated. Thanks to Tom Goodfellow, David Jackman, and Davison Muchadenyika for their feedback on an earlier draft.

References

Alexander, J., McGregor, J., and Ranger, T. O. (2000). *One Hundred Years in the Dark Forests of Matabeleland, Zimbabwe*. Oxford: James Currey.
Auret, D. (1995). *Urban Housing: A National Crisis*. Gweru: Mambo Press.

Banks, N., Lombard, M., and Mitlin, D. (2020). Urban informality as a site of critical analysis. *Journal of Development Studies* 56(2): 223–238.

Bayat, A. (2000). From 'dangerous classes' to 'quiet rebels': The politics of the urban subaltern in the global South. *International Sociology* 15(3): 533–557.

Bond, P. (1998). *Uneven Zimbabwe: A Study of Finance, Development and Underdevelopment*. Trenton, NJ: Africa World Press.

Bond, P., and Manyanya, M. (2003). *Zimbabwe's Plunge: Exhausted Nationalism, Neoliberalism and the Search for Social Justice*, 2nd ed. London: Merlin.

Caldeira, T. (2017). Peripheral urbanization: Autoconstruction, transversal logics and politics in cities of the global South. *Society and Space D* 35(1): 3–20.

CCJP and LRF (1997). *Breaking the Silence, Building True Peace: Report on the Disturbances in Matabeleland and the Midlands, 1980–1989*. Harare: Catholic Commission for Justice and Peace and Legal Resources Foundation.

Chaeruka, J., and Munzwa, K. (2009). *Low Cost Housing Development in Zimbabwe: An Assessment of the Effectiveness of the Regulatory Framework*. Harare: UN-Habitat and Government of Zimbabwe.

Chamunogwa, A. (2019). The negotiability of state legal and bureaucratic authority in Zimbabwe. *Review of African Political Economy* 46(159): 71–85.

Chamunogwa, A. (2020). The making of a system of partisan authority on commercial farmlands in post-2000 Zimbabwe. In B-. M. Tendi, J. Alexander, and J. McGregor (eds), *The Oxford Handbook of Zimbabwe Politics*. Oxford: Oxford University Press. https://academic.oup.com/edited-volume/35414/chapter-abstract/303157954?redirectedFrom=fulltext

Chaterjee, P. (2004). *The Politics of the Governed: Popular Politics in Most of the World*. New York: Columbia University Press.

Chatiza, K. (2010). Can local government steer socio-economic transformation in Zimbabwe? Analysing historical trends and gazing into the future. In J. de Visser, N. Steytler, and N. Machinguta (eds), *Local Government Reform in Zimbabwe: A Policy Dialogue*. Bellville, South Africa: Community Law Centre, University of the Western Cape, pp. 1–30.

Chatiza, K. (ed.) (2016). *The 2013 Constitution of Zimbabwe as the Basis for 'Tsunamic' Reform of Local Government*. Gweru: Midlands State University and Commonwealth Local Government Forum.

Chatiza, K., and Mpofu, S. (2014). *Independent Mid-term Evaluation of the Harare Slum Upgrading Project*. Harare: Dialogue on Shelter, Zimbabwe Homeless People's Federation, and City of Harare, Zimbabwe.

Chatiza, K., Makanza, V., Musekiwa, N., Paradza, G., Chakaipa, S., Mukoto, S., Kagoro, J., Ndlovu, K., and Mushamba, S. (2013). *Capacity Building of Local Government for Service Delivery*. Harare: Government of Zimbabwe and United Nations Development Programme.

Chaumba., J., Scoones, I., and Wolmer, W. (2003). From jambanja to planning: The reassertion of technocracy in land reform in south east Zimbabwe? *Journal of Modern African Studies* 41(4): 533–554.

Cheeseman, N., and Klaas, B. (2018). *How to Rig an Election*. New Haven, CT: Yale University Press.

Chigudu, S. (2020). *The Political Life of an Epidemic: Cholera, Crisis and Citizenship in Zimbabwe*. Cambridge: Cambridge University Press.

Chirisa, I., and Muhomba, K. (2013). Constraints to managing urban and housing land in the context of poverty: A case of Epworth settlement in Zimbabwe. *Local Environment: The International Journal of Justice and Sustainability* 18(8): 950–964.

Chirisa, I., Bandauko, E., and Mutsindikwa, N. (2015). Distributive politics at play in Harare, Zimbabwe: Case for housing cooperatives. *Bandung Journal of Global South* 2(1): 1–13.

Chirisa, I., Gaza, M., and Bandauko, E. (2014). Housing cooperatives and the politics of local organization and representation in peri-urban Harare, Zimbabwe. *African Studies Quarterly* 15(1): 37.

Chitekwe-Biti, B. (2009). Struggles for urban land by the Zimbabwe Homeless People's Federation. *Environment and Urbanization* 21(2): 347–366.

Chitekwe-Biti, B., and Mitlin, D. (2001). The urban poor under threat and in struggle: Options for urban development in Zimbabwe 1995–2000. *Environment and Urbanization* 13: 85–102.

Chitekwe-Biti, B., Mudimu, P., Masimba Nyama, G., and Jera, T. (2012). Developing an informal settlement upgrading protocol in Zimbabwe: The Epworth story. *Environment and Urbanization* 24(1): 131–148.

City of Harare (2018). State of the City address by Mayor, Councillor Bernard Manyenyeni, 11 April.

Cliffe, L., Alexander, J., Cousins, B., and Gaidzanwa, R. (2011). An overview of fast track land reform in Zimbabwe: Editorial introduction. *Journal of Peasant Studies* 38(5): 907–938.

Dialogue on Shelter (2014). *Harare Slum Profiles Report*, 2nd ed., March. Harare: Dialogue on Shelter and Zimbabwe Homeless People's Federation.

Dorman, S. (2016a). 'We have not made anybody homeless': Regulation and control of urban life in Zimbabwe. *Citizenship Studies* 20(1): 84–98.

Dorman, S. (2016b). *Understanding Zimbabwe: From Liberation to Authoritarianism and Beyond*. Oxford: Hurst.

EU (2014). *EU Roadmap for Engagement with Civil Society 2014–2017*. Harare: European Union.

Goodfellow, T., and Jackman, D. (2020). Control the capital: Cities and political dominance. ESID Working Paper no. 135, Effective States and Inclusive Development Research Centre, University of Manchester.

Government of Zimbabwe (2005). *National Housing: Circular Number 70 of 2004- New Housing Standards*, 14 January. Harare: Government of Zimbabwe.

Government of Zimbabwe (2015). *Harare North Housing Cooperative Compliance Audit Report, 16 July*. Harare: Ministry responsible for Local Government, Public Works and National Housing.

Government of Zimbabwe (2019). *Summarising Findings and Recommendations of the Commission of Inquiry into the Matter of the Sale of State Land in and around Urban Areas since 2005*. Harare: Government of Zimbabwe.

Hammar, A., McGregor, J., and Landau, L. (2013). Displacing Zimbabwe: Crisis and construction in Southern Africa. *Journal of Southern African Studies* 36(2): 285–299.

Hammar, A., Raftopoulos, B., and Jensen, S. (2003). *Zimbabwe's Unfinished Business: Rethinking Land, State and Nation in the Context of Crisis*. Harare: Weaver Press.

Holston, J. (2008). *Insurgent Citizenship: Disjunctions of Democracy and Modernity in Brazil*. Princeton, NJ: Princeton University Press.

Holston, J. (2009). Insurgent citizenship in an era of global urban peripheries. *City and Society* 21: 245–267.

IDAZIM (2010). *Local Governance in Transition: Zimbabwe's Local Authorities during the Inclusive Government*. Harare: RTI International and Institute for a Democratic Alternative in Zimbabwe.

Jones, J. (2010a). 'Nothing is straight in Zimbabwe': The rise of the *kukiya-kiya* economy 2000–2008. *Journal of Southern African Studies* 36(2): 285–299.

Jones, J. (2010b). Freeze! Movement, narrative and the disciplining of price in hyperinflationary Zimbabwe. *Social Dynamics* 36(2): 338–351.

Kamete, A. (2007). Cold-hearted, negligent, and spineless? Planning, planners, and the (r)ejection of 'filth' in urban Zimbabwe. *International Planning Studies* 12 (2): 153–171.

Kamete, A. (2009a). In the service of tyranny: Debating the role of planning in Zimbabwe's urban 'clean-Kameup' operation. *Urban Studies* 46(4): 897–922.

Kamete, A. (2009b). For enhanced civic participation in local governance: Calling tyranny to account in Harare. *Environment and Urbanization* 21(1): 59–67.

Kamete, A. (2012). Interrogating planning's power in an African city: Time for reorientation? *Planning Theory* 11(1): 66–88.

Kamete, A. (2013). Missing the point? Urban planning and the normalisation of 'pathological' spaces in southern Africa. *Transactions of the Institute of British Geographers* 38(4): 639–651.

Kamete, A. (2018). Pernicious assimilation: Reframing the integration of the urban informal economy in southern Africa. *Urban Geography* 39(2): 167–189.

Kriger, N. (2003). *Guerrilla Veterans in Postwar Zimbabwe: Symbolic and Violent Politics 1980–1997.* Cambridge: Cambridge University Press.

Kriger, N. (2012). ZANU(PF) politics under Zimbabwe's 'Power-sharing' Government. *Journal of Contemporary African Studies* 30(1): 11–26.

Lund, C. (2006). Twilight institutions, public authority, and local politics in Africa. *Development and Change* 37(4): 685–705.

Maringira, G., and Gukurume, S. (2020). Youth patronage: Violence, intimidation and political mobilization in Zimbabwe. APN Working Paper no. 28, African Peacebuilding Network, New York.

Marongwe, N. (2009). Interrogating Zimbabwe's fast track land reform and resettlement programme: A focus on beneficiary selection. PhD thesis, University of Western Cape.

Marongwe N., Mukoto S., and Chatiza, K. (2011) *Scoping Study of Governance of Urban Land Markets in Zimbabwe.* Harare: Urban Landmark.

Mbiba, B. (2017a). Idioms of accumulation: Corporate accumulation by dispossession in urban Zimbabwe. *International Journal of Urban and Regional Research* 41(2): 213–234.

Mbiba, B. (2017b). On the periphery: Missing urbanization in Zimbabwe. *Africa Research Institute: Counterpoints*, 27 March. Available at: https://www.africaresearchinstitute.org/newsite/publications/periphery-missing-urbanisation-zimbabwe/, accessed 30 July 2019.

Mbiba, B. (2022). The mystery of housing demolitions in urban Zimbabwe. *International Planning Studies* 27(4): 320–335.

McGregor, J. (2013). Surveillance and the city: Patronage, power-sharing, and the politics of urban control in Zimbabwe. *Journal of Southern African Studies* 39(4): 783–780.

McGregor, J., and Chatiza, K. (2019). Frontiers of urban control: Lawlessness on the city edge and forms of clientelist statecraft in Zimbabwe. *Antipode* 51(5): 1554–1580.

McGregor, J., and Chatiza, K. (2020). Partisan citizenship and its discontents: Precarious possession and political agency on Harare City's expanding margins. *Citizenship Studies* 24(1): 17–39.

Mitlin, D. (2014). Politics, informality and clientelism: Exploring a pro-poor urban politics. ESID Working Paper No. 34, Effective States and Inclusive Development Research Centre, University of Manchester.

Mlambo, A. (1997). *The Economic Structural Adjustment Programme: The Case of Zimbabwe, 1990–1995.* Harare: University of Zimbabwe Publications.

Muchadenyika, D. (2015). Land for housing: A political resource—Reflections from Zimbabwe's urban areas. *Journal of Southern African Studies* 41(6): 1219–1238.

Muchadenyika, D. (2020). *Seeking Urban Transformation: Alternative Urban Futures in Zimbabwe*. Harare: Weaver Press.

Muchadenyika, D., and Williams, J. (2017). Politics and the practice of planning: The case of Zimbabwean cities. *Cities* 63: 33–40.

Musekiwa, N., and Chatiza, K. (2015). Rise in resident associational life in response to service delivery decline in urban councils in Zimbabwe. *Commonwealth Journal of Local Governance* 16/17: 120–136.

Mutongwizo, T. (2014). Chipangano governance: Enablers and effects of violent extraction in Zimbabwe. *Africa Peace and Conflict Journal* 7(1): 29–40.

Mutwiza-Mangiza, N. (1991). Financing urban shelter development in Zimbabwe: A review of existing institutions, problems and prospects. *Habitat International* 15(1–2): 51–68.

Muwanga, N. K., Mukwaya, P. I., and Goodfellow, T. (2020). Carrot, stick and statute: Elite strategies and contested dominance in Kampala. ESID Working Paper no. 146, Effective States and Inclusive Development Research Centre, University of Manchester.

Pasirayi, S. C. (2021) Urban activism in local governance in Harare: Doctoral thesis (PhD), University of Sussex. Unpublished.

Patel, D. H., and Adams, R. J. (1981). *Chriambahuyo: A Case Study in Low Income Housing*. Gweru: Mambo Press.

Potts, D. (2006). Restoring order? Operation Murambatsvina and the urban crisis in Zimbabwe. *Journal of Southern African Studies* 32(2): 273–291.

Potts, D. (2011). 'We have a tiger by the tail': Continuities and discontinuities in urban planning in Zimbabwe. *Critical African Studies* 4(6): 15–46.

Raftopoulos, B. (2004). Nation, race and history in Zimbabwean politics. In B. Raftopoulos and L. Sachikonye (eds.), *Zimbabwe: Injustice and Political Reconciliation*. Cape Town: Institute of Justice and Reconciliation, pp. 181–194.

Raftopoulos, B. (2006). The Zimbabwean crisis and the challenges for the left. *Journal of Southern African Studies* 32(2): 203–219.

Raftopoulos, B. (2009). The crisis in Zimbabwe 1998–2008. In B. Raftopoulos and A. Mlambo (eds), *Becoming Zimbabwe*. Harare: Weaver Press, pp. 201–232.

Raftopoulos, B., and Phimister, I. (eds) (1997). *Keep on Knocking: A History of the Labour Movement in Zimbabwe 1900–1997*. Harare: Baobab Books.

Raftopoulos, B., and Sachikonye, L. (eds) (2001). *Striking Back: The Labour Movement and the Postcolonial State in Zimbabwe 1980–2000*. Harare: Weaver Press.

Rakodi, C. (1995). *Harare: Inheriting a Settler-Colonial City—Change or Continuity?* Chichester: John Wiley and Sons.

Resnick, D. (2014a). *Urban Poverty and Party Populism in African Democracies.* Cambridge: Cambridge University Press.

Resnick, D. (2014b). Urban governance and service delivery in African cities: The role of politics and policies. *Development Policy Review* 32(1): 3–17.

Sawyer, L. (2014). Piecemeal urbanisation at the peripheries of Lagos. *African Studies* 73(2): 271–289.

Scoones, I., Marongwe, N., Mavedzenge, B., Murimbarimba, F., Mahenehene, J., and Sukume, C. (2010). *Land Reform in Zimbabwe: Myths and Realities.* London: Zed Press.

UN (2005). *Report on the Fact-Finding Mission to Zimbabwe to Access the Scope and Impact of Operation Murambatsvina by the United Nations Special Envoy on Human Settlement Issues in Zimbabwe, Mrs Anna Kajumulo Tibaijuka.* Nairobi: United Nations.

Zamchiya, P. (2013). The role of politics and state practices in shaping rural differentiation: A study of resettled small-scale farmers in south-eastern Zimbabwe. *Journal of Southern African Studies* 39(4): 937–953.

8

Beautification, governance, and spectacle in post-war Colombo

Iromi Perera and Jonathan Spencer

8.1 Introduction

In the immediate aftermath of its 2009 victory over the rebel Liberation Tigers of Tamil Eelam (LTTE), the government of Sri Lanka launched a major programme aimed at the 'beautification' of the island's largest city, Colombo. Trees were cut, pavements restored, colonial buildings uncovered, and new public spaces opened up. Low-income communities were faced with the threat of eviction from their homes in the city centre and relocation into new tower blocks in more peripheral locations. The source of this flurry of activity was the President's brother, former soldier Gotabaya Rajapaksa. Soon after the end of the war, his Ministry of Defence took over administrative responsibility for urban planning and development, with the creation of the Ministry of Defence and Urban Development—and army personnel oversaw the early waves of eviction. When the Rajapaksas were defeated in elections in 2015, it was hoped the clear-out of the urban poor would cease. But the policy continued until late 2019, when Rajapaksa was returned to power, this time as President himself.

Yet the state's assault on the urban poor was not quite the pacification exercise it might at first appear. Central Colombo was not a site of past or future challenge to the regime—which is not to say that the Rajapaksas were popular in the city. Central Colombo has been a stronghold of the rival United National Party (UNP), but despite Sri Lanka's turbulent postcolonial history, until recently it has not been a place of major disruption or protest. In the eyes of the Rajapaksa regime, it was not so much dissenting as dissonant: a colonial city with more Tamils and Muslims than Sinhala, more Christians and Muslims than Buddhists. The beautification programme spoke to a rather different audience, the overwhelmingly Sinhala Buddhist new middle class of the expanding suburbs. In this respect, it might be read as a generative

Iromi Perera and Jonathan Spencer, *Beautification, governance, and spectacle in post-war Colombo*. In: *Controlling the Capital.* Edited by: Tom Goodfellow and David Jackman, Oxford University Press. © Oxford University Press (2023). DOI: 10.1093/oso/9780192868329.003.0008 intervention, in our editors' terms, intended to create—or, minimally, to recognize and acknowledge—a new political group in the peri-urban middle class, and align it with the interests of wealthier professionals and, of course, the military.

In 2022, that emergent political force, the new middle class of the suburbs, initiated the first major protests as the country's economy was showing signs of imminent collapse. With long daily power cuts, accelerating inflation, and shortages of essential goods, groups of protestors started to appear along suburban roadsides. After a confrontation close to the President's private residence in the suburbs, protest shifted to a central site on Galle Face Green, abutting the Presidential Secretariat. The protestors' rallying cry was 'Gota go home' and their encampment on Galle Face became known as Gota-GoGama (GGG, 'Gota go village'). As the protests grew, Mahinda Rajapaksa resigned as Prime Minister in May. In July, a huge crowd broke into the presidential palace; soon after, Gotabaya Rajapaksa himself resigned. Our central argument in this chapter, written before these recent events, is that while Colombo had *not* been a centre for insurgency in post-independence Sri Lanka (because insurgency flared in more peripheral parts of the country), it was a key site for political spectacle, some of it (like the 1983 anti-Tamil pogrom) violent. In 2022, spectacle morphed into insurgency as the crowds at GGG succeeded in forcing out an authoritarian President.

This chapter tells the story of post-war beautification in the context of a longer history of urban politics and protest, and with special attention to those moments, like the 1983 pogrom, when national-level conflict impacted directly upon the city. Our purpose is not simply to argue a negative case against the broader thrust of this collection. It is true that Colombo is not in a simple sense an insurgent city which poses a serious threat to the exercise of state power. It does have an important history of sporadic moments of significant political violence, and that history, which we reconstruct in Section 8.2, does provide our entry into the comparative questions we wish to explore. Those questions take as their point of departure the idea of treating the links between authoritarianism and the urban as a kind of diagnostic—what other relations come into focus if we make this our start? What ancillary questions might it provoke? In Section 8.2, we describe Colombo's place in Sri Lanka, and the way in which it has been the centre of an officially unacknowledged urban expansion in recent decades. In Section 8.3, we trace its political presence during the war years, a presence increasingly at odds with the broader trends of mainstream politics. Rather than acting as a straightforward political resource, Colombo during the war became the stage for acts of spectacular violence. In the post-war years of Gotabaya Rajapaksa's beautification drive, it then became the site for a new kind of experiment in authoritarian governance without politics. In 2022, it became the setting for unprecedented spectacular protests, which, in the short term at least, exposed the weaknesses in the Rajapaksas' politics of dominance by beautification.

Before going further, it might be helpful to say a little more about the history of parties and politics in Sri Lanka. From the 1950s to the 2010s, power changed hands between two major parties, the right-of-centre UNP and the slightly left-of-centre Sri Lanka Freedom Party (SLFP). In 1956, a populist coalition led by the SLFP won a landslide election victory on a tide of Sinhala nationalist fervour. In 1977, the UNP won another landslide victory, ushering in the so-called 'open economy' and rewriting the Constitution with the creation of a powerful executive presidency. The period of UNP rule from 1977 to 1994 also saw conflict with the minority Tamil community escalate into a state of civil war, a war which only ended with the crushing of the separatist LTTE in 2009. In the late 1980s, intervention from India to impose a peace settlement led to further insurgency by Sinhala youth, led by the leftist-nationalist Janatha Vimukthi Peramuna (JVP) (People's Liberation Front).[1] From 2004 to 2022, the Rajapaksa family dominated the political landscape, employing a cocktail of appeals to Buddhist nationalism, deft deployment of patronage, and a great deal of brute authoritarianism, to maintain power.

8.2 Colombo in war and peace

Statistically, Colombo presents a paradox. Officially, Sri Lanka has a very low level of urbanization, and the area officially designated as the city of Colombo itself has a modest population of just over half a million. But recent studies indicate that the levels of *de facto* urbanization are far higher than official figures suggest. Spatial analysis by UN-Habitat for a 2018 report suggested instead that Sri Lanka has experienced one of the world's highest rates

---

[1] Discussed in these terms, 'parties' in Sri Lanka easily gain a misleading sense of concreteness and stability: in practice, each of the two major parties has been an unstable coalition linking key big men (women are massively unrepresented in the higher levels of party politics), each of whom has his own, personality-based, following (Peiris 2018). In the machinations that led to the defeat of Mahinda Rajapaksa's government in 2015, the SLFP split, and the Rajapaksas reconstituted their support base in the form of a new party, the Sri Lanka Podujana Peramuna (SLPP) (Sri Lanka People's Front). In the lead-up to the 2019 presidential election, won by Gotabaya Rajapaksa on the SLPP ticket, the UNP split, with the son of a former President, Sajith Premadasa, emerging as the leader of another new alliance, the Samagi Jana Balawegaya (SJB) (United People's Power). In short, beneath the surface of party politics lies a shifting and volatile network of clientelist ties, out of which particular politicians might be seen to be mobilizing particular combinations of interests at particular moments.

of urbanization in the past two decades (UN-Habitat 2018).[2] Expansion, though, has occurred not within the boundaries of urban local government, which determine government assessments of urbanization, but in the steady expansion of suburban and peri-urban sprawl. This expansion is very clear from the three maps in Fig. 8.1, which show the levels of *de facto* urbanization over a twenty-year period, from 1997 to 2017. Densely urban areas have expanded north along the coast, and east into neighbouring districts areas like Kotte/Sri Jayawardanapura, Maharagama, and Homagama. Insofar as there is recognition of this huge urban expansion, it comes in the form of plans for something called the Western Province Megapolis, an idea which at once acknowledges and simultaneously denies this pattern of rapidly expanding urbanization. According to the 2015 Masterplan, only about 2 million people live in Colombo and its suburbs: the 'majority of the population [of 5+ million in the region] are living in villages scattered across the flat areas' (Masterplan 2015: 9).

Taking into account this unacknowledged growth, a very different picture emerges. Colombo municipality had a population in 2012 of 561,314. If we add the contiguous municipalities of Dehiwala to the south and Kotte to the west, that figure increases to 889,000. But with the 'fringe' area included, the population becomes 6,081,000 (UN-Habitat 2018: 38), or a little short of a third of the national population—not perhaps a megacity to compare with Jakarta or Mumbai, but a great deal more substantial than the official population of half a million, or the Masterplan's 2 million for the city and its suburbs. However calculated, Colombo dwarfs the island's other urban centres: the official city population is five times higher than the next biggest city (Kandy), while the UN-Habitat expanded figure for the Colombo conurbation is sixteen times bigger than the next (Galle). Economically, Colombo is habitually called the country's 'powerhouse'. A high proportion of Sri Lanka's economic growth has been concentrated in Western Province, which includes Colombo, and it also boasts the country's lowest poverty rates.

There is a reasonably straightforward political-economic history behind these figures. Colombo was established at first as a trading centre, especially for Muslim traders working down the coastline of the Indian subcontinent.

---

[2] Official figures for the urban–rural divide in Sri Lanka are narrowly based on the boundaries of administrative areas classified as 'urban'. Changes in those boundaries in the 1970s and early 1980s created an artificial 'drop' in the area officially designated as 'urban'; subsequent censuses reinforced these static boundaries (UN-Habitat 2018: 14). The reanalysis in the 2018 UN-Habitat report is based on analysis of land use patterns from satellite images; the methodology is described in more detail in an annex to the report (UN-Habitat 2018: 165). In effect, this recent UN-Habitat methodology absorbs some of the criticisms of the use of official measures of the urban advanced by Brenner and Schmid (2014), without attempting a major rethink of the theoretical presumptions of the very idea of the urban. That is a matter for another day.

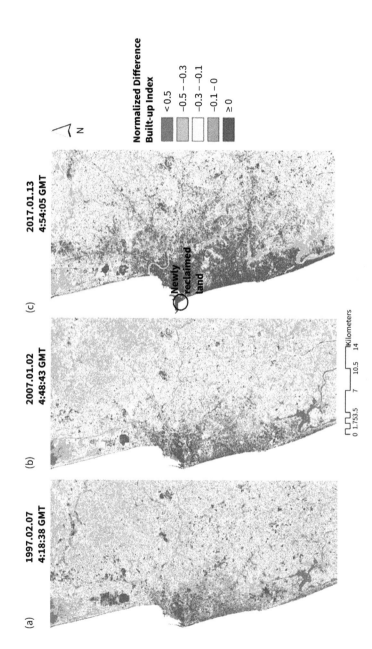

Fig. 8.1 Growth of urban area, Western Province

Source: Ranagalage et al. (2017). Published under a CC BY 4.0 International license: https://creativecommons.org/licenses/by/4.0/.

In the sixteenth century, the Portuguese took over the city as a military and trading base. The Dutch consolidated Colombo's position as an administrative hub for their territories on the island, and when the British gained control of the entire island in 1815, Colombo was already the established capital. Growth was steady through the nineteenth century and early part of the twentieth century. The island's export crops made their way out through Colombo's port, rich traders from different Indian communities—Chettiars, Bohras, Memons, Parsis—established themselves in the city, while South Indian labourers supplied much of the workforce in the docks, and in the domestic spaces of the city's colonial middle class (Moore 1997; Meyer 2003; Sivasundaram 2017). With the rise of Sinhala Buddhist nationalism as a political force in the mid-twentieth century, Colombo became increasingly associated in the popular imagination with commerce, the foreign, and the inauthentic. It was perhaps in partial response to this perception, and to camouflage his own government's enthusiastic embrace of global capital, that in the early 1980s President J. R. Jayawardene announced the shift of government business to a 'new' capital, Sri Jayawardanapura, established on the site of an old kingdom in an eastern suburb of Colombo. Parliament and most government departments now operate from there, but the new city is indistinguishable from the surrounding urban sprawl which quickly enveloped it, and 'Colombo' remains the usual signifier of the centre of political and cultural life on the island.

This colonial and commercial history is sedimented clearly enough in the demography of central Colombo. In the 2012 census, only 37 per cent of the population were Sinhala (compared to 75 per cent nationally), 32 per cent were Tamil, and 29 per cent were Muslim. There were small but culturally significant clusters of Malays, Burghers, Chetties, and others. In religious terms, Buddhists and Muslims had almost equal numbers (31 per cent), followed by Hindus (23 per cent) and Christians of various sorts (15 per cent). Again the variation from national figures is striking (Buddhists 70 per cent, Hindus 12 per cent, Muslims 10 per cent, Christians 8 per cent). In Sri Lanka, urban centres are centres of trade, and as such, in the recent past were likely to be ethnically heterogeneous, marked by the presence of mosques and churches alongside Buddhist temples. Central Colombo is the clearest expression of this. In contrast, the new suburbs are strikingly homogeneous in ethnic and religious terms: Sri Jayawardanapura-Kotte is 85 per cent Sinhala; Maharagama is 96 per cent Sinhala; Homagama—further inland—is 98 per cent Sinhala. The equivalent proportions of Buddhists in the population of these districts are 77 per cent, 92 per cent, and 96 per cent. In their apparent lack of diversity, the expanding suburbs that have grown since the early 1990s can perhaps be read as non-centres of a new way of being urban.

It is important to hold on to the haziness that blurs our understanding of the new suburbs and their occupants. The prevailing social imaginary in Sri Lanka still divides the world into cities and villages, with nothing in between. The Masterplan imagines 4 million villagers living in what the UN-Habitat report identifies as essentially urban areas. When asked where you are from, the standard question is 'Where is your village?' Everyone 'has' a village; no one, it seems, 'has' a city. One way to understand what follows is as a story in which the inhabitants of these suburbs gradually discover themselves as a cultural and political presence.

Colombo is perhaps as important for its symbolic properties as for its actual politics, standing, as it does for many people, as a complex signifier of class and distance. In the 1970s and 1980s, two radical youth movements challenged the state head on—the young separatists of the LTTE in the north, and the leftist-nationalist JVP in the predominantly Sinhala south. For both, 'Colombo' stood above all as a symbol of privilege and exclusion. *Kolamabata kiri, apata kekiri* was the best-known JVP slogan: 'Colombo gets the milk, we get *kekiri* [a kind of gourd].' Within Colombo, certain districts (Colombo 7), and certain schools (Royal, St Thomas's), stand as particularly condensed expressions of privilege. In a BBC documentary about the LTTE from the early 1990s, a young cadre, eyes shining with injustice, tells the camera, 'If you look at schools in Colombo, they have *marble* lavatories' (BBC 1991).[3]

Politically, Colombo has long been thought of as a UNP town. In the 2019 presidential election, for example, it held out against the national trend, with the defeated candidate from the successor to the UNP, Sajith Premadasa, receiving 73 per cent of the vote in Colombo West and Colombo North, and 80 per cent in Colombo Central. The longer history, though, has been a great deal more complicated than these figures suggest. In the 1956 landslide win for S. W. R. D. Bandaranaike's nationalist–populist coalition, Colombo returned leading figures from the Communist Party and the Trotskyist Lanka Sama Samaja Party—Pieter Keunemann, Vivienne Gunawardena, and Colvin de Silva. By 1970, when Bandaranaike's widow Sirimavo herself won a landslide national victory, Colombo was being represented by a combination of UNP MPs and figures from the Old Left parties. But in 1956, Colombo elected a UNP mayor—the first in an unbroken line, as the UNP has gone on to

---

[3] One helpful reviewer of an early version of this chapter thought it important to remind readers that Colombo schools do not actually have marble lavatories. On the JVP insurgencies, see Uyangoda (2003), Hughes (2013), and Moore (2021).

dominate Colombo local government. Over this period, UNP mayors have been Tamil, Muslim, and Sinhala in turn.

Although the UNP is generally held to be right of centre, more or less pro-Western, and pro-market, this characterization is disturbed, like everything else in the polity, by the dynamics of Sinhala Buddhist nationalism. In the 1930s, the most charismatic political figure in Colombo city was A. E. Goonasinha, a labour leader who gradually shifted from class politics to ethnic politics in the course of his career (Jayawardena 1985). Ranasinghe Premadasa, the most important political figure to emerge from postcolonial Colombo politics, started his career in Goonesinghe's Labour Party, leaving it for the UNP in the mid-1950s. After a spell as Deputy Mayor, Premadasa was elected as an MP, becoming Prime Minister to J. R. Jayawardene as President in 1978, and succeeding to the presidency itself in 1989, before dying at the hands of an LTTE suicide bomber in 1993. Premadasa is a fascinating figure—of low-caste origin, he worked his way doggedly up the system from working-class city politics to the presidency, the first (and still the last) politician to achieve this. Middle-class liberals usually remember him for his part in the country's slide into long-term war and authoritarian rule, but for many of the Colombo poor he was, and still is, a hero. His commitment to Jayawardene's pro-market policies was tempered by his background as an organizer working with Colombo's low-income communities. His most impressive legacy was the 'million houses' programme, which provided for either new houses for the poor, or the upgrading of services and tenure for residents of the low-income settlements in the city (known as *wattes* in Sinhala) (Royo-Olid et al. 2018).

In electoral terms, Colombo pursued an apparently steady course through the 1980s and 1990s, even as the country as a whole tore itself apart. In an election conducted in the shadow of the JVP insurrection in 1989, the UNP won the biggest share of the vote in every polling division in Colombo district. In 1994, when Chandrika Kumaratunga's People's Alliance finally put an end to seventeen years of UNP rule nationally, that share dipped, but the UNP continued to dominate the central areas of the city. By 2004, when the UNP government was defeated again by Kumaratunga's alliance, Colombo city was even more of an outlier from national trends, with the UNP getting over 70 per cent of the vote in a string of polling divisions in the city centre.

But something quite unprecedented happened in the 2004 election. A new party dominated by Buddhist monks, the Jathika Hela Urumaya (JHU), fielded 200 monks as candidates in the national election. Seven monks were directly elected, and two additional JHU members (one not a monk) were added from the national list. What is of most interest at this point in our argument is the spatial distribution of the JHU vote. Of the seven directly elected monks, six came from the three contiguous Western Province divisions, Colombo, Gamapaha (immediately north of Colombo), and Kalutara (south of the city). Within the divisions, the vote was very unevenly distributed—an unimpressive 10 per cent in central divisions in the city proper, but closer to 30 per cent in the expanding, all-Sinhala suburbs like Maharagama, where the UNP was pushed into third place. A new political force had found its voice: it was the sound of the suburbs, middle class (but only just, in many cases), aspirant, fiercely nationalist, and deeply ambivalent (but never indifferent) in its attitude to the modern and the foreign (DeVotta and Stone 2008).

8.3 City and spectacle: One pogrom, two funerals, and many killings

In this section, we focus on the city as a site of certain sorts of spectacle, specifically killings and funerals. Neither this, nor the section that follows, is intended as a comprehensive account of its topic. Instead we want to isolate certain particularly important incidents and chains of events which we think might tell us something of wider significance about the uses of violence in the city. The twenty-six-year civil war, for the most part, did not run its course in the city: urban violence was sporadic rather than endemic. But the city provided the setting for some of the most spectacular acts of violence of the past forty years, and in the form of mass funerals, some equally spectacular responses, and these are our focus here.

There are a number of possible claims for the exact time and place when Sri Lanka's long civil war started, but one of the most plausible candidates is the Kanatte cemetery in Borella, south-west of the city centre, on the evening of 24 July 1983. The previous day, in Jaffna, far to the north, the LTTE had pulled off its most audacious attack yet, killing thirteen soldiers in an ambush on the edge of town. On the 24th, the bodies of the soldiers were flown to Colombo for a joint funeral at the main cemetery. What happened that evening is much disputed—the flight was late, a crowd gathered and started to grow restive, the funeral was cancelled, and the bodies were subsequently released to the families of the killed men. What had become a large crowd then spilled out of the cemetery, and the first attacks began on Tamil shops.[4] A curfew was imposed from Monday the 25th. In the week that followed, attacks on Tamils

---

[4] Earlier accounts of the 1983 violence can be found in Manor (1984) and Piyadasa (1984). Divergent interpretations of the events can be found in Kapferer (1988) and Spencer (1990). Rajan Hoole's (2001)

and their property ebbed and flowed across the city, and spread to other towns in the south of the island.

The attacks of what is remembered as 'Black July' seemed to alternate between moments of considerable planning and organization, and chaotic moments of rumour-fuelled panic (Nissan 1984; Spencer 1984). At the time, two explanations for the organized aspects of the violence were presented. The government, while claiming that 'the people' had expressed its unhappiness with the separatists in the north, also managed to blame the violence on three left-wing parties, which were immediately proscribed. Others blamed the ruling UNP: the motive was also clear enough (and even said out loud by one or two UNP politicians)—to teach the Tamils in the north a lesson. The consequences of the July violence were huge. Many Tamils with money and connections left the island to form the nucleus of the large Sri Lankan Tamil diaspora now to be found in cities like Toronto, London, and Paris. Of those who stayed behind, young men joined the separatists in their hundreds, turning what had been a minor security irritant into the first stirrings of a civil war. But there was no direct repetition of the kind of violence unleashed on the Tamils of Colombo in 1983. Although the LTTE desperately wanted to provoke some kind of a repetition, in the form of further riots or pogroms, it never happened—presumably because the powerful decided it should not happen. There was, however, one perverse consequence of the attempted ethnic cleansing of the city. As the situation in the north worsened, many better-off Tamils moved from Jaffna to the safer environment of Colombo. Others, who stayed, tried to send their sons there to keep them safe from the twin dangers of forced recruitment into the LTTE and harassment by the security forces. For many young men, in particular, Colombo became a kind of waiting-room for eventual departure to Canada, the UK, or Australia. Despite the exodus to Europe, Australia, and North America, however, the Tamil proportion of the Colombo population increased through the years of war (Thiranagama 2011: 228–256).

* * *

21 February 1988, Independence Square. One of the biggest crowds ever seen in Colombo has gathered for the funeral of Vijaya Kumaranatunga, a massively popular Sinhala movie star, but latterly as well known for his political work alongside his partner, Chandrika Kumaratunga, the daughter of

---

careful sifting through of the available evidence is now the essential point of departure for anyone trying to get a sense of what happened and why.

Sirimavo Bandaranaike.[5] The coffin is only partially open: Kumaranatunga's head is covered to conceal the damage inflicted by his assassin, who shot him at the gate of his house before fleeing on a motorbike. As the huge crowd watches, Chandrika marks her husband's departure with a raised and clenched fist.

Vijaya Kumaranatunga was the great lost hope of the Sri Lankan left. Good-looking and charismatic, married into the heart of the political establishment, from the early 1980s onwards he became equally well known as a critic of Jayawardene's right-wing government, and as the war escalated, an advocate of a political solution to the separatist crisis in the north. Before his death, he and Chandrika split from the SLFP and formed their own party, the Sri Lanka Mahajana Party (SLMP). He made well-publicized visits to Tamil Nadu and Jaffna, where he met senior LTTE leaders. He welcomed the 1986 Peace Accord imposed on Jayawardene's government by India and, in doing so, became a target for the JVP, which had embarked on a campaign targeting 'traitors' from both the right and the left. As its campaign developed, even funerals were threatened: mourners for its victims were ordered not to attend. But there was no prospect of shutting down Vijaya's funeral, given his popularity (Jeyaraj 2020).[6]

The second JVP insurrection was fought most bitterly in rural and semi-rural areas, in the island's so-called 'deep south', and in the villages around Kandy. The war with the LTTE was also fought far away from the city. But the targeted assassination became an increasingly frequent weapon, and as often as not, Colombo was the site for the killing: Ranjit Wijeratne, Minister of Defence, in 1991; President Premadasa, mingling with the crowd at a May Day rally in 1993; UNP presidential candidate Gamini Dissanayake at an election rally in 1994; the Tamil academic and politician Neelan Thiruchelvam in 1999; Ketesh Loganathan, a Tamil human rights worker and critic of the LTTE in 2006; Foreign Minister Lakshman Kadirgamar, shot the same year by a sniper while entering the swimming pool at his Colombo house. These were all the work of the LTTE, and the spectacle of the killing would be followed by the spectacle of the funeral. The list of those killed by the JVP in and around Colombo in the 1980s is less grand and more mixed: Daya Pathirana, leader of the (anti-JVP) Independent Student Union; various government MPs; a popular TV presenter; the Vice-Chancellor of Colombo University.

---

[5] For most of his cinema career, Vijaya used the long version of his surname, Kumaranatunga; his widow has used a shorter version, Kumaratunga.

[6] As political alignments changed in the 1990s, it became more comfortable for those around Vijaya to claim that his killing was the work of the government, rather than the JVP.

In the mid-2000s, with a Norwegian-brokered ceasefire between the government and the LTTE looking increasingly threadbare, a rather different pattern emerged. The Tamil journalist Dharmeratnam Sivaram was bundled into an unmarked vehicle in April 2005; his body was discovered the next day in a high-security zone near Parliament; Jaffna MP Nadarajah Raviraj was murdered later that year as he drove to work. Key figures in the government war effort, notably army chief Sarath Fonseka and Gotabaya Rajapaksa himself, narrowly escaped assassination attempts in central Colombo. As the war approached its end in 2009, the abductions and killings escalated. The Sinhala journalist Lasantha Wickrematunge was killed in his car on his way to work in January 2009; in an editorial written shortly before his death, and reprinted round the world, he said, 'When finally I am killed, it will be the government that kills me.' But 'government' itself was hardly singular in those days—different figures in the security forces and the government were allegedly running their own separate death squads; Sivaram's death was blamed on a former Tamil militant group which had long ago crossed to the government's side; other deaths and disappearances, like that of the Vice-Chancellor of Eastern University, Ravindranath, were blamed on a breakaway group from the LTTE, the Tamil Makkal Viduthalai Pulikal, which had aligned with the government in 2004. Still others were attributed to shadowy groupings from the security forces.

In many of these years, Colombo felt quite far away from the war which was being fought in the north and east of the island. Tourists stayed at the five-star hotels, and restaurants and clubs opened, catering to the country's expanding middle class. Defence spending mushroomed, as did the number of young men and women working in the security forces. The recruits into the swollen security forces did not, on the whole, come from economically strong areas like Colombo: they came from poor rural areas like Moneragala, Hambantota, and Polonnaruwa, areas where at the time as many as half the households might be drawing some of their income from security-force employment (Venugopal 2018).

Occasionally, though, something would happen to shatter the complacency. In 1987, a bomb killed over 100 people at the main bus stand in Pettah. Fifty-two died in the suicide bombing which killed the presidential candidate Gamini Dissanayake in 1994. A huge bomb killed ninety-one, and caused massive damage to the Central Bank, in 1996. Sixty-four were killed in a train bombing in Dehiwela the same year. In response, Colombo acquired a carapace of security: checkpoints on main roads, vehicle checks at VIP functions. A high-security zone was established around the Presidential Secretariat in the Fort. In the second half of the 1990s, traffic ground to a halt after a section of the main north–south road, which runs past the official residence of the Prime Minister, was closed altogether. But other, less visible, modes of securitization were also instituted. Tamil residents were required to register with the police, and arbitrary stops and detention were a regular threat. The lodging houses where young men from the north and east took shelter from the threat of LTTE recruitment were the subject of surveillance and always likely to be raided at any time. But for all this—and this is a distinction that might be contested—Colombo was always pre-eminently a site for the *staging* of occasional moments of spectacular violence. There was never a sense that it was a *strategic* part of either the rebels' or the government's military thinking. Unlike towns in the north, no part of the city was every held by anti-government forces, there were no no-go zones, and there were never any street fights for territory.

This concern for spectacle was most apparent in a last bizarre episode in the final years of the war. In 2007, as the LTTE lost ground to government forces in the east of the country, Sri Lanka reached the final of the cricket World Cup, which was being played that year in the West Indies. As Colombo focused on sport, with the entire city glued to late-night television coverage of the game, the LTTE launched an air raid on the city. Two of its light planes successfully bombed an oil storage facility outside the main urban area. Chaos ensued, as the government shut down the city's power supply just as the match was getting going. Rumours flew, causing many members of the security forces to fire futilely into the night, thereby adding to the panic. The LTTE's light planes escaped. A Reuters report at the time concluded with a trenchant comment:

> 'It was a dirty thing to do', Colombo security guard Sarath Leelaratna said of the attack. 'Everyone in the country was watching the match. To do this on a day like that is dirty'. (Reuters 2007)

Sri Lanka lost the game. But even so, the government of Sri Lanka was winning the war, not especially in Colombo, but in the arid scrub landscape south of Jaffna, known as the Vanni. This was the quintessentially peripheral region, from which the LTTE had successfully resisted both the Indian and the Sri Lankan military for so long, and this was where the final defeat occurred.

8.4 From defence to beautification

If the war started in the early 1980s, it reached an impasse in the second half of the 1990s, followed by a pause occasioned by the Norwegian intervention in 2001. Then, events started to speed up from early 2004 onwards. The death

of a popular Buddhist monk, Reverend Gangadowila Soma, had first provoked a spate of attacks on Christian churches, then another huge funeral
in the centre of Colombo, and then the foundation of a new political party
dominated by hardcore nationalist monks, the JHU. It is widely believed that
the size of the crowd at the funeral persuaded President Kumaratunga to call
an early election. In the parliamentary election in April 2004, the incumbent
UNP was defeated, further weakening the already fragile peace process. A few
weeks earlier, the LTTE had split, with the eastern leadership breaking away
and, eventually, taking refuge with the government security forces. In retro-
spect, that can be seen as the decisive moment in the LTTE's slow journey to
total defeat. The tsunami of December 2004 brought an army of international
relief workers; the promised aid to the country which might have acted as the
carrot to bring the LTTE and the government back to the negotiating table
instead proved to be more of a wedge that drove them even further apart.
In 2005 Mahinda Rajapaksa was elected President and immediately started
ramping up the military pressure on the LTTE.

Rajapaksa's brother, Gotabaya, a former army officer who had settled
in the USA, returned to help in his brother's election campaign. He was
appointed Permanent Secretary to the Ministry of Defence immediately after
his brother's victory, and swiftly oversaw a major change in tactics. After an
exchange of ever-more serious provocations, the war proper restarted in July
2006. Within a year, the LTTE had been completely driven out of the east.
Through 2008 and the first half of 2009, the LTTE was forced to cede ever
more territory as the government forces overwhelmed its former strongholds.
Finally, in May 2009, the remnants of the LTTE were surrounded on a strip
of beach near Mullaitivu on the north-east coast, accompanied by several
hundred thousand civilians who had been forced to join them in their final
retreat, effectively playing the role of human shields for what was left of the
LTTE fighting force. The LTTE's leader, Prabakharan, was killed, other leaders disappeared in the chaos of the surrender, and the war was finally and
comprehensively over.

We want to focus briefly on the institutional story that enabled the government victory. First of all, there was a huge rise in military expenditure after
Rajapaksa's 2005 election to the presidency, followed by a counter-intuitive
climb after the 2009 victory over the LTTE (Spencer 2016). The number of
personnel employed by the security forces continued to increase after the
fall of the LTTE. Between 2005 and 2009, Gotabaya Rajapaksa's Ministry
of Defence grew ever bigger in its capacity and its cost. Gotabaya Rajapaksa
himself, despite his apparent role as a senior civil servant, used the ministry
as the stage to build his own cult of personality alongside the figure of his

brother, the President. The ministry's elaborate website produced a flow of news stories about the achievements of the armed forces, accompanied by appropriate quotes from the omnipresent Permanent Secretary. What was to be done with the defence establishment that expanded so fast in the last years of the war? One answer was to repurpose it. For a time there were frequent reports of soldiers farming land in the occupied areas of the north and the east, opening businesses like tourist hotels and roadside restaurants. But as well as this commercial activity, the military started to take an increasingly visible role in routine areas of governance.

In April 2010, the Urban Development Authority (UDA), a government agency originally created by Premadasa in the lead-up to his Million Houses programme in the late 1970s, was brought under the Ministry of Defence. The newly created Ministry of Defence and Urban Development, with thousands of military personnel at its disposal, took responsibility for the transformation of Colombo into a 'world-class city'. The UDA, which had overseen an impressive but relatively little-known programme of community-based upgrading of under-serviced settlements across the city, became transformed into something rather different. Military figures were drafted in to provide a new kind of leadership. The Ministry of Defence website, which had blossomed as a highly coloured vehicle for the view from the military command in the final years of the war, now started to report regularly on new developments in Colombo. 'Beautification' was the promised direction of travel and the figure of the Secretary to the Ministry of Defence was to be seen everywhere (Fig. 8.2). In what follows we draw heavily on Gotabaya Rajapaksa's speeches of the time, all reported in full on the Ministry of Defence website.[7]

Urban development, broadly understood, was the responsibility of a bewildering number of state agencies, from the Colombo Municipal Council, to the Ministry of Construction, Engineering Services, Housing and Common Amenities, home of smaller agencies like the National Housing Development Authority, to the UDA itself. But in the years after 2010, all were eclipsed by the newly animated UDA. In the 2013 budget, four years after the war, there was an almost 19 per cent increase in the Ministry of Defence allocation— by far the highest for any ministry. Within this there was an 86.3 per cent increase for the UDA, although it accounted for only 4.7 per cent of the entire Ministry of Defence budget. Of this, more than half was allocated for building projects in Colombo and Hambantota, the district from which the Rajapaksa family came into the political fray (Ratnayake and de Mel 2012).

---

[7] For this chapter, we use copies of the speeches downloaded from the Ministry of Defence website when they were first made available. None of them are now available anywhere on the web.

Fig. 8.2 Gotabaya Rajapaksa overseeing new park development in Colombo, 2013

Source: photo originally available on Ministry of Defence website.

The creation of the post-war world-class city involved two key projects— the Urban Regeneration Project, by the government of Sri Lanka, and the Metro Colombo Urban Development Project, a joint project with the World Bank. The URP aimed to transform public spaces in Colombo through its beautification programme, but also to relocate 65,000 families from their cur- rent 'under-served' settlements to high-rise complexes built by the UDA. This would require the dispossession of anything between 350,000 and 500,000 people. Much of the work that was planned for Colombo centred around making the city more attractive, or at least comparable with the 'world-class' aesthetic associated with cities like Singapore and Dubai. This included the renovation of heritage properties, and making the city greener, with better public spaces, the removal of pavement hawkers, better garbage and sewage management, attracting well-known luxury developers and hotel chains to invest in condominium and hotel developments, and the relocation of gov- ernment buildings. These 'urban fantasies', in Watson's (2013) terms, were commercially driven and aimed at a middle- and upper-income market; the fantasy was of a city free of poverty, unemployment, and congestion, where global capital was welcome and could operate without constraint. Beautifi- cation also involved the acquisition of large parcels of valuable land for a 'public purpose', which turned out to be high-end condominiums and mixed development projects (Perera 2019).

In early May 2010, the Urban Development Authority undertook the first of its military-backed evictions when bulldozers accompanied by armed soldiers demolished the homes and businesses of a small lower-middle-class community on Mews Street in Colombo's Kompannyaveediya area (also known as Slave Island) on a Saturday afternoon. Their homes were demolished to make way for the expansion of a school for children of military officers. The twenty-one houses that were demolished were permanent structures and all the residents had deeds to their property. The evicted community lost all their belongings, including official documents such as birth certificates and national identity cards, in the eviction process and subsequently filed a Fundamental Rights case shortly thereafter.[8]

The beautification projects under the URP saw pavestone sidewalks created, parks landscaped, colonial-era buildings that had been previously used as army barracks, or had been unused, renovated into high-end shopping complexes. It became a Colombo that the middle class and tourists alike loved, with spaces not only to shop, but for recreation. The outdoor spaces for recreation—walking and cycle paths, small cafés—emerged in the suburbs as well, where boundaries around paddy fields and protected mangrove sites were landscaped and paths created. The creation of these spaces for the suburban middle class, who had previously had no such outdoor spaces for recreation, unlike in central Colombo, was welcomed by residents, who to date regularly exercise and dine there. The military were ubiquitous in Colombo—landscaping, building, cleaning, and undertaking many of the tasks more commonly associated with the municipal workforce. Various disciplinary regimes—from 'jay-walking' fines to the 'environmental police' to controlling access to the city—were in place, and public spaces were constantly under surveillance by the military and police (Centre for Policy Alternatives 2014; Amarasuriya and Spencer 2015; Nagaraj 2015; Abeyasekera et al. 2019). The accelerated post-war development drive focused on making Colombo a world-class city and the 'centrepiece of Sri Lanka's economic revival', a 'preferred destination for international business and tourism', and the driving force of Sri Lanka's development.[9] In his speeches made between 2011 and 2014, Gotabaya Rajapaksa spoke of providing the urban poor with

---

[8] News media were barred from covering the eviction, which took place in broad daylight, with journalists later reporting that the military 'destroyed pictures taken by photojournalists at the site where the UDA demolished houses. An abusive brigadier was heard ordering Army personnel to delete the pictures and remove video cassettes of TV journalists' (Centre for Policy Alternatives 2014: 27–28). In 2020, after almost six years of litigation and living in rental premises, the former residents were given apartments in the UDA-built high-rise buildings, which they received free of charge in lieu of compensation.

[9] Gotabaya Rajapaksa, 'Full text of the speech delivered by Secretary Defence at National Conference on Architecture 2012', 23 February 2012, at the Bandaranaike Memorial International Conference Hall.

a 'domestic environment to achieve social mobility' and of relocating them to 'less obtrusive sites that will not impact the city's image'. The lack of enforced regulation, flooding, the shortage of land for middle-income housing, and many other issues were blamed on the urban poor and were used to justify the relocation of whole communities so that they would 'no longer disfigure the city'.[10]

In keeping with the regime's ideological orientation, Colombo's urban renewal was also crafting an affective landscape that could mobilize elite and mass loyalty around ethno-religious and national sentiments (Anand 2006; 'A Correspondent' 2013). The ethno-religious symbolism of some of the key post-war infrastructure projects in Colombo is clear—for example, in the $104 million Nelum Kuluna (Lotus Tower; see Fig. 8.3), funded through a loan from the EXIM Bank of China, and the state-of-the-art Nelum Pokuna (Lotus Pond) performance theatre, built in the shape of an open lotus flower and also funded by China. The lotus flower is a familiar Sinhala Buddhist icon, as well as the party symbol of the SLPP, the new political party formed by the Rajapaksas in 2016. As Watson (2015) comments, one important vehicle for promotional narratives in aspiring global cities is the built environment, which not only has to be 'modern' but also has to display an iconic architectural identity.

In a 2011 interview, reflecting on the government's defeat in Colombo local government elections, the historian and activist Nirmal Dewasiri astutely identified the political dynamic informing the Ministry of Defence project to beautify Colombo:

> The government knows that Colombo cannot organize itself as a separate opposition to it … The political power of the country rests not in the hands of the people who live in Colombo but those who come to Colombo in the morning and leave Colombo in the evening. The formation of an authority that supersedes the authority of the Colombo Municipal Council will be attractive to the floating population that comes in and goes out of Colombo. Therefore the opinion of those who live in Colombo does not matter to the government. (Dewasiri 2011)

The audience for the performative politics of urban beautification was not the people living in the city, it was the people who come into the city every day. Colombo has a daily floating population of over half a million that commutes to their offices and belong to the new urban sprawl. As noted previously, these middle-class commuters were overwhelmingly Sinhala Buddhist, and

[10] Gotabaya Rajapaksa, 'Current plans for the city of Colombo', Sujata Jayawardena memorial oration, 1 December 2011.

Fig. 8.3 Colombo Lotus Tower
Source: Iromi Perera.

were most obviously impressed by the promise of the beautification project. In 2022, they also became the vanguard of the protest movement that brought the Rajapaksas down.

But what of the people who *were* living in the city? For a time in 2012 and 2013, Gotabaya Rajapaksa seemed to be everywhere, giving speeches to bodies of architects, planners, software engineers (Amarasuriya and Spencer 2015). Each speech laid out his vision for the city, and for the country at large.

In an interview in 2012, Rajapaksa explained his role as the chief architect of Colombo's post-war development plans:

> We have started a programme to remove unauthorized constructions such as slums and relocate them into proper housing. We cannot allow these people to live under such low standards ... We must give them the opportunity to live well. With that, discipline will also come to them. It is not that they don't like to live like that.

When unpopularity was mentioned, he replied, 'Yes, but we are not throwing people out of their homes. We always look after them but they must understand, this is for their benefit. We have to do such programmes for the advancement of the people and the country' (Business Today 2012).

Between 2010 and 2014, many low-income communities were forcibly evicted from their homes by the military, including some under a World Bank-funded project that was rehabilitating the canal banks and drainage infrastructure in Colombo (Perera 2015). After the electoral defeat of the Rajapaksas in 2015, the forcible evictions stopped but communities continued to be moved to the high-rise buildings with very little choice in the process. Colombo's low-income communities are ethnically diverse such that, without explicit ethnic targeting, Muslim and Tamil communities were most affected. All the documents the communities were given to sign, including documents related to housing, were only available in Sinhalese and not Tamil (despite a constitutional provision to the contrary). Many Muslim communities found themselves living in Sinhala-majority areas where the tower blocks had been built, far from the closest mosque.[11]

The Megapolis Masterplan covering 2015 to 2019 went beyond Gotabaya Rajapaksa's original framing, by calling the various housing complexes for the urban poor a 'creation of secondary cities within the city of Colombo'. It was essentially segregation through housing—the urban poor were to be moved into the outskirts, as there would be no place for them or their aesthetic in the world-class city that would be central Colombo. The new high-rise complexes spanned twelve to fourteen floors, with some housing 300–500 apartments, and some large enough for around 1,200 apartments (Fig. 8.4). All affected communities received housing in the tower blocks, following the

[11] The selection of communities for relocation was primarily driven by the value and location of the land they lived on, but it was also tied into a broader strategy of aesthetic dominance. There was a particular 'look' for the world-class city that Gotabaya Rajapaksa was aiming for, including a certain shade of white for the outside of buildings. The colourful versatility of the low-income settlements therefore did not fit this aesthetic; nor did the early tower blocks whose balconies became sites of creative display. Later blocks had no balconies to disrupt their uniform exteriors.

'house for a house' policy, although the authorities most times counted multiple households living in one multistorey structure as 'one house', which led to overcrowding in the new flats until additional flats could be received after discussion with the UDA. Each flat came at a 'subsidized' price of around US$6,000, to be paid in monthly instalments over twenty to thirty years, in addition to utility bills. While this was a huge burden on relocated communities even before the Covid-19 lockdowns, their inability to work for many months in 2020 and 2021 due to several strictly imposed lockdowns left many with accumulated arrears in payments to the UDA. The economic crisis of 2022 has also hit these families hardest: unable to put one meal on the table, and threatened by the authorities for massive arrears in utility bills (Colombo Urban Lab 2022).

For the majority of the families that have been, or will be, relocated to the high-rise apartment complexes, Colombo is their home

Fig. 8.4 New UDA housing development
Source: Iromi Perera.

(Abeyasekera et al. 2019). It is where most have lived for generations, setting down roots and incrementally building their homes over time. A city-wide survey of low-income settlements in 2012 showed that around 90 per cent of the houses fell into the category of 'permanently upgraded' (Sevanatha 2003). People have been registered to vote for years from these addresses, have paid rates and taxes, and have diverse paper trails, often kept meticulously to show their connection to the land and their house. Labelling them as 'slum and shanty dwellers' or even 'encroachers' renders invisible their history in the city, and the decades of political bargaining that have provided for various services (Perera 2020). A powerful state narrative not only painted these communities as illegal, but also portrayed a dismal living environment, one that was derelict and affected by floods and mosquito-borne diseases, and riddled with drugs and crime. This was a key factor in the lack of pushback from middle- and upper-class Colombo (particularly those living in the suburbs, at whom beautification was aimed), where it was often believed that the 'asset' of an apartment given to the urban poor would simply lead to a vast improvement in their quality of life.

In a speech to a World Bank event in Colombo in March 2012, Gotabaya Rajapaksa seamlessly linked the challenge of social cleansing to economic gains:

> It has been observed that relocating the urban poor to high-rise buildings causes several problems. The people find it very difficult to adjust to their new environment. They typically lack an interest in preserving these buildings properly, and their attention to cleanliness is not as great as it should be. Because they are from the low-income segment of society, they would find it difficult to maintain the high-rise buildings properly even if they had an interest in doing so. As a result, the cost of maintaining these buildings ultimately devolves onto the government. With the initial construction cost of these buildings also being very high, this makes relocating low-income segments to high-rise buildings a very costly exercise. However, because the shantytowns and slums tend to be low-rise buildings sprawled over large extents of land, one of the great benefits of the relocation programme is that it will release a lot of prime land in Colombo for commercial and other developments, including the creation of more public spaces.[12]

According to the UDA, 15,769 families had already been moved to the high-rise blocks by mid-2019. With new funding of US$280 million made available by the Beijing-based Asian Infrastructure Investment Bank from 2019

---

[12] Gotabaya Rajapaksa, 'Full text of the keynote speech delivered by Secretary Defence at the South Asia Region Urbanization Knowledge Platform', 20 March 2012, at Cinnamon Grand, Colombo.

onwards, the project continues. While the URP's aim of making Colombo beautiful and free of slums and shanties is endlessly replayed in the largely state-controlled media and public forums, it is important to remember that, unlike many other South Asian cities, Colombo has never had large sprawling slums. The UDA's own data show that the working-class communities who are being relocated under the URP constitute 50 per cent of Colombo's population but only occupy 10 per cent of the land mass of the city.

Here we must contrast the political implications of the new order for the poor after 2010, with the trajectory they had followed since the late 1970s. As well as improving access to services, the original UDA had employed community mobilizers to work with the poor as active citizens, stabilizing their legal position on the land while improving their housing conditions. The history runs deeper still: this is a policy that carries through key principles in Patrick Geddes' original plan for Colombo from 1921 (Geddes 1921). The displacements and evictions that have followed the end of the war in 2009 treat the poor as passive miscreants, lacking both political voice and political aspirations, but desperately in need of the kind of improvement that 'discipline' might bring—in short, as something much less than full citizens participating in the life of the city.

8.5 From beautification to insurgency

In the years immediately after the war, Colombo was not simply the site for new experiments in housing. There were other kinds of social cleansing at work, some visibly the work of the state, others less obviously so. One early move was a 'war' on alleged underworld figures, which involved the arrest of many men from minority communities. Pavements were cleared of hawkers. Stray dogs were rounded up and disappeared. Traffic lights started working and, with the threat of military intervention against transgressors, were somewhat reluctantly obeyed for the most part. Three-wheeler drivers were forced to use meters rather than make up fares as they went along.

In January 2015, Mahinda Rajapaksa called an early presidential election, only to be defeated by a coalition led by his former cabinet colleague, Maithripala Sirisena. Defeat in parliamentary elections followed in October. Rajapaksa won a mere 18 per cent of the vote in Colombo Central, and only a little more in the other Colombo city polling divisions. Electorally, his government's experiment in urban development would seem to have been a striking failure—or so it seemed at the time. With the electoral defeat of the Rajapaksas in 2015, the UDA was moved out of the Ministry of Defence and into the Ministry of Megapolis, where it became the responsibility of another interesting political figure, Champika Ranawaka, a technocratically inclined hardline nationalist, with a political base in the new suburbs of the Colombo. The programme of evictions and resettlement continued, though in a more muted, less flamboyant mode. Ex-military figures retained key positions in the UDA, although the military were no longer directly involved in the evictions themselves. Some of Gotabaya Rajapaksa's initiatives have settled in as permanent changes in the city—the traffic lights still work, and are still for the most part obeyed. Others feel less secure in the long term: the shopping complexes in restored colonial buildings like the Racecourse are much reduced, with many retail units empty and seemingly only the fast-food outlets thriving. The biggest urban infrastructure project of the Rajapaksa period, the $1.4 billion Port City, which aims to create a new financial hub on 2.6 square kilometres of reclaimed land, has gradually taken shape. It is driven, like other building work in the city, by major Chinese investment (Ruwanpura et al. 2020).

Gotabaya Rajapaksa himself took the time out of office to build his own campaign for the next round of presidential elections. He positioned himself, not as the authentic voice of the rural heartlands, as to some extent his brother Mahinda had done, but as the front man for a new kind of constituency, urban professionals, and equally important no doubt, those who aspire to be urban professionals. Eschewing both the ubiquitous national dress of mainstream Buddhist politicians, and uniforms and medals that might seem too overtly militaristic, he cultivated an appropriately professional look: crisply pressed shirts and ties for formal occasions, chinos and polo shirts for less formal ones. Widening cracks in the coalition government made his political task easier, and the terrorist bombings in churches and tourist hotels in Easter 2019 further highlighted the dangers of a divided and inept government, and the attractions of an apparently strong and decisive figure for whom any appeal to 'security' was something of a trump card. In November 2019, he won in the first round with 52 per cent of the votes, against his main opponent Sajith Premadasa's 42 per cent. Although he only did a little better than his brother in 2015 in the central polling divisions in the city (16 per cent in Colombo Central, 23 per cent in Colombo North and Colombo West), he swept the surrounding suburbs with over 65 per cent of the vote in Homagama, Kesbewa, and Maharagama.

Although many parts of our story are familiar across South Asia, where the lure of the 'world-class city' has captivated political elites in every country in recent decades, there are distinctive aspects of the Sri Lankan version. Although speculative capital has driven a programme of demolition and building across Colombo at an accelerating rate since 2000, there is still a distinctive political and aesthetic story to be told about the post-war years and Gotabaya Rajapaksa's project of 'beautification'. Beautification was the main means by which Rajapaksa himself remade his own public image, from the man who had military oversight of the brutal last stages of the war, to a man with a vision of a city for the new middle classes, brought about through military discipline, technical competence, and indifference to the niceties and delays of urban politics. This was, in the phrase we used earlier, an experiment in governance without politics. The city provided a stage for Rajapaksa to project an image of himself as a man who gets things done. The things that were done were the shiny new signs of the world-class city. The people living in the city were not the intended audiences for this project, and there is little sign from the 2019 election results that they are any happier with it than they were when Mahinda Rajapaksa was defeated in 2015. But the voters of the suburbs, urbanized rather than urban, seemed to have bought into the project with more obvious enthusiasm.

As the former soldier who had overseen the final defeat of the LTTE, Gotabaya was able to promise renewed security (after the Easter bombings), and a more efficient (because less 'political') technocratic approach to government. What he actually delivered was an averagely chaotic approach to the pandemic combined with impressively incompetent management of the economy. By early 2022, a sovereign debt crisis long in the making rendered the country almost bankrupt. Acute shortages of foreign currency led to shortages of everyday necessities like cooking gas and fuel, as well as long daily power cuts. The protests that built up into the *aragalaya* started unspectacularly in the middle-class suburbs of Colombo in early 2022, when groups of neighbours started to gather in silent protest by the roadside in the early evenings. In April, a larger protest took place near the President's private residence and was mercilessly crushed by the security forces. Undaunted, a call went out for the protestors to regroup at Galle Face in central Colombo. Over the weeks that followed, a permanent tent village grew (Fig. 8.5), with a library, cinema hall, and improvised showers hacked from the external pipework of the luxury Shangri-La Hotel. In the evenings, the crowds grew enormously as protestors came in to chant and dance and simply enjoy the carnivalesque atmosphere. The crowd was mixed, with families bringing children and elderly relatives, though the leadership was overwhelmingly young. The police and army, on the whole, stood back and watched passively. The main slogan was 'Gota Go Home' (an allusion to the President's previous existence as a green-card holder in Los Angeles) and the city became known as GotaGoGama (Gota go village). Condensed in that slogan was a fury at the

Fig. 8.5 Tent village, May 2022
Source: Chulani Kodikara.

entire political elite of all parties, whose corruption and incompetence had brought the country to its knees.

By the first week in May, the country was entirely focused on the struggle being played out nightly at Galle Face, and on the more mundane everyday struggle to survive in the face of ever-worsening shortages. As pressure mounted on the Rajapaksas, rumours spread of a rift between the brothers, with Gotabaya hoping that Mahinda resigning as Prime Minister would take the pressure off him. What followed between 7 and 10 May had a strangely choreographed feel to it. On the 8th, Mahinda Rajapaksa made a pilgrimage to the Buddhist city of Anuradhapura, where he was met with jeers and catcalls. The next morning he held a rally of his party faithful in the grounds of his official residence. The participants were fired up by speeches before marching out to attack the protestors at GotaGoGama just up the road. That in turn brought thousands of people out to protect the protestors. Mahinda's supporters were chased away, their vehicles attacked. By mid-afternoon, Mahinda Rajapaksa had resigned. Two months later, an even bigger protest ended with the storming of the presidential palace and, eventually, Gotabaya's resignation.

The story is far from over as we make the final revisions to this chapter, but these recent events have a certain sense of completion about them. In the long run, Colombo has been most conspicuous as a site of political spectacle, including spectacular violence, but actual, regime-threatening insurgency had bubbled up far from the city, in the badlands of the Vanni and in the rural strongholds of the 1980s JVP. In 2022, Galle Face Green, classically the site of Independence Day parades and celebrations of victory over the LTTE, hosted the most spectacular protests ever seen in Sri Lanka, and in the end brought down a President and a Prime Minister. Colombo was the city in which Gotabaya Rajapaksa had auditioned for the role of President, using the UDA to develop a style of technocratic and disciplined domination. Elected to the presidency, he delivered a broken economy, and it was his most fervent supporters among the new middle class of the Colombo suburbs who first took to the streets in protest against him. In the months of agitation that followed, it was quietly announced that the UDA had suspended all its large-scale projects in Colombo. It is safe to conclude that Gotabaya's experiment in authoritarian beautification has not been a success.

Fig. 8.6 Boundary of the Port City project, 2018
Source: Iromi Perera.

Acknowledgements

This chapter was originally commissioned as a working paper by the Effective States and Inclusive Development programme at the University of Manchester. We are grateful to Tom Goodfellow and David Jackman for their patience, encouragement, and excellent editorial advice, and to an anonymous reviewer of an earlier version. We also draw on projects supported by the British Academy and the Economic and Social Research Council, both as part of the Global Challenges Research Fund, and acknowledge our collaborators on these projects, Asha Abeyasekera, Dileepa Witharana, and Vraie Cally Balthazaar.

References

Abeyasekera, A., Maqsood, A., Perera, I., Sajjad, F., and Spencer, J. (2019). Discipline in Sri Lanka, punish in Pakistan: Neoliberalism, governance, and housing compared. *Journal of the British Academy* 7(s2): 215–244.

'A Correspondent' (2013). Cementing hegemony: Politics of urban transformation in post-war Colombo. *Economic and Political Weekly* 48(34): 22–26.

Amarasuriya, H., and Spencer, J. (2015). 'With that, discipline will also come to them': The politics of the urban poor in postwar Colombo. *Current Anthropology* 56(S11): S66–S75.

Anand, N. (2006). Disconnecting experience: Making world-class roads in Mumbai. *Economic and Political Weekly* 41(31): 3422–3429.

BBC (1991). Suicide Killers: Terrorism in Sri Lanka. Available at: https://vimeo.com/304944042, accessed 26 March 2020.

Brenner, N., & Schmid, C. (2014). The 'urban age' in question. *International Journal of Urban and Regional Research* 38(3): 731–755.

Business Today (2012). Commitment, dedication, achievement: Interview with Gotabaya Rajapaksa. May. Available at: http://www.businesstoday.lk/article.php?article=6188, accessed 5 May 2020.

Centre for Policy Alternatives (2014). *Forced Evictions in Colombo: The Ugly Price of Beautification.* Colombo: Centre for Policy Alternatives.

Colombo Urban Lab (2022). From bad to worse: Understanding and supporting Colombo's urban poor families in crisis. May. Available at: http://www.csf-asia.org/understanding-and-supporting-urban-poor-families-in-colombo-in-crisis/, accessed 7 November 2022.

DeVotta, N., and Stone, J. (2008). Jathika Hela Urumaya and ethno-religious politics in Sri Lanka. *Pacific Affairs* 81(1): 31–51.

Dewasiri, N. M. (2011). CMC defeat: Is it a challenge to the government? Interview with Lankadeepa, 18 October, trans. by Minna Thaheer. Available at: https://www.pressreader.com/sri-lanka/daily-mirror-sri-lanka/20111103/296911090694515, accessed 5 May 2020.

Doble, H. (2013). Chandragupta Thenuwara's 'beautification'. Groundviews, 2 August. Available at: https://groundviews.org/2013/08/02/chandragupta-thenuwaras-beautification/, accessed 18 May 2020.

Efroymson, D., and Fernando, U. (2013). Public space and quality of life: A case study of Mount Lavinia Beach. Available at: https://healthbridge.ca/dist/library/Public_Space_and_Quality_of_Life_A4_format.pdf, accessed 31 March 2023.

Geddes, S. P. (1921). Town Planning in Colombo: A Preliminary Report. Ceylon: H. R. Cottle, Government Printer.

Hoole, R. (2001). Sri Lanka: The Arrogance of Power: Myths, Decadence and Murder. Colombo: University Teachers for Human Rights (Jaffna).

Hughes, D. (2013). Violence, Torture and Memory in Sri Lanka: Life after Terror. London: Routledge.

Jayawardena, K. (1985). Ethnic and Class Conflicts in Sri Lanka: Some Aspects of Sinhala Buddhist Consciousness over the Past 100 Years. Colombo: Social Scientists Association.

Jeyaraj, D. B. S. (2020). Charismatic actor-politician may have changed the nation's destiny. Daily Mirror (Colombo), 15 February. Available at: http://www.dailymirror.lk/opinion/Charismatic-actor-politician-may-have-changed-the-nations-destiny/172-183175, accessed 31 March 2023.

Kapferer, B. (1988). Legends of People, Myths of State: Violence, Intolerance, and Political Culture in Sri Lanka and Australia. Washington, DC: Smithsonian Institution.

Manor, J. (ed.) (1984), Sri Lanka in Change and Crisis. London: Croom Helm

Masterplan (2015). The Megapolis Western Region Master Plan 'From Island to Continent'. Colombo: Megapolis Western Region Planning Project.

Meyer, E. (2003). Labour circulation between Sri Lanka and South India in historical perspective. In C. Markovits, J. Pouchepadass, and S. Subrahmanyam (eds), Society and Circulation: Mobile People and Itinerant Cultures in South Asia, 1750–1950. New Delhi: Permanent Black, pp. 55–88.

Moore, M. (1997). The identity of capitalists and the legitimacy of capitalism: Sri Lanka since independence. Development and Change 28(2): 331–366.

Moore, M. (2021). The insurrectionary JVP and the Sri Lankan state. Polity 9(1/2): 51–61.

Nagaraj, V. K. (2015). 'Beltway bandits' and 'poverty barons': For-profit international development contracting and the military-development assemblage. Development and Change 46(4): 585–617.

Nissan, E. (1984). Some thoughts on Sinhalese justifications for the violence. In J. Manor (ed.), *Sri Lanka in Change and Crisis*. London: Croom Helm, pp. 175–186.

Peiris, P. (2018). Changing dynamics of the party–voter nexus. In A. Shastri and J. Uyangoda (eds), *Political Parties in Sri Lanka: Change and Continuity*. Delhi: Oxford University Press, pp. 71–91.

Perera, I. (2015). Evicted under the World Bank's watch. *Sunday Times FT*, 24 May. Available at: https://www.sundaytimes.lk/150524/business-times/evicted-under-the-world-banks-watch-149983.html, accessed 7 November 2022.

Perera, I. (2019). *Land Acquisitions for a Public Purpose in Post-war Sri Lanka*. Sri Lanka: Law and Society Trust.

Perera, I. (2020). 'We can't feel the earth beneath our feet anymore': Dispossession and high-rise living in Colombo. *Polity* 8(1/2): 51–57.

Piyadasa, L. (1984). *Sri Lanka: The Holocaust and After*. London: Marran.

Ranagalage, M., et al. (2017). An urban heat island study of the Colombo metropolitan area, Sri Lanka, based on Landsat data (1997–2017). ISPRS International Journal of Geo-Information 6(7): 189, https://doi.org/10.3390/ijgi6070189.

Ratnayake, Jayani, and de Mel, Nishan (2012). *Sri Lankan Budget 2013: Increasing Assistance, and Vulnerability*. Colombo: Verité Research.

Reuters (2007). Air raids and Gilchrist dampen Sri Lankan party. 29 April. Available at: https://www.reuters.com/article/uk-cricket-world-lanka-reaction-idUKCOL13056420070429, accessed 31 March 2023.

Royo-Olid, J., Fennell, S., et al. (eds) (2018). Building, owning and belonging: From assisting owner-driven housing reconstruction to co-production in Sri Lanka, India and beyond. European Union. Available at: https://publications.europa.eu/en/publication-detail/-/publication/6495c9ee-f909-11e8-9982-01aa75ed71a1/language-en, accessed 31 March 2023.

Ruwanpura, K. N., Brown, B., and Chan, L. (2020). (Dis)connecting Colombo: Situating the megapolis in postwar Sri Lanka. *Professional Geographer* 72(1): 165–179.

Sevanatha (2003). The case of Colombo, Sri Lanka. Understanding Slums: Case Studies for the Global Report on Human Settlements, Urban Slums Report. Available at: https://www.ucl.ac.uk/dpu-projects/Global_Report/pdfs/Columbo.pdf, accessed 18 May 2020.

Sivasundaram, S. (2017). Towards a critical history of connection: The port of Colombo, the geographical 'circuit', and the visual politics of new imperialism, ca. 1880–1914. *Comparative Studies in Society and History* 59(2): 346–384.

Spencer, J. (1984). Popular perceptions of the violence: a provincial view. In J. Manor (ed.), *Sri Lanka in Change and Crisis*. London: Croom Helm, pp. 187–195.

Spencer, J. (1990). Collective violence and everyday practice in Sri Lanka. *Modern Asian Studies* 24(3): 603–623.

Spencer, J. (2016). Securitization and its discontents: The end of Sri Lanka's long post-war? *Contemporary South Asia* 24(1): 94–108.

Thiranagama, S. (2011). *In My Mother's House: Civil War in Sri Lanka*. Philadelphia, PA: University of Pennsylvania Press.

UN-Habitat (2018). *The State of Sri Lankan Cities 2018*. Colombo: UN-Habitat.

Uyangoda, J. (2003). Social conflict, radical resistance and projects of state power in southern Sri Lanka: The case of the JVP. In M. Mayer, D. Rajasingham-Senanayake, and Y. Thangarajah (eds), *Building Local Capacities for Peace: Rethinking Conflict and Development in Sri Lanka*. Delhi: Macmillan India, pp. 37–64.

Venugopal, R. (2018). *Nationalism, Development and Ethnic Conflict in Sri Lanka*. Cambridge: Cambridge University Press.

Watson, V. (2013). African urban fantasies: Dreams or nightmares? *Environment and Urbanization* 26(1): 215–231.

Watson, V. (2015). The allure of 'smart city' rhetoric: India and Africa. *Dialogues in Human Geography* 5(1): 36–39.

9
Conclusions

Within and beyond urban dominance

Tom Goodfellow and David Jackman

As Covid-19 spread across the world in early 2020, the place of cities in society was brought into sharp relief. Mounting case numbers and death tolls led to divisive debates about the most effective and appropriate public health responses, with cities at the epicentre of government action and the economic disruption that ensued. The severity with which Europe, much of Latin America, and particularly the USA were affected also raised questions about the capacity of democratic systems to deal with such emergencies, and whether more authoritarian and indeed repressive modes of governance could leverage their strengths to better protect their citizens and economies. For many, Covid-19 has spurred on the centralization of power with increased surveillance and suspension of rights (Brown et al. 2020), and been accompanied by a 'deglobalization' that supports the nationalist ideologies often underpinning authoritarianism (Cooper and Aitchison 2020). Among our cases, ruling elites in Harare, Lusaka, and Kampala were accused of using the Covid-19 pandemic as a pretext for increased repression in the face of protest, with devastating effects in Kampala in November 2020. These events served as an important reminder of the questions that animate this book.

The preceding chapters have explored the political strategies deployed by dominant ruling coalitions in capital cities, and their urban development consequences. The decision to focus on countries with a dominant regime—rather than choosing to explore the relationship between capital cities and political strategy in more competitive democratic contexts—was motivated by a need to better understand the urban dimensions of the 'authoritarian turn' around the world. Yet it was also spurred by an interest in questions of socioeconomic development, the relationship of which to authoritarianism is an uncomfortable and contested topic. The reality is that many (though by no means all) countries that have made significant progress on key development indicators in recent decades have been characterized by dominant political

Tom Goodfellow and David Jackman, *Conclusions.* In: *Controlling the Capital.* Edited by: Tom Goodfellow and David Jackman, Oxford University Press. © Oxford University Press (2023). DOI: 10.1093/oso/9780192868329.003.0009 settlements. This dominance is often underpinned by authoritarian practices and repression, but can also involve more generative and even developmental processes. Striving for urban dominance can involve the ramping up of repression, surveillance, and violence against political opposition *simultaneously* with major investments in infrastructure, job creation, and service provision. Countries such as Ethiopia, Bangladesh, and Uganda have been regularly held up in recent decades as examples of success in economic development and poverty reduction, even while in other circles these countries have been reviled as crucibles of violence and repression. These dual narratives are often two sides of the same coin: the pursuit of dominance. Nowhere are these two sides of the story more evident than in the politically and economically vital context of the capital city.

With this in mind, in this project we selected cases with varying trajectories of socioeconomic development as well as varying levels and longevity of dominance. We chose countries with dominant-party regimes that had been in place for decades (Uganda and Ethiopia), where the attempt to dominate the city politically had been notably more effective in the latter, even though the ruling coalition's dominance was starting to unravel at the national level. We also selected countries that had only recently started exhibiting a shift towards a more dominant political environment (Bangladesh and Zambia), but where this shift was clearly evident in changing approaches towards controlling and manipulating the politics of the capital city (and where the attempt to secure dominance eventually failed spectacularly in the latter). We also commissioned two additional studies: a case of attempts to control a city that has been opposition-supporting for decades in the context of rising authoritarianism and economic meltdown (Harare), and a case in which the city was relatively marginal to the national political settlement but where a concerted strategy to build urban support had been central to a recent authoritarian project (Colombo).

In this chapter, we distil key findings from the comparative analysis of our cases and consider the implications of these for research and policy. We explore, in turn: the position of capital cities in variable geographies of dominance; the role of spaces, institutions, and coalitions in strategies for urban control; the ways in which dominance can be co-constituted by elites and urban populations; the limits of repression and the question of when generative strategies come to the fore; the distinction between 'persistent' versus 'episodic' strategies of dominance; the varying effects of external versus intra-coalitional threats to dominance; and the factors that overall appear to favour more developmental outcomes in the pursuit of urban dominance. Following this, we conclude and reflect on the broader implications of these findings.

9.1 Why capital cities matter in diverse dominance geographies

Capital cities are important everywhere because they symbolize political sovereignty, are home to political elites, drive economic growth, and often house a large percentage of the urban population. They are consequently also places of great political opportunity—for both ruling coalitions and their opponents. The precise ways in which capital cities feature as important in seeking and sustaining political dominance is highly contextual and nuanced, and the magnitude of importance differs markedly across our contexts. In seeking to understand this, we here introduce the concept of *dominance geographies*, which can be thought of at both national and urban scales. The first of these relates to the question of where the city sits within a national political settlement: something affected by a wide range of factors including the city's population size, the degree of urban primacy,[1] and the location of the city in relation to the regional base of the ruling coalition or key opposition groups. These factors influence the extent to which the city has been central to struggles for dominance and whether its population has a privileged position within a national political settlement.

Though capitals and other large cities are increasingly important to political settlements in all urbanizing contexts, their role varies substantially depending on whether they have been central to building dominance more broadly, and the extent to which the ruling coalition has a rural base. Understood in relation to risk, the question then is: how central is the capital to the formation and stability of the ruling coalition? In situations where a regime's overall dominance involves a substantial rural stronghold, such as Uganda, Zimbabwe, or Sri Lanka, urban constituents are rarely considered long-term strategic allies, being used for political gain but ultimately treated as expendable. In contrast, urban dominance is crucially important in contexts such as Dhaka and Lusaka, where the loss of it likely means the loss of power nationally. In Lusaka, the Patriotic Front (PF) became a victim of its own success in mobilizing urban constituents. Its success in doing so led to its taking control of major city councils including Lusaka from 2006, which formed a platform for winning at the national level in 2011. Yet having raised the expectations of such a wide range of urban dwellers, the PF needed to develop a more concerted and persistent approach to urban dominance in order to maintain it, and ultimately failed to do so. In Ethiopia, despite the ruling coalition's rural origins in the Tigray region, its focus on building long-term strategic allies

---

[1] This refers to the extent to which the urban population is concentrated in one particular city.

in Addis Ababa was partly a response to the challenges it faced in holding together a political settlement nationally. While the Ethiopian People's Revolutionary Democratic Front (EPRDF) was largely successful in this attempt to dominate the city, ultimately this was insufficient to save a political settlement in a fractured national context where the capital—although very important—was only one among many elements of a complex political jigsaw that needed careful management for dominance to survive.

As well as understanding the role of the capital in relation the ruling coalition and its base, understanding the national dominance geography also depends on the role the capital has played historically in the formation of opposition and the undermining of ruling coalitions. How important has the capital been to political opposition? This can be seen most strikingly at points of historic regime change, in the dynamics of a coup or liberation movement, mass protest, and struggles for democracy. It is common for capital cities to be visible sites of protest, where interest groups take a campaign to the streets to try and leverage strength and gain momentum. Yet capital cities have played notably different roles in major historical political transitions. In the cases of Lusaka, Dhaka, and Addis Ababa, for example, the capital has been foundational to major political movements. Lusaka has been the site of student-led protests, and highly active civil society bodies in the media and churches, pushing against authoritarian rule. Dhaka has been central to how mass movements have formed, setting a precedent for mobilization elsewhere in the country, as has been seen through all major political transitions. Addis Ababa, too, has been the epicentre of student protests since the mid-twentieth century, contributing to the toppling of Haile Selassie's regime in 1974 as well as shaking the foundations of EPRDF rule in 2005. In such contexts, capital cities can have a symbolic and moral significance, where mobilization conjures up images of previous regime changes, and can set a pathway for how political change happens. Two ostensibly similar protests in different capital cities can, then, have radically different political connotations, shaped by the resonances they have in context.

None of the above should be taken to imply that capital cities cannot take on new significance over time, either as sites of contention, or as new sources of authority for the ruling coalition. All of our cases indicate fluidity and new opportunities. One clear example of this is the case of Colombo, which went from being relatively marginal to the geography of the national political settlement prior to 2009, to being a central site in an effort to build political dominance. This, as Perera and Spencer show in Chapter 8, is partly because of increased awareness of urbanization and the new significance of the suburban population in the greater Colombo area. Indeed, Colombo illustrates a situation in which the increased importance of the capital in the national 'dominance geography' is closely connected to the second scale of dominance geography that our cases highlight—that is, the spatiality of dominance *within* a city. It is often the case that particular geographical areas within a city become a focus of struggles for dominance, either because of their socioeconomic, ethnic, or religious character, or because of a general feeling of spatial exclusion that provides opportunities for mobilizing support. In the case of Colombo, the relatively homogeneous (largely Sinhala and Buddhist) 'new suburbs' thus provided a key locale for the Rajapaksas' efforts to build dominance. Here, and in some of other cases, particular geographic configurations within the city have been central to dominance strategies and their success or failure—as we explore further below.

9.2 Challenges of control: Spaces, institutions, and coalitions

Our cases reveal that the nature of urban interventions intended to generate support and control opposition is highly diverse and multifaceted, often emerging from the contingencies of particular historical moments, and influenced by a multitude of factors. From cooperatives to skyscrapers, social protection systems, legal changes, and security interventions, a huge range of measures have direct political import in authoritarian settings. Yet behind this diversity we can discern a common set of challenges to controlling capital cities. These relate to particular *spaces*, *institutions*, and *coalitions*.

Spaces

This project was premised on the argument that we need to move beyond the level of the nation state when we think about the construction of political dominance, authoritarianism, and political settlements. Our cases challenge us to go further. Not only does attention need to be given to a city, but also we need to examine particular sub-municipal places and spaces that for varied reasons have a disproportionate significance for ruling coalitions. Images of urban protest often draw attention to central squares, avenues, and junctions; however, in a number of cases here, the spatial strategies evident in efforts to dominate capital cities focus on urban peripheries. This has been most evident in Harare and Colombo, as sites for notable generative interventions.

In Harare, efforts to secure dominance were particularly marked in settlements on the periphery, where bureaucratic authority had not yet been established and where, consequently, the ruling elite was able to build pockets of support through land-based patronage in an opposition-leaning city. McGregor and Chatiza, in Chapter 7, thus characterize these areas as 'dominated locales' within an opposition-supporting city, where residents engaging in opportunistic and often desperate survivalist tactics contributed to the ruling coalition's dominance by enmeshing themselves in ZANU(PF) structures and strategies in order to access land. This idea of 'dominated locales' is, we suggest, a more useful and nuanced concept than the more common term 'strongholds' in contexts where dominance in a particular area is relatively fragile, and contingent on processes of establishing often transitory coalitional dominance rather than a solid foundation of party support.

In Colombo, areas outside the urban core also played a key role in a very different way. Through the years of civil war, Colombo felt quite removed from the conflict, but in the meantime the city was quietly growing into a metropolis, swollen by the new middle classes, tourism, and the growing security forces themselves. Subsequently, efforts by the Rajapaksas to win over a new class of middle-class suburbanites have characterized politics since 2009, in what was historically seen as a town loyal to the United National Party—their main opposition. This courting of the suburbs clearly contributed to Gotabaya Rajapaksa's electoral success in 2019, reflecting the growing importance of this constituency: the difference between his levels of support in the city centre (16 per cent) and the suburbs (65 per cent) illustrate the starkness of this divide. The shift towards co-opting the middle-class suburbs explains Colombo's major programme of urban 'modernization' and 'beautification' in recent years, even if this ultimately proved inadequate to secure Rajapaksa's dominance, as the major protests leading to his removal in 2022 demonstrated. In Kampala there have also been signs of increased attention towards the urban periphery, as the National Resistance Movement (NRM) unsuccessfully focused significant efforts in the run-up to the 2021 election attempting to regain support in Wakiso district, the increasingly urbanized zone surrounding Kampala that had been lost to the NRM for the first time in 2016. Our cases thus suggest that the political manoeuvres in the expanding metropolitan fringes surrounding capital cities should attract our attention as much as the projection and contestation of power in central streets and squares. These apparently peripheral areas are, perhaps increasingly, often where dominance is won and lost.

Institutions

A second set of challenges revolve around existing democratic and electoral institutions. In many of our contexts, the ways in which political dominance has been sought or established have been highly authoritarian, yet elections still play real and important roles in the political life of the nation. It is well established that formal institutional democratic frameworks—such as the existence of political parties, election commissions, ballots, and even observers—should not be mistaken for the values of liberal democracy in action, or necessarily taken as a positive signal for the character of politics to come. Yet in only very few contexts globally do ruling coalitions have such a firm grip on power that opposition cannot make advancements through elections, or at least unsettle those in power. As such, it is not only coups or insurgencies that are a threat to authoritarian regimes, but changes at the ballot box that filter through despite the myriad efforts to control elections— a reality in many 'hybrid' political contexts (Cheeseman and Klass 2018). Because it is difficult to shut down democracy completely, the manipulation of nominally democratic institutions of governance is often central to strategies of dominance. These manipulations can manifest 'horizontally' through the deliberate fragmenting of authority or finding new ways to reduce checks and balances, or 'vertically' through the realignment of powers held by different tiers of governance in decentralized systems.

The recentralization of urban governance has been a notable feature in several cases, in response to failures to dominate the city through the electoral process. This was particularly evident in Kampala with the creation of the centrally appointed Kampala Capital City Authority from 2011; in Harare where the powers of the Ministry responsible for Local Government were used to weaken the opposition-controlled City Council in the 2000s; and in Colombo where a new Urban Development Authority was created in 2010, accountable to the Ministry of Defence and superseding Colombo Municipal Council. The immediate effects of this can sometimes appear quite positive if it results in central government resources being channelled into urban infrastructure and services; yet these investments and the new authorities supervising them can later be neglected or even sabotaged if they do not ultimately help in securing political dominance. In this way, the five-year project in Kampala to build the new authority's capacity to 'modernize' the city through infrastructure and regulation was progressively undermined after 2016, in a new effort to co-opt informal workers through populist overtures and forbearance.

Our cases also indicate more conventional examples of meddling with urban elections, such as in Colombo in 2011 when the Rajapaksa government illegally delayed the Colombo Municipal Council elections. In Dhaka, municipal elections have been similarly delayed in some instances, and conducted under highly dubious conditions, often boycotted in the process by opposition parties. Meanwhile, in Addis Ababa the opposition Coalition for Unity and Democracy won the 2005 mayoral election, but the ruling coalition immediately acted to reverse this gain in a range of ways. In addition to the massive and violent repression unleashed, the Addis Ababa case demonstrates a different kind of legal-institutional manoeuvring, in the form of the sudden expansion in local council seats after 2005 (from fifteen to 300), making it virtually impossible for the opposition to compete. This kind of institutional manipulation is also important in terms of how we analyse dominance strategies, because it reveals the limitations of conventional co-optation/repression binaries.

Coalitions

The final and arguably most important challenge we identify across our cases is that of controlling and sustaining particular urban political coalitions. The question of who is or is not included within a ruling coalition is a complex one, and clearly coalitions change over time as groups enter or exit explicit or tacit bargains with the ruling elite (Whitfield et al. 2015). Ruling coalitions can also vary substantially in how encompassing they are—in other words, in terms of what Kelsall et al. (2022) term the breadth of the coalition's 'social foundation'—and how this breadth varies over time. Ruling elites adopt 'coalitional strategies' (Whitfield et al. 2015: 11) to manage opposition, but are not always fully in control of the scope of their coalition. A ruling coalition will usually need to involve a range of violence specialists, such as state security agencies or other coercive urban groups. Yet they may also encompass particular interest groups that they can appeal to through generative interventions in order to solidify urban control or win an election, attempting to expand their social foundation at key moments in the political cycle.

In Zambia, for instance, Sata began by mobilizing the urban poor but increasingly turned to Lusaka's middle classes and civil society movements as a means of further building his urban base in advance of his success in winning power in 2011. Broadening the coalition's social foundation in this way in order to gain power comes with significant risks: when urban informal workers and urban middle-class professionals are crucial to a ruling coalition's rise to power, they can also be its potential undoing when it becomes difficult for the government to meet the (often conflicting) expectations of these groups in office. The mobilizing power of these urban groups is thus a double-edged sword. Consequently, ruling elites that win power democratically through bringing certain groups into their coalition can sometimes harshly repress the same groups to try and maintain dominance. Nowhere was this more evident than in the case of Lusaka under the PF, where market vendors were courted and then tolerated in the PF's first years of rule before being repressed after 2016, and civil society and media figures were both co-opted and increasingly repressed as the ruling elite became increasingly divided and threatened.

Different forms of generative and repressive measures are also associated with different types of coalition. The case of Colombo illustrates how a major new suburban middle-class constituency was drawn into the social foundation of Rajapaksa's coalition alongside an empowered defence force that needed to be kept well occupied after the end of a long civil war. This particular coalition resulted in a dominance strategy centred on military-led urban beautification and securitization. The continued loyalty of groups brought into the coalition is particularly important in the case of security forces, especially when dominance relies quite heavily on coercion. Sophisticated forms of repression require an empowered and loyal coercive apparatus, something that the Awami League (AL) in Dhaka has recently achieved to an unprecedented degree as the security and police forces have been thoroughly politicized and processes of high-tech surveillance have been institutionalized. Yet, as we explore below, to persist over time requires a coalition that reaches beyond the groups who specialize in coercion. In particular, when the levers of repression are turned on large segments of the urban population whose expectations have been raised by prior co-optation, as in Lusaka, the ruling coalition's legitimacy can rapidly unravel. With the uneasy transition to President Lungu after Sata's death, and a deteriorating economy, support for the PF drained from its new urban constituents, prompting a shift towards repression of the very same groups. Treating urban groups as 'disposable allies', through episodic strategies (defined below) and an increased reliance on coercion, ultimately amounted to a failed dominance strategy as the 2021 Zambian election showed.

A common challenge identified across our cases is that of the urban youth and their role within ruling coalitions or rival coalitions. Often digitally literate, well connected, motivated ideologically and politically, young people frequently bear the brunt of urban pressures, from a lack of jobs and opportunities to poor living standards. Controlling young people appears to be a perennial concern for ruling coalitions, and one made more of a challenge when the leadership and origins of a regime appear distant and out of touch, appealing to ideas that motivated previous generations but have less currency with the young. The case of Addis Ababa is particularly significant in relation to the relatively successful mobilization of urban youth under the ruling coalition. As Gebremariam shows in Chapter 4, this took place both through forms of cooperative empowerment that involved building the organizational capacities of urban groups including young people—through Urban Consumers' Cooperatives (UCCs)—as well as through more top-down forms of coercive distribution in the case of making access to the Revolving Youth Fund dependent on party membership.

In practice, the crafting of dominance unfolds at the intersection of spaces, institutions, and coalitions, and the relationships between these evolve over time. In Chapter 5 on Dhaka, for example, Jackman highlights the historical importance of earlier shifts in the urban political economy for the emergence of an authoritarian coalition. Here, urban gangsters prominent in particular urban neighbourhoods were effectively institutionalized as a mode of governance and rule, and it took significant urban upheaval to bring them under control, and for conditions to be set for the political dominance seen today. The nature of interventions is closely shaped not only by the challenges posed in sustaining urban coalitions, but also by the opportunities that are presented by particular historical legacies and inheritances. In Sri Lanka, for example, the ruling party inherited a large and politically crucial security infrastructure from decades of intense conflict. There is a sense in which the urban interventions seen in Colombo were closely shaped by the merging of the Ministry of Defence with the Urban Development Authority, which served as a means by which the ministry could have budget increases and a role to play in peacetime, and reflected how power was configured within that coalition.

9.3 Co-constituting dominance

While this volume has (for reasons stated at the outset) focused primarily on ruling elite strategies for dominance, it has also challenged our initial framing of dominance as being built through strategies and interventions crafted from the top down that are either contested by the urban population, or somehow just absorbed by them. In fact, we can see in several cases the *co-constitution*

of dominance by segments of the urban population as they actively seek to
engage the ruling coalition in projects with overlapping interest, even if these
shared interests may be fleeting and shot through with power imbalances. As
noted above, dominance is always predicated on coalitions, and urban social
groups exercise their agency to varying degrees on entering such coalitions.
In this regard, the framing of top-down control and bottom-up contestation
as a dialectic can miss some of the more subtle and mutually constructed ways
in which dominance is built and undermined. The production of dominance
is thus not simply about the strategies of the dominant and how they are
received, but about *terrains of negotiation* in which people attempt to deploy
and bargain with their political value in exchange for often meagre gains as
they navigate urban life (Goodfellow 2020).

The mutual construction of dominance is evident in very different ways in
the cases of Addis Ababa, where the co-constitution of dominance was *sec-
toral* in nature, and Harare, where it was more *spatial*. In the former, as noted
above, the UCCs themselves lobbied for an increased role in the distribution of government-subsidized food, a project that benefited them but was
clearly also in line with the ruling elite's agenda to extend its levels of control over the urban population after the upheavals of 2005. This produced a
shared agenda that built the increased presence of the party into the lives of
urban consumers, and over time started to look more like coercive distribution. In Harare, meanwhile, the decision of communities in the vulnerable
and fragmented urban peripheries to mobilize ZANU-PF support was a tactical manoeuvre in an opposition-leaning city. It was partly driven by fear
and limited room for manoeuvre, but nevertheless was more mutually initiated than is suggested by the idea of an elite-led strategy or intervention.
Thus, while top-down strategies for the building and maintenance of dominant authority certainly exist, a range of mutually crafted forms of dominance
also unfold in order to make the capital city manageable not only for ruling
authorities but for urban groups themselves who are struggling to survive.
This leads us to the question of whether ruling coalitions can rely exclusively
on coercion to maintain dominance, and when coercive strategies are forced
to give way to more generative approaches.

9.4 The limits of repression

A crucial question in the study of authoritarian settings relates to the role
of coercion and the conditions under which violence and coercion become
(or cease to be) the primary means through which dominance is achieved

and maintained. Common images of authoritarian regimes cracking down on citizen protests or opposition politicians easily give the impression that visceral coercion is commonplace. Yet it is worth recalling Arendt's formulation that 'Violence can always destroy power; out of the barrel of a gun grows the most effective command, resulting in the most instant and perfect obedience. What can never grow out of it is power' (Arendt 1969: 53).[2] The point here it that violence can be deployed in the pursuit of dominance, but cannot in itself generate the power needed to secure continued dominance over time; hence it tends to reach its pitch in the process of establishing dominance, or when dominance is slipping from a ruling coalition. Though violence can wield unparalleled repressive force, the maintenance of dominance over time always requires generative interventions as well. This is especially the case in urban areas, where density of social organization can enhance the capacity for groups to mobilize demands, and heightened visibility limits the extent to which violence can be the sole mechanism of control. The case of Harare illustrates this well, because while the devastating violence of Operation 'Clean the Filth' clearly damaged the opposition's ability and willingness to mobilize by generating significant fear, it also damaged regime legitimacy. This level of violent coercion was not something that could keep being repeated. For the ruling coalition to grow its power in the urban peripheries actively, rather than just attempting to destroy that of others, it needed to deploy generative clientelist strategies in the form of providing access to land and housing alongside its continued repression.

Urban dominance always involves a balance of repressive and generative interventions. Comparative analysis of our cases suggests that there is no *general* rule regarding the changing use of repressive versus generative interventions over time. This depends on varying pathways to power, the history of institutionalization within the ruling party and the opposition, the nature and timing of crises faced by the ruling coalition, and the relative success of earlier strategies for dominance. The balance between strategies depends on the nature of the political settlement, but inevitably it changes over time because political settlements themselves change over time, in response to the growing or diminishing power of particular groups. Moreover, experimentation with different strategies and tactics can create positive and negative feedback loops that shape future interventions. Thus, shifts in strategy may simply be a consequence of a previous approach yielding decreasing returns, running out of steam or being fiercely contested; but it may also

---

[2] This is the centrepiece of her argument that 'violence and power are opposites', and 'violence appears where power is in jeopardy, but left to its own course it ends in power's disappearance' (Arendt 1969: 56).

be a consequence of changing demographics, electoral cycles, or a shift in international influence within a country.

Rather than necessarily changing the balance of repressive relative to generative measures, electoral cycles tend to influence the intensity of both, with pre-election periods exhibiting heightened coercion and tactical co-optation. For example, in Kampala the year or so before a general election involves enhanced attempts to buy support in informal settlements, alongside spectacular displays of coercive power. In periods after elections, we see more strategic efforts such as administrative restructuring and legal manoeuvring—for example, the passing of legislation to reduce the power of elected officials—as well as the institution of the 'social media tax' targeted at 'idle chatter' among urban middle classes. Similarly in Ethiopia, the ruling party hugely increased the number of council seats after the 2005 election, raising major obstacles to the opposition's electoral prospects.

Despite the lack of an overall, generalizable pattern regarding the changing balance of repression and generativity over time, we do see significant trends across our cases. In some cases there are clear shifts, with building and maintaining dominance marking distinct phases. In cases with a particularly *successful* approach to urban dominance over a sustained period, this appears to involve a shift from more purely repressive measures towards greater use of generative ones. In Addis Ababa, for example, the violent coercion used immediately after the 2005 election crisis helped to establish the ruling EPRDF's dominance of the city, but also further damaged its legitimacy. Consequently, a strategy of long-term generative interventions, in the form of mass housing, infrastructure, subsidized food, and youth employment schemes, was central to maintaining dominance. Similarly in Dhaka, the intense repression of political opposition seen in the early years of AL rule has—largely because of its success—given way to greater focus on development as a centrepiece of the regime's legitimacy and urban interventions. The increased recourse to developmentalist discourses in addition to a legitimizing discourse of securitization in Dhaka reflects the limits of violent coercion and surveillance as strategies that can secure dominance long into the future.

Yet, even in cases where the emphasis on development achievements (supported by some concrete indicators of progress) suggests a gradual shift towards more generative ways of maintaining dominance, it is crucial that we do not miss the more subtle and covert forms of repression that continue and often grow as ruling coalitions seek to stabilize their dominance. Herein lies the paradox of maintaining dominance over extended periods of time: while on the one hand, coercion becomes increasingly *insufficient* over time for reasons discussed above, it simultaneously becomes increasingly *necessary* because opposition tends to grow rather than lessen when a ruling coalition holds power for long periods. This leads to increased dependency on the coercive apparatus of the state. However, any coalition requires a degree of legitimacy in the public eye, which flagrant and continuous repression of opposition can easily undermine. A common finding across our cases was thus the increased use of coercive techniques that are hidden from public eyes. This can mean, at one end, increased recruitment of, and budgets for, informers, or at the other, the deployment of technologies and surveillance systems. A small example from Lusaka was the introduction of Chinese-funded CCTV cameras pointed to popular locations where student protests start, protests which have in turn been crucial in previous transitions in power. A more grandiose example from Dhaka was plans for a citywide surveillance system enabled by Chinese technology. These more discreet modes of control are intended to prevent physical conflict emerging in the public sphere, giving the illusion of peace.

9.5 Persistent and episodic strategies

As the previous sections have indicated, looking at our case studies comparatively reveals not only spatial stories about differences in 'dominance geographies', but also temporal ones in terms of how the pursuit of dominance proceeds over time. In some cases this involves the progressive evolution of a coherent set of dominance strategies, while in others it involves abrupt and ruptural shifts and reorientations. Looking across our cases and extending some of the points made above, we can thus make a distinction between strategies that are more persistent and concerted over time, and those that are more fragmentary and episodic. *Persistent* strategies tend to involve developmentalist discourses, sustained co-optation, and coercive distribution whereby public goods are delivered through party channels. Such distribution can mobilize political allegiance in ways that are consistent with longer-term economic development goals. This developmentalist rhetoric is, however, often accompanied by the incremental enhancement of surveillance and closure of political space. Addis Ababa under the EPRDF after 2005 provides probably the clearest example of a persistent dominance strategy among our cases, witnessed for example in the successive versions of youth employment programmes over more than a decade, described by Gebremariam in Chapter 4. While it is highly debatable whether these schemes were economically effective (Di Nunzio 2019), they were consistent in their approach to urban youth and this did yield clear political dividends at the city level: even when the regime was unravelling nationally, Addis Ababa itself has been virtually untouched by protest since 2005.

In contrast, *episodic* approaches commonly attempt (successfully or otherwise) to mobilize the support of a range of urban groups, including urban informal workers, middle-class groups, and those living in spatially excluded peripheries, in ways that raise expectations beyond what can be delivered. Without a clear enough development strategy behind them to mobilize developmentalist discourses, episodic cases often produce swings between populist discourses and discourses of urban securitization. Accordingly, the very same groups targeted for generative interventions in populist moments are then periodically subject to violence, intimidation, and arbitrary arrest. This characterizes the situation in Kampala and Lusaka over several decades, and has been particularly notable with respect to policy towards street vendors. In both cities, ruling coalitions have veered between populist co-optation of vendors and 'modernization' projects aimed at middle-class support, on the one hand, and violent crackdowns on street vendors, on the other. In Lusaka, this was exacerbated by the disorderly transition from Sata to Lungu that led to various internal disagreements and ad hoc policymaking. In some cases, the reasons for episodic interventions are less straightforward. In Harare, for example, there was a shift from allowing the urban peripheries to be governed 'lawlessly' by party barons towards one of bureaucratic recognition and incorporation, but in ways that were patchy and uneven depending on the perceived political 'value' of the residents and their capacity to mobilize politically.

The degree to which we see persistent rather than episodic strategies depends less on the specifics of the ruling coalition, or on whether it achieved power democratically, than on the overall balance of power in the city and how it is organized. In Addis Ababa, strong legacies of concerted urban uprising and collective action through general strikes have helped to produce institutionalized and relatively consistent government responses, with both repressive and generative elements. In Dhaka, where student movements have been historically strong, there are also signs of a broadly similar strategy of persistent (if technologically evolving) repression, alongside ongoing attention to progress on key development indicators. In contrast, the episodic approaches in Kampala and Lusaka are explicable in part as responses to diverse and uncoordinated demands from different constituencies—supported by relatively vibrant urban media that amplify these demands in real time—with the result being haphazard and conflicting interventions, guided to a significant extent by electoral cycles. Fig. 9.1

	Generative	Repressive
Cases characterized by **persistent** strategies	Clientelism often takes the form of long-term public goods delivery, deployment of developmental rhetoric, and potential for sustained progress towards urban economic development and social inclusion	Heightened sophistication in surveillance, repression tied to public goods delivery (coercive distribution), and reduced need for overt violence by state security over time
Cases characterized by **episodic** strategies	Populist rhetoric accompanied by inconsistent clientelist tactics, passive co-optation, and forbearance, particularly in pre-election period	Alternate co-optation and coercion of the same groups at different points in time, reliance on overt violent policing, and of violence in pre-election periods

Fig. 9.1 Persistent and episodic strategies

summarizes the kinds of generative and repressive interventions typical of persistent and episodic strategies.

9.6 Urban strategy and external versus intra-coalitional crises

Another important aspect of strategies for dominance relates to the nature of the specific threats a given ruling coalition faces. In authoritarian contexts, threats are often conceptualized in two ways. First, there are threats seen as originating from outside the ruling coalition—for example, in a mass uprising or the mobilization of a group of rival elites. Dealing with these has been termed 'the problem of authoritarian control' (Svolik 2012: 4). A second set of threats is seen as originating *inside* the ruling coalition, from 'individuals from the dictator's inner circle, the government, or the repressive apparatus' (ibid.). Though the former is often portrayed as the predominant risk, for Svolik the real threat lies within, as relatively few regimes end by mass uprising, and even in cases when they do it is often factional splits within the ruling coalition that enable these uprisings to succeed. Indeed, the tendency to position and study authoritarianism in relation to democracy can give the impression that the greatest threat to any authoritarian government is democracy, when it is more likely to be other authoritarians (Wallace 2019). Political settlements literature similarly portrays risk in this manner, concerned with the balance of power within a ruling coalition, and the stability of dominance over opposition. In practice, political threats often cannot be neatly boxed into 'internal' or 'external', with many groups acting in a liminal space or as 'contingently loyal' (Kelsall et al. 2022), and with actors and historical processes deeply interlinked in ways that challenge internal/external binaries: think, for example, of how opposition movements and internal dissent within a political coalition often grow together and crescendo into change. Yet the heuristic of external versus internal threats is useful for thinking about the broad sources of instability and how these are interpreted and responded to.

Based on the case studies presented here, we suggest—very tentatively, given the small sample—that while a ruling coalition facing a significant *external* threat often turns towards generative interventions, when facing crises *within* the ruling coalition there is a tendency to lean more on coercion alone. This is likely because of the difficulty in mobilizing effective generative interventions during an internal coalitional crisis, as well as the insufficiency of repression alone in dealing with major external threats. In Harare, for example, when threatened by surging urban support for the opposition Movement for Democratic Change (MDC), ZANU-PF initiated informal land-based generative clientelism on the urban periphery to win back urban support, alongside its continuing repression of opposition figures. This is not to deny the extent of violent coercion, but to highlight that, at the moment when the external threat to ZANU-PF rule looked existential from 2008 to 2013, there began a particular effort actively to win support in the urban peripheries. After 2013, when the external MDC threat receded but ZANU-PF was riven with internal splits, these generative measures were curtailed as the dominant faction sought to regain control through regularizing and repressing settlements in which it was threatened by other factions.

In Kampala, an internal coalitional crisis also saw a shift in approach towards the motorcycle-taxi (*boda boda*) sector, which is demographically very significant in the city. While this sector has often been subject to generative measures including regulatory forbearance, when it became drawn into factional splits among state security agencies this led to a ramping up of repression. However, the most striking case of a repressive shift in response to internal crisis was in Lusaka, where the death of President Sata without an anointed successor led to factional splits and a botched transition that precipitated greater reliance on surveillance and coercion.

9.7 Urban dominance and development

In drawing this book to a close, we again need to reflect on the question of development outcomes, and when the pursuit of urban political dominance can actually deliver socially and economically progressive outcomes that raise the standard of living across urban society. Although, historically, development processes have often been bound up with attempts to secure political dominance, the relationship between the two is far from given. History suggests that the majority of dominance projects are *not* developmental; even if they create opportunities through generative interventions, these are often episodic, short-lived, or counteracted by other factors. As others have argued, it has usually been when a ruling elite faces an existential threat and is thus fighting not just for dominance but for its very *survival*, and this comes together with a concerted project to ramp up capitalist productivity, that sustained development has occurred (Doner et al. 2005; Harrison 2020). Yet we cannot escape the fact that efforts to promote development are often linked to dominance strategies and, if successful in development terms, are thus likely to further dominance projects as well. The fundamental challenge for policymakers and practitioners concerned with development is that interventions designed to improve development outcomes—in terms of infrastructure, social protection, poverty reduction, and so forth—have a political significance that is often, at least in part, intended to shore up an authoritarian ruling coalition. It is important not to brush over the complexity in motivations that can drive ruling coalitions in attempts to improve urban conditions. Yet not all efforts to improve such conditions have meaningful results, and they are often outweighed by the sheer force of repression.

In this respect, generative interventions can be more or less 'developmentalist', in the sense of involving efforts to build support through long-term strategies of socio-economic advancement, rather than short-term populist appeals to sectional groups. In urban contexts, a significant factor in determining whether generative interventions are more likely to be persistent and developmental appears to be the nature of urban opposition. Based on the cases presented in this book, we suggest that *contexts with a long history of relatively well-organized urban opposition, pre-dating and external to the current ruling coalition, are the most conducive to persistent generative strategies and, potentially, sustained development progress.* Thus in Ethiopia, where the regime was seriously threatened by widespread urban revolt in 2005, which in some respects built on longer histories of urban activism, relatively developmental strategies such as urban food subsidies and employment generation became central to strategies for dominance. In Dhaka, where the history of organized urban mobilization has also been strong, the regime is under increasing pressure to respond with sustainable interventions to address urban grievances. Recent student-led movements have precipitated shifts and promises for policy changes on access to state employment and road safety, and these pressures for developmental interventions are likely to increase in Dhaka. By contrast, in Kampala urban opposition has been evident in elections and waves of protest, but not yet in the form of sustained social movements with potential to overthrow the regime or overcome it electorally. In this context, generative responses have been more sporadic and arbitrary, consisting of elite co-optation, short-term favours for specific groups, and 'forbearance' in the face of government regulation, rather than programmatic public goods provision. As the 2021 election showed, violent coercion has compensated for the limitations of these approaches.

Unfortunately, however, more developmental forms of generative intervention in the face of concerted urban opposition do not necessarily mean less repression. Indeed, developmentalist approaches often come with repression, though the nature of that repression may be different from other cases. Large-scale episodic repressive interventions can disrupt both developmentalist narratives and the achievement of development outcomes, meaning that persistent, often insidious, and increasingly sophisticated forms of repression (as in the rise of digital surveillance in Dhaka) are better for providing the stability and narrative required for persistent generative interventions. This is not a comfortable conclusion to reach, and it does not make the repression any less pernicious. There are other routes to development—but in this book we have been looking purely at dominant political settlements where authoritarian practices were part of the selection criteria, and in such cases we see that persistent approaches to development and repression often go together. In cases where urban opposition has been fragmented historically and lacked continuity, such as Kampala, there is less need for more penetrative and sophisticated forms of repression, and a reliance on blunter and more episodic instruments of surveillance and coercion.

9.8 Conclusions

The foregoing prognosis may seem gloomy and fraught with normative concern. Echoing analysis elsewhere that presents development as exacting, strategic, fraught with risk, and often brutal (Harrison 2020), development emerges from the above as a story of strategically persistent generativity alongside persistent repression. But it is important here to remind ourselves of three things. First, as noted above, although capitalist development always involves some conscious allocation of pain and gain (ibid. 15), heavy repression is neither the only nor necessarily the most effective path to developmental progress; notwithstanding the authoritarian turn, the debates on the prospect for 'democratic developmental states' continue to play out, and many more democratic and competitive contexts observe significant development progress around the world (Mkandawire 2010; Nem Singh and Ovadia 2018). Second, there is reason to believe that over time, if persistent developmental political projects yield dividends, the need for repression to secure dominance lessens. Perhaps more importantly in the long run, the perceived need to secure political dominance itself gradually abates because opportunities to prosper become less dependent on dominating the political space. Of course, there will always be some desire on the part of ruling authorities to control city populations, but many societies survive and indeed thrive with vertically divided authority, in which the refusal of cities to be dominated does not result in relentless campaigns to make them submit.

A third point from which we might draw optimism is that the pursuit of dominance is often self-defeating in the end. Although this can play out in different ways and over very different time frames, cases such as Lusaka and Colombo have shown that even the most energetic efforts to dominate city populations politically can overreach themselves and collapse, while in Kampala national dominance does not translate into urban control, and in Addis Ababa urban dominance could not prevent national collapse. In this respect, while we cannot be certain what the politics of future cities will look like—particularly in these times of turmoil and constant technological revolution—we can be pretty sure that authoritarian domination of cities will never come easily.

This book has made no attempt to resolve important questions about the state of democracy in urbanizing regions of the global South, or to project seriously into the future regarding whether cities will ultimately fulfil the originating promise with which they are often associated: the promise of democracy. What it has done is to put debates about urbanization and its political consequences, including with respect to state-building and development, into conversation with debates on authoritarian politics and the 'authoritarian turn'. The vast majority of the literature in the latter field has taken cities and their qualities as spaces for the production and contestation of dominance for granted, while the former debates have tended to focus on the liberatory potential of urban movements and protests without fully accounting for what they are up against. As our case studies have shown, what they are up against can be formidable—and not only in terms of the repressive and coercive apparatus of the state, but also a range of other strategies to reshape political coalitions, reconfigure spaces, and manipulate institutions. Whether and how urban populations can engage with these shifting, often sophisticated strategies of dominance in order to build coalitions for cities in their own image must be a subject for future research.

References

Arendt, H. (1969). *On Violence*. Orlando, FL: Harcourt.

Brown, F. Z., Brechenmacher, S., and Carothers, T. (2020). How will the coronavirus reshape democracy and governance globally? Carnegie Endowment for International Peace. Available at: https://carnegieendowment.org/2020/04/06/how-will-coronavirus-reshape-democracy-and-governance-globally-pub-81470, accessed 31 March 2023.

Cheeseman, N., and Klaas, B. (2018). *How to Rig an Election*. New Haven, CT: Yale University Press.

Cooper, L., and Aitchison, G. (2020). The dangers ahead: Covid-19, authoritarianism and democracy. Conflict and Civil Society Research Unit, LSE.

Di Nunzio, M. (2019). *The Act of Living*. New York: Cornell University Press.

Doner, R. F., Ritchie, B. K., and Slater, D. (2005). Systemic vulnerability and the origins of developmental states: Northeast and Southeast Asia in comparative perspective. *International Organization* 59(2): 327–361.

Goodfellow, T. (2020). Political informality: Deals, trust networks, and the negotiation of value in the urban realm. *Journal of Development Studies* 56(2): 278–294.

Harrison, G. (2020). *Developmentalism: The Normative and Transformative within Capitalism*. Oxford: Oxford University Press.

Kelsall, T., Schulz, N., Ferguson, W. D., Vom Hau, M., Hickey, S., and Levy, B. (2022). *Political Settlements and Development: Theory, Evidence, Implications*. Oxford: Oxford University Press.

Mkandawire, T. (2010). From maladjusted states to democratic developmental states in Africa. In Edigheji, O. (ed), *Constructing a Democratic Developmental State in South Africa: Potentials and Challenges*. Cape Town: HSRC Press, pp. 59–81.

Nem Singh, J., & Ovadia, J. S. (2018). The theory and practice of building developmental states in the Global South. *Third World Quarterly* 39(6): 1033–1055.

Svolik, M. W. (2012). *The Politics of Authoritarian Rule*. Cambridge: Cambridge University Press.

Wallace, J. (2019). Authoritarian turnover and change in comparative perspective. Oxford *Research Encyclopedias: Politics*. Available at: https://doi.org/10.1093/acrefore/9780190228637.013.636, accessed 31 March 2023.

Whitfield, L., Therkildsen, O., Buur, L., and Kjær, A. M. (2015). *The Politics of African Industrial Policy: A Comparative Perspective*. Cambridge: Cambridge University Press.

Index

elites/repressive states 'protection
pacts', 15
party-political domination, 4–5, 173, 235
political settlement and, 8
pursuit of dominance as
self-defeating, 253
resources and, 11–12
ruling coalition and, 5–6, 8, 9, 11–12
twenty-first century, 4
urban dominance and development, 250
urban political resistance and, 3–4
see also dominant political settlement
political dominance strategies, 6–7, 15,
234–235
authoritarian regimes and, 6–7, 30–31
balance of generative/repressive
interventions, 244–247
conceptual framework, 20, 30, 45*f*
contention and control, 15–16, 45–46
development as persistent dominance
strategy, 247–248, 252–253
generative interventions, 20–22, 31–33,
37, 40–41, 45*f*, 46, 77–79, 249–250
generative interventions as
'developmentalist', 251–252
intimidation, 31, 33–34
lower-level/grassroots actors and, 32,
173–174
'persistent' vs 'episodic' strategies of
dominance, 22, 242, 247, 249*f*, 251–252
political settlements approach and, 46
repressive interventions, 20–22, 30–33,
40–41, 45*f*, 46, 77–79, 127–128,
249–250, 252
ruling coalition and, 11–17, 32, 34,
37–38, 45–46
specific groups targeted for, 46
'strategies of subversion', 13–14, 41
surveillance, 31, 33–34
top-down strategizing, 11, 45–46,
243–244
urban strategy and external vs
intra-coalitional crises, 22, 249
violence, 20, 31, 42–43, 244–245
see also co-optation; political dominance
strategies: case studies; political
dominance strategies: typology;
repression
political dominance strategies: case studies

Addis Ababa, 20–21, 86, 90–91, 96–111,
247–249
Colombo, 19–20, 203–204, 225, 227–228,
242
Dhaka, 21, 118, 125–126, 131, 139–140,
248–249
Harare, 21–22, 172–175, 177–182,
185–186, 194–196, 248
Kampala, 20, 52–53, 55, 58–77, 78*f*,
248–249
Lusaka, 21, 144–145, 148, 151–156, 161,
166, 248–249
see also political dominance strategies
political dominance strategies: typology, 20,
32–33, 45–46, 45*f*, 46
coercive distribution, 20, 33, 36
legal manoeuvres, 20, 33, 40
legitimizing discourses, 20, 31, 33, 42
violent coercion, 20, 33
see also coercion; co-optation; political
dominance strategies
political parties, 8
authoritarian durability and, 5
Bangladesh: party-political competition, 118–123, 125, 128,
139–140
Harare: party-political
domination, 173–175
party-political domination, 4–5, 173, 235
political violence, *see* violence
populism, 248
definition, 44
as legitimizing discourse, 44
populist parties, 148
Sri Lanka, 205, 209–210
Zambia, 145, 158–159
ZANU(PF) (Harare/Zimbabwe), 172, 182
power
cities, state-building, and, 8
political settlement and, 7
spatiality and, 6
state power and cities, 8–9 n5
urban power, 8–10
violence and, 244–245
Premadasa, Ranasinghe, 210, 213, 217
Premadasa, Sajith, 205 n1, 209–210, 226
Prosperity Party (Ethiopia), 19, 86 n1,
112–113
protests, 2–3
age of 'mass protest', 1–2